A desire for beauty

秋山瘦入雲林畫

丁卯仲夏雲樵屋主退石

Lê Thành Khôi

A desire for beauty

Photography by the author

HORIZONS DU MONDE

Front cover
Adam Totalik.
Two Flying Geese.
Caribou antler.
H: 19cm x L: 25cm.
Spence Bay, Canada.

Preciding page
Dream stone: *Autumn*
mountains in the forest
***of clouds.* Mid-summer**
1867 (or 1807).
The Hermit of clouds.

Back cover
Mother-of-pearl
pendant
representing a bird
inlaid with shell.
H: 8.5cm. Guangala,
Ecuador,
100 B.P.- 800.

Art Design: Bruno Leprince
Translation: Chrisoula Petridis
Lithography: Compo Rive Gauche, Paris
Printing: Grafiche Zanini, Bologne

© Lê Thành Khôi for the text and illustrations, Paris 2000
Published by the Association "Horizons du Monde", Paris
ISBN : 2-9515181-1-0
Printed in the European Community

Contents

Art and Beauty   6

The idea and the real   10

Matter and form   21

The universal and the particular   34

Purity of Line   49

The unity and diversity of ways of thinking   49

Abstraction and representation of nature   58

Representation of the human figure   78

Harmony of Color   97

Societies and significations   97

Pictorial colors and monochrome   104

The magic of ornamentation   114

Movement and Rhythm   131

On a flat or curved surface   132

Three-dimensional expressions   142

The garden: the art of space and time   160

The Face of the Invisible   167

Looking and silence   168

Impulses of life and death   188

The ephemeral and the eternal   205

Index   220

Bibliography   222

Really there is no East, no West,
Where then is the South and the North?
Illusion makes the world close in,
Enlightenment opens it on every side.

Buddhist Song

*B.P.: Before Present

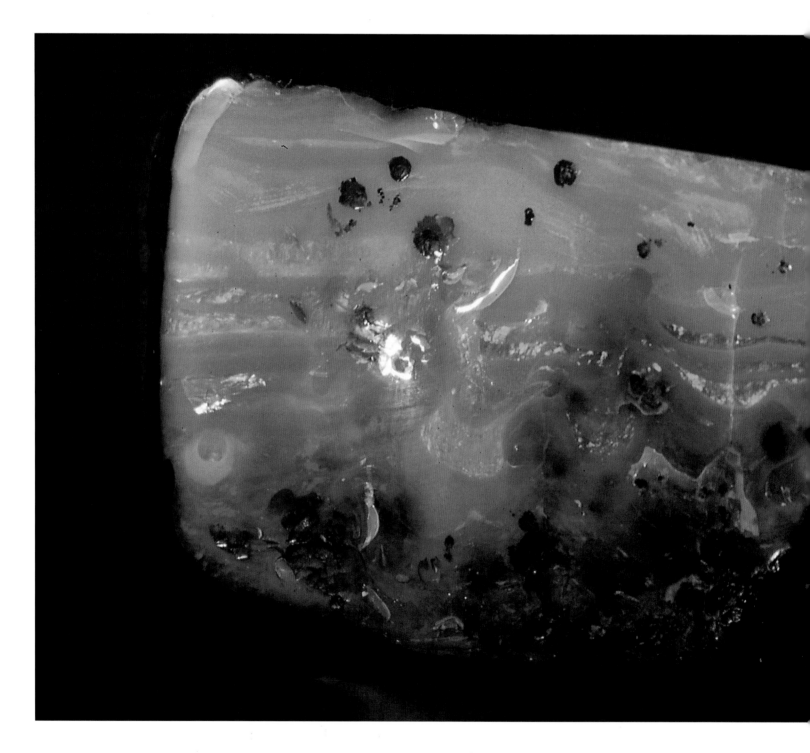

"There is a sleeping song in all
things that dream endlessly
and the world will begin to sing
if you find the key word"
(Joseph von Eichendorff).
Polished opal boulder.
H: 8.5 cm x W: 4.5 cm. Australia.

Art and Beauty

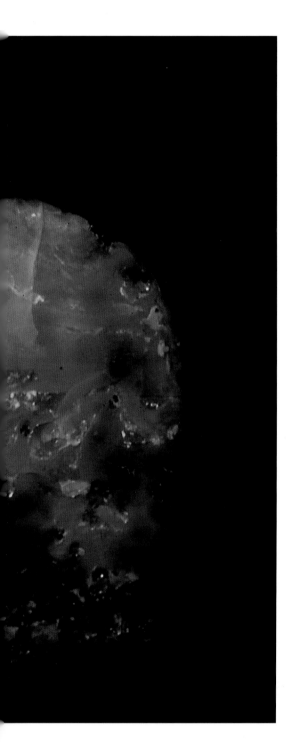

Beauty gets bad press in certain circles. André Malraux wrote, "It makes our relationship to art unintelligible." Traditionally described as "what it pleasing," as what, according to Kant, provokes "disinterested pleasure," beauty has been repudiated by many contemporary artists. Unable to find a set of criteria, Malraux thought that, "today, beauty is that which has survived." Which, strictly speaking, means nothing: ugliness has also survived. Of course, his way of thinking is understandable – it is time that separates out the "beautiful" works from the others. But we do not know why they are beautiful.

We would like to carry out this search in the light of world history. Is there, despite the diversity of cultures and aesthetics, common ground for the appreciation of beauty? We are not speaking of art. Today, we no longer think that the goal of art is beauty. A distinction must be made between the work and its subject, which may be something repugnant (Rembrandt's *Flayed Ox*), banal (Van Gogh's *Room* in Arles), sad (Dürer's *Old Woman*), ugly (Sharaku's portraits of Kabuki actors) or strange or aberrant (many of the masks from Africa or Oceania). Rodin spoke of the alchemy of art: "When Velázquez painted Sebastian, the dwarf of Philip IV, he gave him so moving a gaze that we are able to read in it immediately the painful secret of this infirm creature forced, in order to make a living, to give up his human dignity, to become a toy, a living bauble… And the more the martyrdom of the consciousness housed in this monstrous body is poignant, the more the artist's work is beautiful" (46-52). According to Rodin, in art, only that which has character is beautiful; that is, "the intense truth of any natural sight, beautiful or ugly, and even that which could be called a *double truth*, that of the interior translated by that of the exterior." Inversely, "that which is false, artificial, which seeks to be pretty or beautiful instead of being expressive is ugly." The artist who embellishes nature "creates ugliness because he is lying."

Henry Moore distinguished between "beauty," which aims to satisfy the senses – which was not his goal – and "vitality" – which was. There is "in it a pent-up energy, and an intense life of its own, independent of the object it may represent… a power of expression… which is more moving and goes deeper than the senses" (quoted in Read, 1964, 163). Of course, it is possible for one not to share this opinion, which is founded on the traditional concept of beauty ("in the Greek or Renaissance sense") and makes vitality a component of beauty. Picasso, the 20th century's greatest inventor of forms, was looking less for beauty than for a way of exploring all the possibilities of expressing his inner demon. But while the great artist can transform ugliness into beauty, the same is not true for less capable practitioners. On the other hand, activities believed initially to be solely utilitarian sometimes result in works more beautiful

Sickle with iron blade and curved wood handle covered with copper bands. W: 46 cm. Cambodia.

Milk pot.
Wood.
H: 27 cm.
Rwanda.

than those intended to be "artistic" such as photographs of mineral, crystalline and metallic structures, microorganisms, or projections into space of mathematical equations – real abstract paintings or sculptures such as Plücker's conoid at the Palais de la Découverte in Paris.

If beauty is not necessarily found in "art," especially in our era when some people take pleasure in the morbid and the obscene, it may be discovered on the contrary in what is not usually considered "art," in the humble objects of everyday life, in the decoration of the body, in the ephemeral paintings that African and Asian women draw on walls, in the earth and in the sand, in the natural objects that the human hand may or not have refashioned in order to find some resonance in them: the branch of a tree, a creeper, a rock or a pebble. Max Ernst, working with Alberto Giacometti on blocks of granite from the moraines of Forno, wrote to his friend Carola Giedion-Welcker: "Wonderfully polished by time, frost and weather, they are in themselves fantastically beautiful… why not, therefore, leave the spadework to the elements and confine ourselves to scratching on them the runes of our mystery?" (Giedon-Welcker, 300)

Should we not call art all the material productions through which human beings give meaning to their lives, despite or because of their poverty? It is precisely because their existence is difficult that they seek every occasion to introduce a bit of grace to it, by decorating their temples, the color of their clothes and their furniture, the shape of their tools, the rhythms of their music and their dances and even up to the doors of their tombs. The Toraja of Sulawesi (Celebes) carve the head of a water buffalo on these doors; the water buffalo is the animal which conducts the dead towards the afterworld.

The useful is not necessarily the antithesis of the beautiful; on the contrary, how many times has it been observed that the most functional lines are also the most pleasing to look at? That in so-called traditional society, design is not separated from production as it is in modern industry, is not a stranger to it: the craftsman passes the culture with which he is imbued into his creations. He takes joy in the finishing of the object in his hands.

For millennia, art was not disassociated from life. All members of the community participated in its ritual, poetic and musical activities, weaving their clothing, decorating their homes, manufacturing their tools; only certain objects, endowed with magical powers, necessitated the intervention of a specialist. The desire for beauty in everyday life is so natural that, after decades of ignorance, industry became aware that "ugliness does not sell" and that even the most ordinary objects had to be both functional and pleasing to the eye. On a larger scale, there is a need for a reintegration of the arts into community life so that the individual is no longer "one-dimensional," but will fully develop all his faculties. The process will be even more enriching if it will be able on the one hand to reject the elitist notion of creation reserved to a few areas for the entertainment of a minority and on the other to open itself

Skirt (*pasin*) in cotton and silk, border with multicolored geometric and animal motifs. 90 x 66 cm. Laos, Samneua region. Early 20th c.

Loom pulley topped
with a female head.
Wood.
H: 22.5 cm x W: 5.9 cm.
Guro, Ivory Coast.

up to the contributions of all civilizations, that it, assume its intercultural responsibility in a world where technology and the economy have done away with borders.

Yanagi Soetsu, who militated in favor of a revival of traditional Japanese crafts, wrote, "To me, the greatest thing is to live beauty in our daily life and to crowd every moment with things of beauty. It is then, and then only, that the art of the people as a whole is endowed with its richest significance. For its products are those made by a great many craftsmen for the mass of the people, and the moment this art declines the life of the nation is removed far away from beauty. So long as beauty resides in only a few articles created by a few geniuses, the Kingdom of Beauty is nowhere near realization… These works of people's art are simple and unassuming. It is a quality that harmonizes well with beauty. That which is truly beautiful is often simple and restrained… The Japanese have a special word *shibui* to express this ideal beauty… Etymologically, *shibui* signifies "astringent," and is used to designate a pro-found, unassuming and quiet feeling… [It] is the final criterion for the highest form of beauty. It is, moreover, an ordinary world, and is repeated continually in our casual conversation. It is in itself unusual that a whole nation should share a standard word for aesthetic appraisal" (quoted in Leach, 25-27).

The idea and the real

The rejection of beauty encountered in the contemporary West is explained in part by the normative idealism that dominated this field for a long time and by the confusion of this notion with those of truth and goodness. The person initially responsible for this was Plato. In one of his early dialogues, he asserted that beauty per se exists: it adorns all other things and makes them appear beautiful when this form is added to them (*Hippias major*, 289d). Beauty per se is a transcendent and eternal Idea (*eidos*) that is more or less reflected in perceptible instances of beauty. Man recognizes them because his soul caught a glimpse of the Ideas in the past and remembers them. Plato was interested in founding a City of Justice in which each individual carries out his hierarchically determined functions. The philosopher governs because he is the only one who has knowledge of the Good. While music (excluding annoying rhythms) encourages moderation and harmony, the poet and the painter cannot teach virtue because "their works are valueless from the point of view of truth, as they deal with the basest element of the soul and not with the best." The theory of Ideas thus results in the confusion of Beauty, Truth and Good as norms because it chases all deviants out of the Republic. Plato listed all the seductive qualities of art in order to condemn them in the name of morality.

Aristotle rejected Platonic idealism. His doctrine no longer aims for Good in itself but at that of man whose happiness merges with that of the city. For Aristotle as well, art is linked to political organization. Music and drawing, along with literature and gymnastics, are the foundations of education and in both Aristotle praises imitation (*mimesis*): it is educational and gives pleasure. Art responds to man's need for and pleasure in imitation. The purging (*catharsis*) of emotions by tragedy takes place as a result of the audience's identification with the characters. The two authors more or less agree on the definition of beauty. For Plato, beauty is constituted by "measure and proportion" (*Philebus*); for Aristotle, it lies "in measure and in order" (*Poetics*).

The Renaissance established the Greco-Roman model and the imitation of nature

Betel box in hammered silver decorated with openwork foliage. D: 18 cm x H: 11 cm. Laos.

Comb decorated with
the busts of two women
joining hands.
H: 11 cm x W: 11.5 cm.
Madagascar.

Khol bottle in silver decorated with floral and plant filigree motifs. H: 24.8 cm. Tunis.

which, as God's creation, leads to beauty. And since cosmic order was thought to be based on numbers (Pythagoras), it was in mathematical and geometrical relationships that harmony and perspective were sought; it was a way of representing and recognizing the power of the divine. While these conventions did not present an obstacle to artistic creativity during this period, the situation changed when painting academies began to develop in the 16th century. Institutionalized teaching led to the establishment of disciplines and of rules that, intended to facilitate learning, became routine and ended up stifling initiative and inventiveness. China, where the first painting academy was founded in the 10th century, had already undergone this experience.

In the early 19th century, Hegel elaborated his *Aesthetics* on the basis of artistic beauty (he excluded natural beauty which he thought inferior as it was not a product of the mind, the spiritual being superior to the natural).

According to Hegel, artistic beauty is "the idea most precisely determined as being an individual effectiveness… configured according to its concept. Thus understood, it is the *ideal*" (*Lectures on Aesthetics*). The ideal is realized historically in specific forms that correspond to as many steps. Greek art represents the classical form where the concept and reality as well as form and content correspond. With Christianity comes the superior form that Hegel calls Romantic; it is superior because spirituality attains a higher degree within it and fulfils itself in the interior. Hegel wanted to draw up a uni-

versal aesthetics. He produced an evolutionist and Eurocentric metaphysics. His concept of beauty has no foundation other than his own thinking from where he deduced his conception of specific forms and periods, the whole subsumed into an evolutionism modeled on European history. The inferiority of other civilizations is an extension of the initial dogma (the *ideal*). Hegel declared it expressly: "The *deficiency of form* thus comes from the *deficiency of content*. If the Chinese, the Indians and the Egyptians, for example, remained for their artistic figures, their divine effigies and their idols in a total absence of form or form that is badly and falsely determined, if they were not able to master true beauty, it is because their mythological representations, the content and the thought that were the basis of their works of art were still undetermined in themselves or badly determined and were not the absolute content in itself" (*ibid*). But what is the "absence of form," "form badly and falsely determined," "real beauty" and the "absolute content" if we do not accept Hegel's *a priori* system?

During the last quarter of the 19th century, views on art were to change progressively. The revolution came with the Impressionists whose two exhibitions (1874 and 1876) were followed by the discovery of the admirable bison of Altamira (1879). The Japanese woodblock print with its bright flat colors made a decisive contribution. "Hiroshige is a wonderful Impressionist," declared Pissarro. From the south of France, Van Gogh wrote to his brother Theo: "Here, after some time, the view changes, one sees

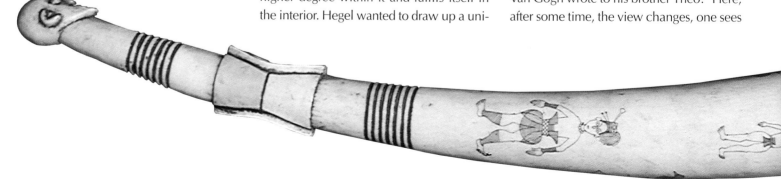

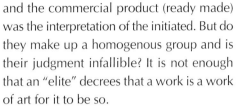

with a more Japanese eye and experiences color differently." About a Hokusai print, he wrote, "These waves are claws, the vessel is imprisoned within, one can feel it."

In the early 20th century, it was Negro art that in turn contributed to a renewal of the visual expression by the Cubists and the Fauves. The Surrealists were more interested in Oceanic art whose fantastic aspect appealed to their desire to explore dreams and the unconscious. André Breton saw in this art the "most exuberant products" of the world of the imagination that "largely eclipse the real world." The fascination for this art led to the reappraisal of Amerindian art. For Henry Moore, Mexican sculpture "seemed true and right. Its 'stoniness,' by which I mean its truth to material, its tremendous power without loss of sensitiveness, its astonishing variety, and fertility of form-invention, and its approach to a full three-dimensional conception of form, make it unsurpassed in my opinion by any other period in stone sculpture."

This period was also that of the contesting of traditional aesthetic criteria. At the same time that Dada shouted "to hell with beauty," Marcel Duchamp exhibited a urinal called *Fountain* in an art gallery. According to Duchamp, "There are very few people who find a urinal marvelous. Because the danger is artistic delight. But people can be made to swallow anything; this is what happened." For Jean Dubuffet, the terms "beautiful" and "ugly" were meaningless. Some authors put forward that what made the difference between the work of art

and the commercial product (ready made) was the interpretation of the initiated. But do they make up a homogenous group and is their judgment infallible? It is not enough that an "elite" decrees that a work is a work of art for it to be so.

The proliferation of "anything" and contradictory "theories" bears witness to the loss of points of reference. The crisis in art is linked to the general crisis of values in a world filled with self doubt which has to face destruction of all sorts that its will to power and desire for profit has triggered. Can we overcome the malaise by clearing the slate of all "isms" and restarting the debate from a different basis: the evaluation of the contributions of all civilizations? Universal art has a very long history and humanity's experience of its divergences and convergences reduces the agitation of a certain number of modern and "postmodern" movements and discourses to insignificance. The first bone into which signs were carved, found in Bacho Kiro in Bulgaria, dates back 50,000 years. The petroglyphs of Panaramitee in Australia with their meanders, circles, dots and arcs date from 5,000 years later.

Since the 1950s, with the recovered independence of Asia and Africa, the expansion of communications and the media, travel and exhibitions, globalization has become more rapid. Minds have been opened to a

better understanding of the other. The term "primitive art" is being replaced, because of its evolutionist and ethnocentric connotations, by that of "primary arts." Of course, prejudice has not completely disappeared. If objects from these cultures were and still are relegated to museums of anthropology or natural history most of the time, the underlying reason is (was) that they were not considered "art" and were too foreign to the Greco-Roman heritage the West has erected as a model and to Christian notions of revelation and original sin. In his book *Primitive Art*, Douglas Fraser wrote, "An object may be extremely handsome and interesting in its own right, yet still not be worthy of the name work of art. Such objects we call crafts. It is true, of course, that primitive man, not having a word for art as such, would not trouble himself over what is and is not 'Art'"(13).

This is a flagrant example of ethnocentrism. The Greeks did not distinguish between art and craft either. For the Greeks, *techne* expressed the ability that allowed man to give shape to something that already existed in nature. Art comes from the Latin *ars* and initially meant "science, knowledge," then "means, method." It only took on its current meaning (the original is still in use) in the middle of the 18th century. No one, however, has given a satisfactory definition of art. As for the beautiful, according to Kant, it cannot be conceptualized. In

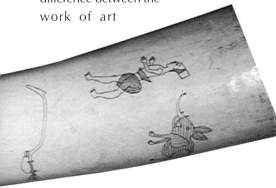

13

France, during the polemic about the creation of the Musée de l'Homme, des Arts et des Civilisations, and the possible exhibition in the Louvre of masterpieces of primary arts, the curator of the Louvre opposed the move because these works "do not speak for themselves." Certain anthropologists point out that they can only be understood in relation to their social and cultural context: they should not be isolated to present only their aesthetic aspect. In fact, this practice is universal and the Louvre only "speaks" to visitors who have been prepared for it by their education – that is, Europeans (or rather some of them) and not the others who only see the beauty of the works. But is not the aesthetic emotion the best starting point for seeking to understand the culture from which they sprang?

The concept of art has gotten considerably larger. Folk art, photography and industrial design have entered the museums. The old European division between the "fine arts" and the "decorative arts" has proved groundless. The aim of the fine arts was the representation of the beautiful, especially plastic beauty (architecture, drawing, painting and sculpture); the decorative arts – also called the "minor arts" – were utilitarian. As if the utilitarian could not be beautiful, as if the decorative did not need to seek out appropriate forms. This division is so open to criticism that several authors have attempted to replace it with less problematic systems. These attempts, although they have not been crowned with success, attest at least that this classification belongs to the past just like that between the "liberal arts" (in which the mind plays the principal role) and the "mechanical arts" (which require manual labor): if what counts is beauty, it may be found everywhere. In reality, this classification is specific to modern Europe and dates back to the Renaissance. Its propagation smacks of ethnocentrism.

Apparently, this division does not exist elsewhere. In ancient Greece, ceramics were as highly esteemed as painting and sculpture. In Egypt, statues and painted bas-reliefs were designed to be integrated into the temple, in relation to its masses, lines and the amount of light it received. South of the Sahara, the arts are divided according to two principal functions: the ritual and the everyday. The ritual includes statues and masks of ances-

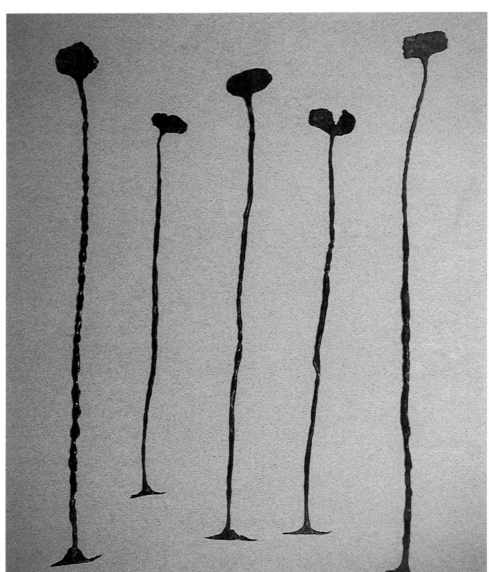

15

tors and spirits; the everyday is made up of objects used in courts and villages: chairs, containers, musical instruments, arms, cloth and jewelry. These are not without symbolic meaning. The Dogon door is decorated with protective mythical figures; the headrest enables the sleeper to communicate with the great beyond. In China, the "four arts" comprised music, poetry, painting and calligraphy. For a long time, calligraphy was considered superior to painting. It should be noted that it has nothing to do with Latin calligraphy, which only sought to decorate letters. On the contrary, Chinese calligraphy is a set of forms and movements whose main aim is to express life; this may only be achieved after a long apprenticeship to develop one's inner personality. Painting included the decoration of ceramics; sculpture included working terracotta, metal and jade. The carving of seals is, unlike in Europe, not considered a minor art. The artist carefully chooses the stone on which he will inscribe characters as elegantly as possible in the different types of script. Famous painters began their careers by practicing this craft. This type of carving was even more important in ancient Mesopotamia where cylinder seals were invented at the same time as writing towards the end of the fourth millennium B.P. for the same reason as in China: the need to authenticate documents. Intaglio engravings, these seals feature a wide variety of subjects: animal friezes, religious or battle scenes and deities. Rolled over wet clay, they reveal "imaginary basreliefs" as the name of a 1973 Paris exhibition suggests. They are only a few inches

Baluster vase in blackish brown stoneware decorated with splashes of ochre. H: 29.5 cm. Henan, China, Yuan period (13th – 14th c.).

Gold pectoral disc
with repoussé circles,
perhaps a stylized face.
D: 13 cm. Flores,
Indonesia.

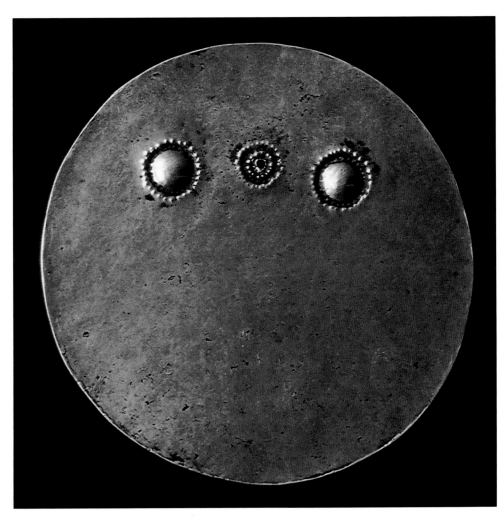

while painters and sculptors only imitate nature, does not occupy the same place in Islam because only God is a creator and because the relationship between solids and voids is less important than that which adorns the walls: mosaics made of stucco or ceramic, calligraphy and arabesques, the wood and mother-of-pearl marquetry of the pulpits.

Living in precarious conditions, the people of Oceania knew how to use all the resources, mainly plant and marine, of their environment to enrich their social and religious life. The "art" of these objects is not independent of their functions. The same remark may be applied to Amerindians whose textiles, ceramics and metalwork, produced with rudimentary technology, have not been surpassed.

The example of pottery demonstrates that the "labor of the mind" is no less considerable in an art qualified as "minor" in Europe than in the so-called "fine arts." In China, the excellence achieved during the Song dynasty (10th-13th centuries) was the result of centuries of research with regards to the material, the firing, the glazes, the decoration, the colors and the synthesis of outside influences from Iran and India and indigenous, Taoist and Confucian designs. The great English potter Bernard Leach, who was born in China and worked in Japan for 11 years, wrote:

"According to the degree to which the vital forces of the potter and that of his culture behind him flow through the process of making, the resulting pot will have life in it or not... Beauty of ceramic form, which is

long, proving that smallness is not incompatible with monumentality.

In Byzantium, sculpted ivory, cloth, objects in precious metals and enamelwork were considered art. In Islam, the art of the book is art *par excellence* because writing is the vehicle for the word of God and the depiction of human beings and animals is prohibited in religious worship so the greatest emphasis is placed on the decoration of the book and of the binding. Conversely, architecture, considered since the time of the ancient Greeks as the principal art in the West because it participates in creation

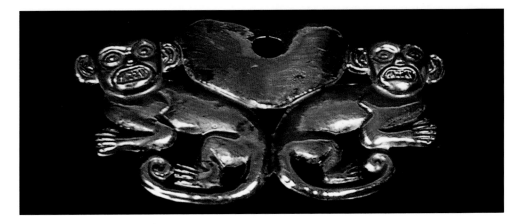

Nose ornament
(*nariguera*) depicting
two monkeys.
Openwork gold.
H: 4.5 cm x W: 9.5 cm.
Mochica, Peru, 400-800.

17

at once subjective and objective, is obtained in much the same manner as in abstract (rather than representational) sculpture. It is subjective in that the innate character of the potter, his stock and his tradition live afresh in his work; objective in so far as his selection is drawn from the background of universal human experience" (Leach, 17-20).

In reality, the difference is between art and industry. Sales oriented, it caters to the tastes of the greatest number of people which risks being an absence of taste. Even if some designers have been able to discover attractive forms and motifs, 90 percent of European industrial production is, according to Leach, "hopelessly bad."

It could even be said that ceramics are superior to painting in the sense that the pleasure offered is not only visual, but also tactile: a bowl or cup invites a caress of a hand to appreciate the regularity or irregularity of the contours, the smoothness or roughness of the material. In China, the emperors created factories whose output was reserved for the court. In Japan, lines of potters succeeded each other alongside those of tea masters who often inspired them. The *raku*, black or red ceramic ware with a thick glaze and sober decoration fired at 750°C, takes its name, "pleasure," from the ideogram engraved on a golden seal that Hideyoshi offered to its inventor Chojiro, who was of Korean descent, in 1598. *Raku* was sought out by tea masters because when they took it in their hands, they took pleasure in its material and the warmth of the beverage. Hegel was wrong indeed to exclude touch from the list of aesthetic sensations.

Jewelry is also an art that fully merits the name. The West only considers it from the angle of its decorative function and social distinction. Actually, it is a universal demand for communitarian and personal identity and not a luxury. The first ornamentation was that of the human body. From the head to the feet, it takes very different forms and sometimes, at first sight, is not very functional. In Africa and India, the heavy bronze anklets of women, which may weigh up to twenty pounds, do not make walking any easier; in fact, they serve as a means of hoarding and as currency in matrimonial transactions. The same is true of the splendid Peul earrings that, although they are much lighter, need to be attached to a red cord passing over the top of the head. In South America, nose ornaments (*nariguera*) sometimes covered the entire mouth; ancient Peruvian nobles had to pierce their earlobes in order to wear golden, lapis lazuli and turquoise discs up to ten inches in diameter which are status symbols. Everywhere, jewelry and clothing class an individual according to ethnicity, birth, sex, age, marital status and function. It also offers protection from evil spirits. Materials of plant and animal origin blend with stones and metals, both ordinary and precious. Jewelry ranges from the most simple, such as Papuan shell pectoral discs, to the most ornate, such as some Berber necklaces made of coral, amber, coins, shells, glass beads, silver hands of Fatima and cloisonné amulets.

Amerindians modeled, molded or lost-wax cast veritable sculptures in gold, silver, tumbaga, shell, lapis lazuli and turquoise – pendants and pectoral discs with stylized animal or human figures, masks and earrings engraved with figures, religious or warrior scenes. More than any other people, Amerindians displayed virtuosity in their use of all the wealth of colors in feathers to decorate the dress of kings, warriors and shamans not only for their beauty, but also for the magical properties that they were alleged to possess: inspiring love or triumphing over an adversary. The people of Oceania fashioned magnificent jewels from tortoiseshell and shells, which also provided them with dye, vessels, tools, arms and currency (cowries).

In several countries in the Americas, in central, south and southeast Asia, textiles are a major art form whose colors and themes may be compared to those of painting. Textiles are not only a status symbol and an element of interior decorating, but are also used in matrimonial exchanges and by the state to reward civil servants and as diplomatic gifts as well as to accompany the dead. The West has recently rediscovered the art of textiles. For a long time, the privileged position of tapestry, considered as the only artistic cloth, made textiles an annex of painting. Because of an increase in knowledge and a better understanding of other cultures – ancient Peru in particular – textiles have been recognized as an art in its own right and a vehicle for meanings and values. Artists are experimenting with various methods in order to create with this very supple material new graphic, pictorial and even sculptural languages (Thomas et al., 1985).

India does not classify the arts but aesthetic sensations in the theory of the *rasas*.

Couple in a garden by the water. In the background, a town at the foot of a mountain under clouds. Miniature on paper. H: 27 cm x W: 20 cm. Kishangar, India, 19th c.

Head of a man, mouth
wide open, long neck.
Terracotta. H: 22 cm,
Base diameter: 8.5 cm.
Sao, Chad, 11th-15th c.

Head of a man, holes as eyes and
mouth; on both sides of the
central bridge, two parallel oblique
lines descend to the upper lip.
Terracotta.
H: 12 cm x W: 9.5 cm. Bura, Niger
Valley, Burkina Faso, 11th-14th c.

Head of a man, ears pricked
up, protruding eyes and
mouth wide open.
Terracotta. H: 12 cm,
Base diameter: 6.5 cm.
Sao, Chad, 11th-15th c.

Head of a man-fish, the human face
punctuated with small triangles,
slits for the eyes and mouth,
surmounted by a fish head with bulging
eyes. Black traces of calcination.
Terracotta. H: 15.5 cm x Max. W: 9 cm.
Sao, Chad, 11th-15th c.

Large jar with neck and
two small handles
decorated with a stylized
frog motif, symbol of
fertility. Terracotta.
H: 35 cm, Neck
diameter: 12 cm.
Yangshao culture. China,
Late 5th – early 4th
millennium B.P.

This term, which means "flavor," is used for the feeling that a literary or visual work inspires. About ten feelings are distinguished: love, gaiety, sadness, furor, heroic exaltation, terror, disgust, marvel, affection and serenity. The erotic feeling (*shringara*) is the foremost *rasa*. It is felt when the artist depicts in the theater, in a poem or in a miniature reunited or separated lovers such as Rama and Sita in the *Ramayana* or in front of the sculptures of couples in Khajuraho or Konarak. In fact, the theory was formed in relation to the theater in the 3rd or 4th century and was extended to poetry and art. In his introduction to his *Lectures on Aesthetics* (1818-1829), Hegel reminds us that aesthetics (from the Greek *aisthetikos*, feeling) means the science of sensibility, the science of feeling and that, when it appeared in Baumgarten's *Aesthetica* (1750-1758), as a new science "in Germany at the time, works of art were considered in relation to the sensations they were supposed to inspire: for example, the sensations of pleasure, admiration, terror, pity, etc."

Matter and form

Each people favors a certain material as a function of its environment, its beliefs, its technology and its economic activities. The material, for its part, influences the form. The artist chooses it according to a certain representation of the work he carries within him. Wood lends itself to all manner of expression while marble lends itself to contemplation. According to Brancusi, "The material should keep its natural life when it is transformed by the sculptor's hand… It must not be submitted to preconceived ideas or forms. The texture itself must command the theme and the form, both of which must emerge from the material and not be imposed from the outside."

For his part, Henri Focillon underlined the reciprocal relationship between the aptitudes of the material and the talent of the artist who gives it life according to his own thinking:

"Materials have a certain destiny or, if you like, a certain formal vocation. They have a consistency, a color, a grain. They are forms and, by the same token, they call, limit or develop the life of art forms. They are chosen not only for the convenience of the work, or, to the extent that art serves the needs of life, for their proper use, but also because they give rise to a particular treatment, because they produce certain effects. Thus their form, entirely raw, arouses, suggests, propagates other forms and, to repeat an apparently contradictory expression, because they liberate them according to their law. But it should be noted without further delay that this formal vocation is not blind determinism because – and this is the second point – these materials, so well characterized, so suggestive and even so demanding as regards art forms on which they exercise an attraction, find themselves in return profoundly changed" (52).

Ceramics is the most widespread art as clay (*keramos* in Greek) exists everywhere; this is not the case with wood and stone. Egypt and Mesopotamia, where the first civilizations developed, constructed their tem-

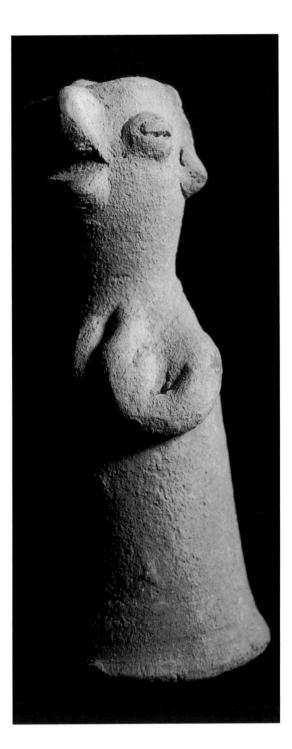

Mother goddess, hands joined between her breasts. Terracotta. H: 15 cm. Pakistan, Bajaur Valley, 2nd millennium B.P.

23

Red vessel with blackened rim. Terracotta with crystallization marks.
H: 12 m x D: 7 cm.
Predynastic Egypt, 4th millennium B.P.

decorated with waves or figurative scenes or bare, the rim blackened by placing the vase upside down in a bed of straw or ashes during or after firing. In China, the Neolithic culture of Yangshao (3000 B.P.) left behind magnificent wheel-thrown pottery made from a paste as thin as an eggshell; of its many forms, the most common is the black and red jar with two handles decorated with geometric (spirals, circles, wavy lines), human or animal motifs which, as elsewhere, symbolize life and fertility and sometimes reappear on bronze vases. In sub-Saharan Africa, if we do not take into consideration the cave paintings and engravings of the San of the southern Neolithic period, the most ancient remains are the terracotta of Nok (6th century B.P.-5th century), Yelwa (2nd-8th centuries) and Ife (11th-15th centuries) in Nigeria, Bura in Niger (9th-10th centuries), of the Sao people in Chad and of Djenne in Mali (11th-15th centuries), sometimes figurative, sometimes abstract in a quite "modern" way. Amerindian potters had no knowledge of the wheel. In the beginning, they modeled, then they molded, without any knowledge of glazing. However, their work has not been surpassed in terms of the variety of painted or incised decora-

ples, the dwelling places of their gods, in brick or in stone because they had little wood. On the contrary, the architecture of India, China and Japan featured wood, which was abundant. Clay is the most malleable material; it takes on any form that man gives it. Man has used clay from ancient times for domestic objects as well as for the walls of his home: the oldest pottery, the product of hunter-gatherers in Japan, is 12,000 years old. In the beginning, clay mixed with sand and shaped by hand was dried in the sun, which made it porous. Later inventions served to make it impermeable (the kiln, the wheel, glaze). But the quality of the object depended primarily on that of the earth. It took centuries for man to realize this, discovering the different types of clay, their composition, the way to prepare them, their

color properties during firing at different temperatures, etc. Europe knew of Chinese porcelain in the early 16th century, but only managed to manufacture it two centuries later in Meissen.

Technical improvements do not necessarily lead to beauty. The elegant forms and decoration of predynastic Egyptian vases (4500-4000 B.P.) were to be lost for a long time: red with carefully polished thin walls

Vessel with a deer head.
Brown terracotta.
H: 18 cm x L: 26 cm.
Vicus, Peru, 300 B.P.-300

tion: human, animal, plant and geometric forms. Even the simplicity of the tools used could stimulate artistic creativity.

After clay, wood and stone are the most common materials. All around the world, men have sculpted their gods and their dreams out of them. The peoples of Africa and Oceania fashioned marvelous objects for daily use by making use of all the resources of wood: forks to make three-legged stools; curves, knots and colors for boxes, cups, spoons, combs, chairs, musical instruments and, in West Africa, pulleys for weaving. Here, provided that the functions of the objects are taken into account, the artist has free reign, whereas when working on statues of ancestors or ritual masks, he is constrained by tradition. By the same token, stone has served, where it is found, in religious worship as well as to beautify everyday life. This Peruvian ceremonial cup is engraved with asymmetric profiles wearing crested headdresses, faces, four-fingered hands, serpents and altars whose meaning is unclear to us.

In Mediterranean Europe, marble has long been the material of choice of the sculptor because of its brilliance, its light reflecting finish and its "grain," comparable to that of the skin. The first civilization flowered in the third millennium B.P. in the Cyclades, which occupied a strategic position between Anatolia, Crete, mainland Greece, Western Asia and Egypt. These islands knew how to make use of the marble with which nature provided them; they worked it with corundum, which is abrasive, obsidian to make incisions and smooth out irregularities and pumice to polish. Cycladic art is celebrated

for the "modern" abstraction of their "idols" whose initially schematic form took on that of a violin before moving on to stylized naturalism. In the 20th century, great sculptors such as Brancusi continued to use marble. Of his *Seal*, a critic wrote: "the white lines in blue-gray marble crisscross the whole body and become like the sound, the powerful voice of the animal. There is such an identification between the animal and the material that one can feel its wet skin vibrate and imagines hearing a sound is coming out of its mouth" (Hulten, in *Constantin Brancusi,* 92).

Jade is another stone that was only used by certain civilizations. Its name comes from the Spanish conquistadors who discovered it in America and called it *piedra de hijada* (flank stone) because, as it was cold to the touch, it was thought to cure lumbar inflammations. *Hijada* became jade and its Latin scientific name is *lapis nephreticus.* Nephrite is the genuine jade. A natural silicate of aluminum, calcium and magnesium, it is softer than jadeite, a natural silicate of aluminum and sodium. Jadeite is more abundant than nephrite in Central America where Olmecs, Nicoyans, Totonacs, Huaxtecs, Mixtecs, Mayas, Teotihuacans and Aztecs successively used it to make masks, statuettes and axes. On the other side of the Pacific, Maoris sculpted *mere*, which chieftains wore around their necks as symbols of their authority, earrings for men, elongated tubes, and *heitiki*, pendants in the shape of a figure whose huge tilted head and protuberant eyes sit directly on top of a body with shortened limbs, out of jade. The most beautiful jades, however, come from China where they have

Stylized human figure: big nose, semi-circular ears, round mouth; three bulges representing breasts and navel. Terracotta. H: 30 cm x Base W: 7.5 cm. Bura, Niger Valley, Burkina Faso, 9th – 10th c.

Oval bowl for food, the
sides incised with
geometric motifs.
Grainy wood, fine dark
brown patina.
H: 7 cm x L: 52 cm x
Max W: 29 cm.
Trobriand Islands,
Huon Gulf.

of good faith because its beautiful internal qualities may be seen from all outside; of the sky because it looks like a shining rainbow; of the earth because its emanations come from the mountains and the rivers [like those of the earth]; of virtue because the tablets and half-tablets made from it are given alone [without any accompanying gifts] by the envoys of princes and because everyone values it."

According to the 1st century *Shuo Wen* dictionary, "*Yu* (jade) is the noblest of stones and possesses four virtues. Charity is symbolized by its brilliant but warm luster, frankness by its translucence which reveals its colors and internal veining, wisdom by its pure and penetrating sound it makes when it is struck, courage by the fact that it may be broken but not bent; finally, it symbolizes equity because it has sharp edges which harm no one."

The most magnificent pieces are the ritual objects from the archaic period, rendered even more beautiful by their sojourn underground, which has left them impregnated with oxides, plant resins and sulfur. The texture and colors of this one evoke a mountain landscape shrouded in mist. In addition to the ceremonial and funerary jades, ornaments (pendants, jewels, pins, belt buckles, etc.) and amulets were also carved out of jade. These types of objects began to proliferate during the Tang dynasty and especially during the Qing dynasty. The use of the wheel, steel and diamonds and the multicolored jade imported from Burma allowed the virtuosity of the sculptor to spread to all fields. But technical finesse

been carved for more than five thousand years, initially using local material, then importing it from Central Asia, Siberia and eventually from Burma, so great was the symbolic value that was attached to it.

Jade filled the most diverse functions: a ritual object used in royal ceremonies, a substance to preserve the corpse it was buried with, an astronomical instrument, a jewel, an amulet and a decorative object. It is a source of fascination because of its color, which ranges from milky white to black via brown, yellow, red and green, with admirable veining, its smoothness and coolness, its hardness and its rareness. It can only be worked with harder stones such as quartz, garnet and corundum. In *The Book of Rites* (*Liji*), which dates from the 4th or 3rd century B.P., Confucius praised jade:

"If the sage attaches little importance to steatite and highly values jade, it is not because steatite is common and jade is rare. It is because the sages of antiquity compared virtue to jade. It is the image of kindness because it is soft and smooth to the touch; of prudence because its veining is fine and compact and it is solid; of justice because it has angles but does not wound; of urbanity because, suspended [from the belt as an ornament], it seems to descend to the earth; of music because clear, high, prolonged sounds which end abruptly are produced when it is struck; of sincerity because its luster is not veiled by its defects or vice versa;

Ceremonial bowl in greenish beige soapstone engraved with a ritual scene.
H: 4.7cm x D: 15.4cm.
Limancarro, Chavin-Cupisnique style, Peru, 900-400 B.P.

could not replace the religious inspiration of ancient times. Jade was now only decorative: this was encouraged by the tastes of the *nouveaux riches* of the Manchu dynasty. The same was true in Mogul India (16th-18th centuries) where cups, bowls and sword hilts were often set with gold and rubies.

Lacquer is a product proper to East Asia. Indian, Burmese and Singhalese lacquer is made with the gum of an insect, the *tachardia lacca*, which is deposited on trees and known as lacquer resin. It does not possess the properties of real lacquer, the sap of the lacquer tree (*rhus vernicifera*) which, originally from China, was transplanted to Viet Nam, Korea and Japan. Lacquer is extremely resistant to water, heat and acids so that, when applied to wood previously coated with varnish or cloth made out of hemp, it serves to both preserve and decorate it. Several coats (up to 30 for the most valuable pieces) are needed and care must be taken that each coat is dried in a humid environment before applying the next one. The quality of the finished object depends on that of the final layer. Lacquer is painted, sculpted and inlaid with gold, silver, bronze and tortoiseshell. The earliest lacquer dates back to the end of the Zhou dynasty (1027-256 B.C.). As early as the Han dynasty (206 B.P.-220 A.D.) their fame spread and they were exported, along with silk, throughout Asia, from Korea to the Mediterranean. The motifs were extremely varied – human, animal or geometric – and of indigenous or foreign inspiration. In Japan, lacquer appeared in the 8th century with the admirable statue of the monk Ganjin. It preserved the tech-

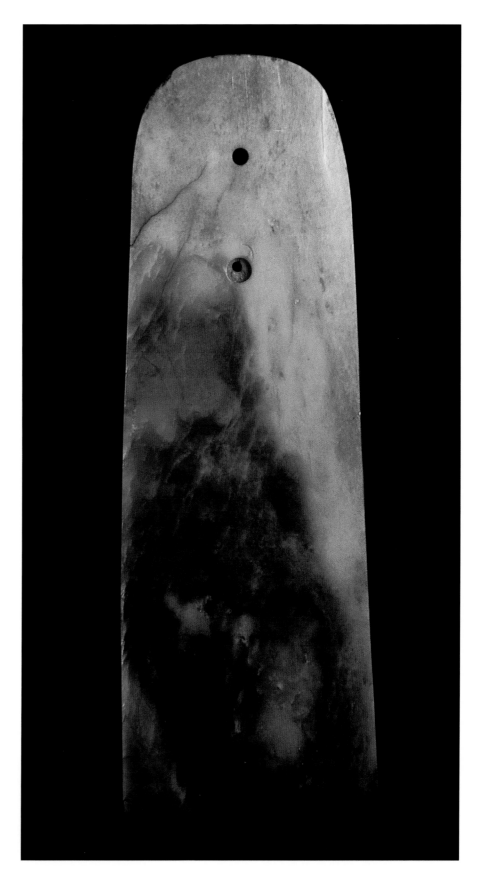

Ceremonial jade of a rusty colour, the holes serving to tie it to a belt.
H: 22.6 cm x Base W: 8 cm.
China, Zhou period.
1st millennium B.P.

30

Eagle pendant with a man's
body, wings outstretched,
holding prey. Gold.
H: 7.7 cm x L: 8.7 cm.
Diqis, Costa Rica, 600-900.

niques that were to be lost in China because of the protection of the nobility and because of the tea ceremony. The most characteristic technique is the *maki-e* in which lacquer is painted with gold or silver powder. In Viet Nam and Korea, lacquer was used essentially to cover Buddhist statues in red and gold. In the 20th century, the school of Hanoi has successfully used lacquer in painting since the 1930s.

While the lacquer tree only grows in East Asia, silk, also Chinese in origin, has spread all over the world. According to legend, the wife of the Yellow Emperor was said to have taught the people "the way of treating cocoons and silk in order to wear it" around the middle of the third millennium B.P. The oldest woven fragments that have been found date from the Shang dynasty (11th century B.P.) which makes the weaving of silk the second oldest art after pottery. Silk is the filament that is unwound from the bombyx of the mulberry tree. Extraordinarily strong, supple and soft, silk soon began to be

exported, first to Korea, Mongolia and Xinjiang, then with the opening of the road through Central Asia towards the West which appreciated the fabric "whose color resembles that of meadow flowers and whose delicacy rivals that of spider webs." Despite the efforts of the Chinese, the secret of silkworm breeding was to spread to India and Iran (2nd-3rd centuries), then to Byzantium (6th century) where several Chinese motifs were borrowed.

Paper, also invented in China (2nd century), has become the most widespread support for all sorts of paintings and drawings. The most interesting example is that of the women of Mithila in Bihar, India, the home of Buddha, who for centuries have been painting the walls of their bridal chamber, wrapping the ritual gifts and drawing magic circles on the ground during religious celebrations. From childhood, the girl learns this art from her mother because it is she who will propose to the boy by sending him a drawing symbolizing sexual union. With a rice

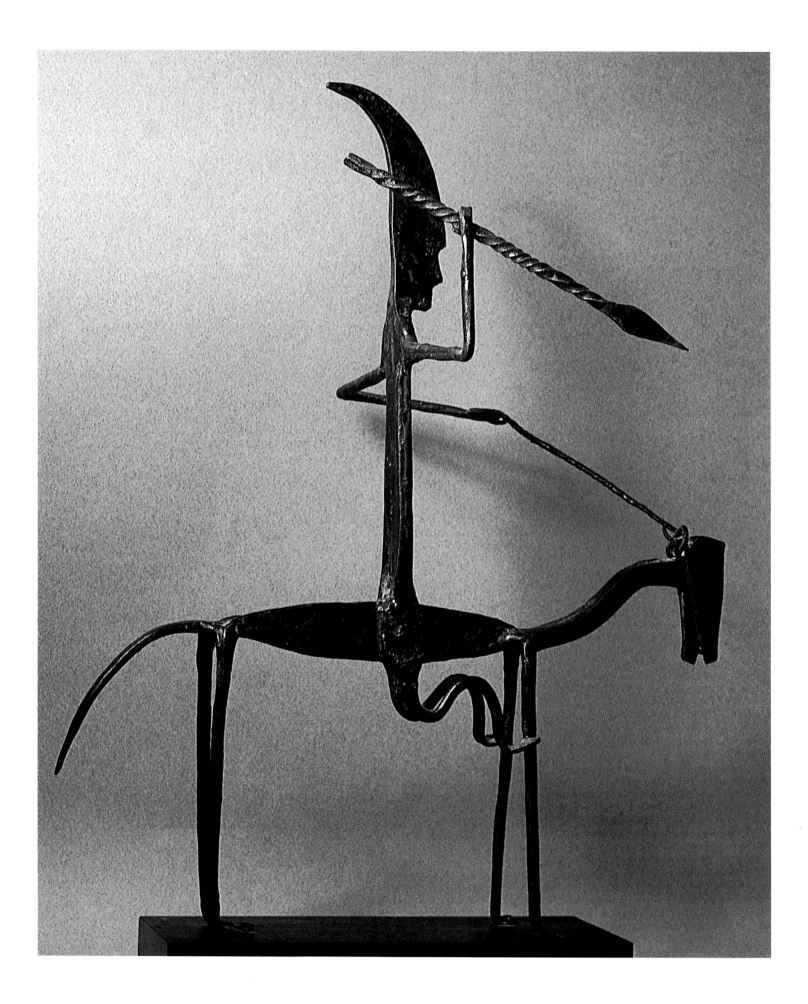

straw and a bit of bamboo wrapped in cotton, she uses black from smoke, blue from indigo, yellow from the carnation or the orpiment and red from sandalwood or iron oxide. The themes are taken from legends involving the gods, the epics of the *Mahabharata* or the *Ramayana*. Today, the tradition is partly aimed at tourists and its palette has been enlarged, but the designs have lost none of their freshness.

Copper and gold were among the first metals to be used for jewelry, arms and prestige objects. The goldsmith's trade made its appearance in Egypt in the fourth millennium B.P. and in Mesopotamia in the third millennium B.P. Strips of gold dating from the 17th-16th centuries B.P. have been found in Peru. Craftsmen developed various techniques which spread north, reaching Mexico around 900: alloys of gold, silver and copper (*tumbaga*) or platinum (La Tolita, Ecuador), lost-wax casting, the inlaying of shells and minerals (turquoise and lapis lazuli) and even a kind of electroplating that allows copper to be plated with gold and silver (among the Moche). The delicacy of the work and the inventiveness of the often fantastic themes of the Amerindians have not been equaled.

The invention of bronze, an alloy of copper and tin, at the end of the 3rd millennium B.P. in western Asia allowed more durable works, most often associated to the worship of the dead, to be cast. Luristan is famous for the objects that nomads buried in the tombs of their chiefs or that farmers presented at their temples: statuettes of genies overcoming monsters, statuettes of goddesses whose

hands are on their bare chests, weapons, harnesses, cups and jewels. The ritual vases, decorated with geometric and stylized animal motifs, used for offerings of food and wine to ancestors of the Shang and Zhou dynasties of China are well known. Bronze would later be used to cast Buddhist statues as well as everyday objects such as this perfectly curved Korean spoon ending in a swallow's tail.

Africa is justifiably proud of the bronzes of Ife and Benin, cast in lost wax, that exalt their kings and queens. This technique is still used by the Akan, the Senufo and the Fon. Bronze is a noble material and every important person owed it to himself to own several objects which he ordered from the blacksmith. They indicated his social status, served as amulets and set out proverbs whose problematic interpretation made the listener feel inferior. The Akan (Ashanti, Anyi, Baule) used figurative and geometric weights to weigh gold dust, pay taxes, and convey sayings and messages for 500 years (1400-1900). Each has several possible meanings of which many have disappeared as the traditions have been lost. For the Ashanti, royal authority was symbolized by the golden stool; a bronze reproduction signified "the king dies, the throne is eternal."

The following are proverbs reported by Niangoran-Bouah.

A tambourine player: "Drummed language goes where no road leads."

A coleopteron (maybug, ground beetle) signifies a need for vigilance. Coleopterons live in the trunks of dead trees. When a farmer wants to prepare his field, he burns

Bamboo flute decorated with rows of triangles painted in reddish brown. L: 82 cm, Vanuatu.

Rider on horse carrying a spear. Iron covered with a rust-resistant coat. H: 36.4 cm x L: 30.5 cm. Bamana, Mali.

33

Painting on paper
of a married couple
on an elephant.
H: 75 cm x W: 55 cm.
Mithila, Bihar, India.

Maya ceremonial
calabash.
H: 25 cm x Diam. 5 cm.
Guatemala, late 19th c.

them. The insects that do not take heed risk death.

A game of *awari* (it consists of circulating pebbles over two rows of compartments): "He who is not free does not play *awari*." Allusion to a king so passionate about the game that he was surprised by his enemies and killed.

Birds on the same pedestal: "When birds of the same species meet, they do not underestimate each other." Advice on modesty for he who might think himself superior to his fellows.

Although more difficult to work, iron was used to create masterpieces of abstraction such as this Lobi antelope. And isn't this Bamana horseman reminiscent of Picasso? His raised right hand holds a lance and he wears imposing headgear. These iron pieces are emblems of power which were the privilege of the chieftains. The material itself secretes an occult energy because of the blacksmith's labor and the magic substances it received at the moment of sacrifice. Placed

around altars, they were taken out and brandished by dancers to the sound of drums during festivals (McNaughton, 125-126).

The calabash is an important fruit in Africa because, soft in consistency, it may be molded by tying when it is growing. Emptied and dried, it is used to store seeds, liquids, clothing and jewelry. It evokes the kitchen, abundance and fertility and is a symbol of woman, the mother and the home. This is why it is decorated with great care, often with geometric or animal pokerwork motifs. The calabash originated in the Americas where the Mayas of Guatemala still used it for their ceremonies at the end of the 19th century: this one, decorated with a procession of priests, was used to hold chocolate or other ritual drinks. Nowadays, the inhabitants of the Andes carve scenes of their work and celebration on calabashes for their own pleasure and for tourists.

In reality, any material, whether rare or ordinary, may be a source of beauty in the right hands.

The universal and the particular

The new millennium allows us to the opposite approach to Hegel: based not on a metaphysical idea, but in the works of all the cultures that are brought into our homes by television, books and CD-ROMs, that we may see in museums, exhibitions and the cinema and even travel in order to contemplate them *in situ*. As Malraux wrote in *La métamorphose des dieux*, "Humanity had only known worlds of art that are exclusive like religions; ours is an Olympus where

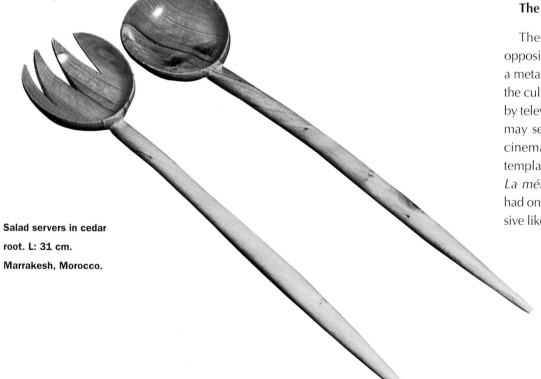

Salad servers in cedar
root. L: 31 cm.
Marrakesh, Morocco.

all the gods and all the civilizations address themselves to all the people who hear the language of art" (34).

The basic hypothesis is that all peoples have an idea of beauty that they realize in various ways according to their beliefs and customs as well as the materials and techniques at their disposal and that some universal criteria may be found in their creations.

This hypothesis is founded on the unity of human kind. It is striking to note how similar from one end of the planet to the other, although the periods do not coincide, the lines of tools in cut or polished stone, pottery for storing food, cave paintings and sculptures of mother goddesses are. It is because the ends are simple and the same everywhere: subsistence and survival and, to this end, the propitiation of invisible forces. There is an accord between thought and gesture to fashion appropriate forms: pointed to strike or pierce, round to contain and conserve. These forms are beautiful and pure because they are reduced to the essential; this quality would be rediscovered by the great artists of our time as they would rediscover the conscious deformation with a view to revealing the hidden. But matter is also beautiful. These Javanese axes from the 5th or 4th millennium B.P. seem to have been lovingly polished after the stone had been chosen with care for its texture and veining.

Fertility is the universal value, whether it is manifested in wall paintings that are sexual in nature or about hunting or in statuettes of mother goddesses or "Venuses" with accentuated breasts, bellies and hips. In South America – isolated for so long from the rest of the world – the oldest ceramic figures found there, in Valdivia, Ecuador (3500-1500 B.P.), are charming female figurines, about four inches tall, sometimes with two heads, always standing and nude, heavy-breasted and wearing headdresses with parallel ridges. During about the same period, the Chinese of Yangshao half-buried large jars which contained their provisions in the earth: the powerful strokes decorating their shoulders depicted frog's legs. Frogs, creatures of the water, symbolized fertility. There is a striking similarity of the hunting and breeding scenes found in the caves of France, Spain, the Sahara, southern Africa and South America: the brushstroke is the same everywhere, only the animals depicted change, not to mention the analogous symbols, notably the hands that are colored or in reserve.

As material civilization develops and economic and social structures become more complex, the arts are diversifying. But cultures do not remain closed: they are constantly influenced by war, trade and travel for religious or political reasons. Borrowed elements are adapted to the environment and spirit of each people: Angkor and Borobudour have no equivalents in India, Korean, Japanese and Vietnamese architecture, painting and ceramics may be differentiated from the Chinese by a certain detail or other; the Indian Gandhara has given Buddha the face of Apollo, except for the smile, but the body remains Indian. The image would be propagated itself, modifying itself each time, in China, Viet Nam, Korea and Japan. Today, after African and Oceanic masks and Amerindian sculpture, Chinese calligraphy and Zen painting are inspiring artists on both sides of the Atlantic.

The convergence of aesthetic judgments is remarkable especially when it occurs outside a community with the same culture and education. Irving Child and Leon Siroto showed photographs of Kwele masks to experts in New Haven, Connecticut – to graduate art students – and Congo-Brazzaville – to sculptors, religious leaders and art connoisseurs. On the whole, there was a correlation in the appraisals of both groups, although there were differences regarding the details. Moreover, the Kwele were not all in agreement about the "fierce" masks. While these masks are instruments of power, it is certain that the dominated do not regard them in the same fashion as the dominating (Joplin, 1971). Such experiments are still rare and their results limited, especially when they are not concerned with the objects themselves but with images of them (commenting on photographs presupposes a familiarity with them): they are nonetheless significant.

Conversely, European art forms have entered the daily culture of the South. These salad servers by a Marrakesh craftsman have lines as beautiful as those by the greatest Swedish designers. They are even more beautiful because cedar root is warmly colored and further enhanced by its veining while steel is cold and the olive tree, so common north of the Mediterranean, has a less discreet texture.

There are, of course, differences. Westerners who know how to appreciate

Wayang shadow theatre puppet. Openwork buffalo leather representing a character from the *Mahabharata*. H: 70 cm, Java, Indonesia.

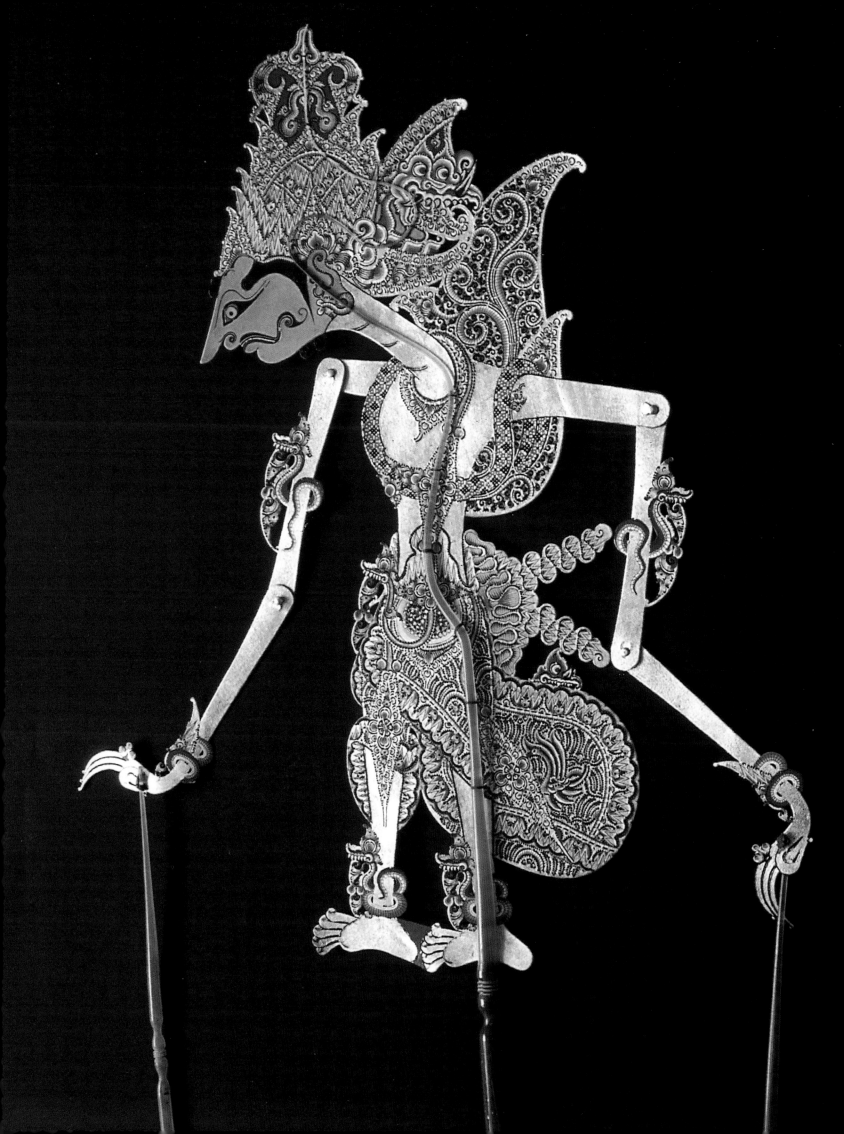

ink painting are rare in comparison to those who appreciate multicolored porcelain. For their part, East Asians have difficulty with Christian art which springs from a vision of the world different from their own. In his *Praise of the Shadow*, Tanizaki Junichiro points out some differences in taste between these two parts of the world:

"As regards Western paper we only have the impression that we are dealing with a strictly utilitarian substance, whereas we have only to see the texture of paper from China or Japan to experience a kind of warmth that puts our hearts at ease. Although equally white, Western paper differs in nature from *hosho* [Japan imperial] paper or white Chinese paper. Rays of light seem to rebound off the surface of Western paper, while the surface of *hosho* or Chinese paper, similar to the downy surface of the first snow, softly absorbs them. Moreover, pleasant to the touch, our papers fold and crumple soundlessly. They are soft and slightly moist to the touch, like a leaf on a tree.

Generally speaking, looking at a shiny object leaves us ill at ease. Westerners use – even at table – silver, steel and nickel utensils that they polish to make them shine while we loathe all that shines in this fashion. Of course we too sometimes use silver kettles, cups and bottles, but we take care not to polish them the way that they do. On the contrary, we enjoy seeing their surfaces get tarnished and, with time, completely blackened; there is scarcely a house where some ill-advised servant has not been reprimanded for having polished a silver utensil covered with a precious patina…

It is the Chinese who appreciate the stone called jade: in effect, does not one have to be East Asian like ourselves in order to find attractive these strangely troubled blocks of stone that imprison in their inmost depths fleeting and lazy glimmers as if air that is centuries old was coagulated within them? What is it then that attracts to a stone like this one, which has neither the colors of the ruby or the emerald or the sparkle of the diamond? I do not know but, looking at the cloudy surface, I feel as if, although this stone is specifically Chinese, its muddy thickness is made of alluvial deposits from the distant past of Chinese civilization, and I must admit that I am not surprised by the Chinese predilection for such colors and substances…

We do not have an a priori bias against all that glitters, but we have always preferred deep, slightly veiled, reflections to superficial and icy sparkle; that is, in natural stones as well as in man-made materials, this slightly altered brilliance that irresistibly evokes the effects of time."

In 1975, after an international symposium on literacy in Persepolis, I took a walk in Luristan and gathered an umbelliferous branch with withered leaves and flowers from the path. In the plane back to Tehran, I held on to it to the bemused surprise of my Iranian and European fellow passengers. Another time, in Viet Nam, I picked up another completely withered branch, with no leaves or flowers, whose form I found interesting. At the airport, while I was waiting for my flight, employees came to admire my branch and compliment me on it. This anecdote is not an attempt to demonstrate

the superiority of a certain group over another; it simply illustrates a difference in sensibility that has nothing to do with education or wealth. The people of East Asia, Chinese, Koreans, Japanese and Vietnamese, have a profound love of nature, most of them for the simple beauty of things – even the poorest grow plants in pots and collect stones – the educated also finding in them literary and philosophical reminiscences. That is why they grow in their gardens the "four friends of the wise man," also known simply as "the four wise men," because of the virtues that they evoke: bamboo, rectitude; the orchid, inner joy; the prunus, purity and chrysanthemum, dignity. The affinity with nature leads to the appreciation of furniture with pure lines that natural wood enhances with only its texture, veining and patina. This furniture attained perfection during the Ming dynasty (15th-17th centuries); it was in contrast to the furniture in the homes of European aristocrats that was overloaded with gold, marquetry and ostentatious sculptures. Another difference is the preference of one group for asymmetry and the preference of the other group for perfect symmetry of decoration. Let us also note the different ways of collecting. In the West, a painting is part of the decor and is exhibited to all onlookers. In East Asia, a painting is rolled up and its owner only shows it to friends whom he knows will appreciate it. The same thing is true of trade: valuable objects are not displayed in the window, but in the back of the shop where only connoisseurs enter.

Beauty has nothing to do with rarity, age

Two-headed red varnish Venus, with ridged headdress. Terracotta. H: 7 cm. Valdivia, Ecuador, 3500-1500 B.P.

or price. Rarity is the result of limited production, destruction due to natural disasters or war, the withholding of work by the artist, dealer or museums. It influences the price which also fluctuates with fashion, the state of the economy (prosperity, depression), investment and speculation. In areas such as African sculpture, Chinese jade, Persian, Indian or Turkish carpets, age is sought out because the matter is more lively and the work more creative even though it may be less technically perfect. In truth, there are always masters and apprentices, works of quality and indifferent ones. A beautiful modern African mask, such as this very expressive Wakamba mask, speaks to me more than a 19th century mask that has only the merit of being old: the artist carved it from a single piece of wood, making use of the knots to fashion the eyes and bridge of the nose. It is true that age, especially when it is associated with long use and burial in the ground, gives wood, jade, ivory and ceramics a marvelous patina that is charming to look at as well as to touch. We cannot really know these objects unless we pick them up, touch and feel them. On the other hand, painting is harmed by time: paper turns yellow, silk and canvas deteriorate and colors lose their brightness. But sometimes a painting that is cracked arouses a more profound emotion in the same way that only a single hand or a headless statue gives free rein to the imagination: Buddha's torso or the *Nike of Samothrace*. Michelangelo's *Pietà Rondanini* is even more touching because it is unfinished. And the simple, rough-hewn bust of Queen

Nefertiti in the Cairo Museum, with its sensuality and intense gaze, is superior to its counterpart in painted limestone in Berlin: it is too perfect, too highly colored and lacks the same liveliness of expression.

Whatever meaning we give to this word and whatever our aesthetic judgment of it, every art form must be analyzed in the same manner, whether the culture is literate or oral, "modern" or "primitive": a work must be explained by the historical and social conditions of its creation, taking into account the specificity of each environment and brushing aside ethnocentric preconceptions. Europe has long denied Africa the sense of beauty, so far were its works from the European ideal inherited from Greece and

Rome. In fact, while some peoples have no word for beautiful and beauty (which does not mean that they do not know it), others do as this Yoruba poem bears witness:

Whoever encounters beauty without looking at it will soon be poor.
Red feathers are the pride of the parrot.
Yellow leaves are the pride of the palm tree.
White flowers are the pride of the leaves…
The rainbow is the pride of the skies.
The beautiful woman is the pride of her husband.
Children are the pride of the mother.
The moon and the stars are the pride of the sun.

Wakamba mask in
***muhuru* wood. H: 55cm.**
Nairobi, Kenya, 1968.

Ifa says: beauty and all kinds of good fortune are on their way.
(quoted in Delange, 1970)

An echo of this song may be found on the other side of the Atlantic in the Navajo *Night Song*:

In beauty, happily I walk
With beauty before me I walk
With beauty behind me I walk
With beauty below me I walk
With beauty above me I walk
With beauty all around me I walk
It is finished again in beauty
It is finished in beauty.
(Berlaut and Kahlenberg, 1)

Like the ancient Egyptians and Greeks, the people of Oceania and Africa link beauty to good and ugliness to badness; the beauty of an object contributes to its function. The Egyptians described a beautiful monument as *menekh*, "efficient work." By the same token, the Chokwe call good work *utombo*, "efficient and well realized." The artist cannot respond to a demand in a mechanical fashion, he needs inspiration. According to an Angolan, "It is not only the brain which directs, but, when one is sculpting, the impulses of the heart are also necessary." Others consider that an object must include a spiritual part to arouse the admiration of a public sensible to its form, meaning and usefulness (Bastin, 40). The sculptor takes into account the tropical light that "accentuates the traits, deepens the hollows even more, hardens and levels the flat sections, affirming them." Jean Gabus met a Hausa blacksmith in Niger who, having finished a dagger, was waiting for the low-angled light of late afternoon in order to judge the qualities and defects of his engraving of the blade. For him it was "the moment of truth" (Gabus, 153). Certain peoples make a division between ordinary tasks and those that must be entrusted to professionals, generally specialized blacksmiths. We could cite names of esteemed sculptors who enjoy a high place in their society. In Cameroon, noteworthy works were made by kings.

Until the 1960s, since "globalization" has affected architecture, painting and sculpture, one could easily identify the works of the world's great civilizations: an African object was easily distinguished from an Amerindian object (differentiating between the Inuit and the Indians of North, Central and South America) or a European, Chinese, Japanese or Islamic object. However, within a general manner of expression which might be attributed to the unity of civilization, there was a more or less considerable multiplicity of forms and styles, even among a single people.

In sub-Saharan Africa, this unity was founded on the predominance of subsistence farming and communal ownership of land, low-level technology, strong family ties, a belief in the correspondence of human order and natural order via the intermediary of ancestors, and the desire for the greatest intensity of life. But the unity of civilization did not prevent the development of a great diversity of styles oscillating between naturalism and abstraction. The We of the Ivory

Coast believe in a supreme being and spirits called *glae* who to act as mediators with humankind. The masks that represent them differ according to their role: the *glae* that entertain (singer, *griot*, beggar) have a realistic human or animal form, those meant to sanction (judge, warrior) have expressionistic, deformed features in order to inspire fear or terror (Gnonsoa, 66-69). For the Ibo, beauty is represented by a white female mask with regular, delicate features and a long, thin nose, the Beast by a composite half-human, half-animal mask with blood-red protruding fangs expressing brutal force (Blier, 107-113). The Dan have about twenty styles and sub-styles in the two main categories of masks for control or entertainment. Masks for entertainment are used during feasts and playlets that are often spiced with social criticism; the masks sometimes have an idealized human face and sometimes a hybrid face with a long beak-shaped nose, a full beard made of monkey hair covering the mouth which has a mobile lower jaw. These are singing masks who recount ancestors' deeds of valor, recall the importance of the hornbill identified with the culture hero who brought humanity the nut of the oil palm, the wealth of this savannah region (Verger-Fèvre).

The Pacific unifies Oceania. But its islands only cover 9 million of its 176 million square kilometers and may be divided into three main groups: Polynesia in the center (from New Zealand to Hawaii and from Fiji, Samoa and Tonga to Rapanui or Easter Island), Micronesia in the northwest (the Marianna, Marshall and Caroline Islands) and Melanesia in the southwest (Australia –

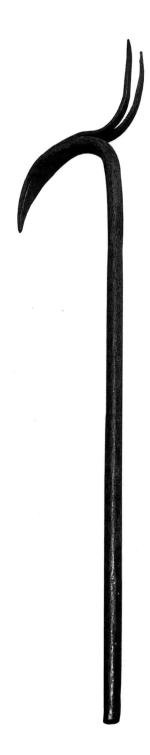

Ritual iron ending in an antelope head. L: 42 cm. Lobi, Burkina Faso.

43

7.7 million square kilometers alone – New Guinea, the Solomon Islands, Vanuatu and New Caledonia). This division roughly defines the cultural areas characterized by common traits: in Melanesia, there is a rather open social structure with societies of initiation whose ranks are marked by the arts; in Polynesia and Micronesia, hereditary hierarchies control them. Within each region innumerable styles flourish; conversely, numerous reciprocal influences due to the antiquity of migrations and exchanges, which allow us to speak of relative unity, may be detected. If we compare Oceania and Africa, which resemble each other in many ways (ancestor and spirit worship, totemism, the division of gender roles, the value of fertility and oral traditions), a statuette, a pole, ceramics, a cloth from one region may be distinguished from the other region without difficulty. The environment (the sea, navigation and vegetation), certain beliefs and techniques explain the abundant phantasmagoria of Oceania (while African art is more closely tied to the earth) and the presence of specific elements: decorated canoe prows, tree fern sculptures and overmodeled skulls.

In the Americas, there was also a highly unified civilization, perhaps even greater than Africa's, because, isolated from the rest of the world, it was not submitted to outside influences. Based on the irrigated cultivation of corn, beans, gourds and cotton, the absence of the wheel and draft animals and elementary technology, it comprised city-states governed by the

priest-kings of a religion that thought of time as a succession of cycles in which the present reflected the past. Despite this unity, a multiplicity of cultures flourished, resulting in an extraordinary diversity of artistic styles: the monumentality of Olmec heads, the abstraction of Mezcala figures, the classicism of Teotihuacan masks, the humor of Colima human and animal statuettes, the baroque Zapotec urns, the sumptuousness of Maya bas-reliefs and the fantastic power of Aztec divinities, to speak only of Mesoamerica.

Conversely, India and China presented a face with less contrast (Europe occupied an intermediary position). This may be attributed to the fact that the unity of civilization there was reinforced by three factors we do not encounter elsewhere, at least, not to the same degree: the unity of the political structure despite periods of division while Oceania, Africa and the Americas were constantly divided between numerous kingdoms and chiefdoms, the unity of the domi-

nant social class – the literate civil servants of China, the Brahmans of India – whose strong ideology was accepted by the population as a whole and, lastly and perhaps above all, the same basic *written* language – Han in China, Sanskrit in India – that was the vehicle for the educational system based on the same books – Confucian classics on one side, the *Veda* on the other. One cannot insist too much on the unifying power of language, writing and education to which Islam, the latest great civilization, also bore witness. The Koran played an analogous role beyond the differences in political and social systems. Western Europe experienced greater artistic unity in the

Middle Ages under the reign of Christianity and Latin than since the Renaissance when the power of the Church began slowly to disintegrate and nationalities began to develop.

But, as stated above, cultural unity has nowhere impeded the diversity of styles, including within a country, however ethnically and linguistically homogenous it is. Thus, the simple architecture of Japanese houses and gardens is celebrated. However, at Nikko, the solid structure of the temple of Tokugawa Ieyasu, Japan's peacemaker, is covered in violent red and gold colors (it is true that the Tokugawa line is a recent one). While the Zen-inspired tea ceremony elevated rustic bowls to the rank of works of art, merchants who made their fortunes in the 17th and 18th centuries preferred shiny Kakiemon porcelain or the even flashier Imari and Satsuma porcelain. And it would suffice to mention the contrast in the same period between the ink painting of literati (*bunjinga*) and the images of "the floating world" (*ukiyo-e*), the most well-known of which are the woodblock prints, the flourishing of which is explained by the same sociological factor, the increasing wealth of the Osaka and Edo (Tokyo) middle classes (*chonin*).

Diversity comes not only from the different ways of thinking of various social groups, but also the materials and techniques at their disposition. The adornment of the body, which is the first visual art form, still exists among peoples who live close to nature while others have covered their nudity under the influence of religious (original sin for Christians) or philosophical doctrines (Confucianism in East Asia). Young Bororo Peul males in Niger use red, black and white makeup on their faces for male beauty contests during annual feasts that also include oratory competitions. Because of their arid or desert environment, the Aborigines of Australia express themselves more through painting than through sculpture, while the people of Oceania have created the most exuberant and most fantastic artistic universe with the local vegetation. And no people has surpassed Amerindian weavers and silversmiths.

Among this abundance of forms, colors and expressions are there ideals that are shared, if not by all, by most civilizations? If the same criteria for beauty are found in different regions and during different moments in history, is this not an objective basis to claim that beauty, contrary to what Kant wrote, can be conceptualized? The notion remains, let us not dissemble, subjective. The criteria that appear to me are those to which I am sensitive because of my education and my culture. The aesthetic emotion I feel in front of an object may not be shared by others, including within the group that produced it. Let us accept it. Did not Baudelaire write, "To be just, that is to have its raison d'être, criticism must be partial, passionate and political, that is made from an exclusive point of view, but from the point of view that opens the most horizons."

This blend of the objective and the subjective reflects, at a higher level, that of the universal and the particular. The universal because each civilization, each people creates beauty. The particular because this beauty is manifested in works whose form and content differ, conditioned as they are by the historical, spiritual, social, economic and technical milieu as well as by the material and the human labor. It seems to me that four qualities are to be found everywhere: purity of line, harmony of color, movement and rhythm, and a sense of the invisible. These are analytical categories. In reality, a beautiful work evokes more or less profound resonances. A pin from Luristan or a Somali headrest assert themselves simply through their lines in the same way that a nomad carpet pleases the eye only because of the harmony of its colors. But Chinese or Arab calligraphy suggests all the rhythm of the world. A Cycladic head or a Yohure mask are not only pure forms, they ask, like the Zen garden of sand and stones, questions about the mystery of life.

Dance mask.
Hard wood,
brown lacquered patina.
H: 24.5 cm x L: 16 cm.
Dan, Ivory Coast.

Bird, protector of the
house. White stone
H: 14cm x L: 26cm.
East Timor.

Purity of Line

A geometric abstraction, the line is doubtless at the origin of art when, in the Paleolithic era, men modeled the first figurines, traced their first signs and drew animals on the walls of their caves. Line delimits a space that color will animate. But, more than fertility statuettes and cave painting, it was the fashioning of axes and the invention of pottery that marked the appearance of the creative being who made tools for living out of stone and clay. As soon as form was born out of formlessness, its beauty has preoccupied humankind.

Every culture would give its own conception of beauty. From the hand that makes things, we would progress to the stylus, the brush, the pen and the quill. A common characteristic was the search for purity, that is, for the essence or what the Chinese call the "internal principle" of things. However, the "essence" is not understood in the same way everywhere. It depends on the dominant ideology meaning the whole of the ideas and beliefs of a society at a given moment of its history. Its transformation into forms is not independent of the materials and techniques at its disposal. The era affects creation without determining it. The great artist is often the artist who breaks with the norm, is ahead of his time and prefigures the future.

The unity and diversity of ways of thinking

The dialectic of unity and diversity may be illustrated by a comparison of two regions particularly rich in terms of their art and the literature about it: China and the West. This is only one example. It does not exhaust the

Tutelary heron decorating the poles surrounding the ancestors' enclosure. Dense wood. H: 117cm. Êdê, Viet Nam.

Mahmud, Calligraphy in the shape of a parrot. Paper. H: 21.5cm x L: 35cm. Isfahan, Iran, 1917.

Ceramic bowl decorated with a brown and yellow crested bird on a cream background. Diam: 17cm. Nishapur, Iran, 10th c.

subject. Universal art is greater than the sum of these two cultures. What is missing, unfortunately, is information, particularly about oral cultures, which will not stop us from mentioning them along the way.

Summing up Chinese thinking about painting (which also applies to sculpture), Li Rihua (1565-1635) wrote:

"For the representation of an object or a scene, it is more important to capture the *shi* (lines of strength) than the *xing* (external form); it is more important to capture the *yun* (rhythm or resonance) than the *shi*; it is more important to capture the *xing* (nature or essence) than the *yun*. The external form is round, square, hollow, flat, etc.; it may be entirely rendered by the brush. The lines of strength reside in the internal thrust which animates the object with its syncopated or continuous, circular or broken movement; the brush can also outline them, but it would be better if it did not do so too completely. In order to give the object an aura, the painter has to take care to integrate the virtual into his work with the brush and the ink. Beyond the lines of strength there is, as we have mentioned, the resonance that only a free and sovereign spirit will know how to capture. As for the essence, it is what links every object (or subject) to its Heaven in itself. The painter apprehends it, not by a solely voluntary act, but by illumination which only comes if he has fully mastered his art.

In painting, it is important to know how to hold back and also to leave out. Knowing how to hold back consists in outlining the contour and the volume of things with brushstrokes. But, if the painter uses continuous or rigid strokes, the painting will be deprived of life. In the tracing of forms, although the goal is to arrive at a plenary result; all the art of its execution lies in the intervals and fragmentary suggestions and thus the need to leave things out. This implies that the painter's brushstrokes are interrupted (not the breath that animates them) better to take on implications. Thus a mountain can comprise unpainted patches and a tree can dispense

50

Pottery fragment decorated with a walking bird incised into a yellow background. 8cm x 8cm. Fostat, Egypt, 12th c.

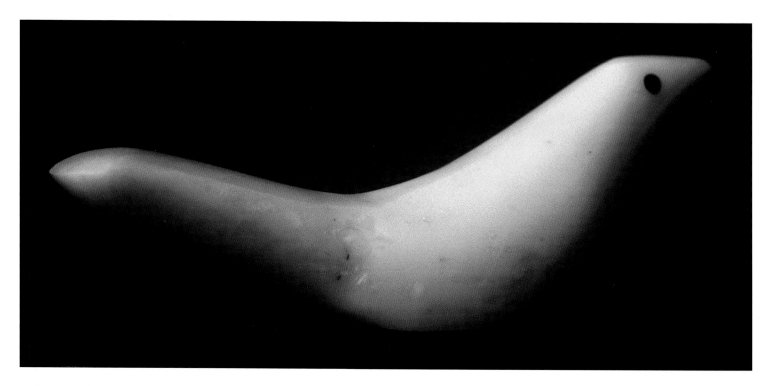

with some of its foliage so that they remain in this state of becoming between being and not being" (in Cheng, 1989, 174-175).

As it is a question of seizing the essence and not the resemblance, the careful style (*gong bi*) is considered inferior to that which "expresses the idea (*xie yi*) without the brush having to go to the end of its course" (Leys, 52), that is, by a minimum of strokes that evoke and suggest.

A remarkable convergence may be found between these ideas and those of contemporary Western artists (in contrast to the illusionists of the past) about the necessity both to observe nature (including man) and transcend it. Picasso, who deformed the real, but always on purpose, said, "I always aim for resemblance. A painter must observe nature but never confuse it with painting. It cannot be translated into painting except by signs."

"Brushstrokes that have no meaning will never make a painting. I too make brushstrokes and sometimes it could even be said that it is abstraction... but they always signify something: a bull, an arena, the sea, the mountain, the crowd... To arrive at abstrac-

tion, one must always start with concrete reality."

"It is necessary for nature to exist in order to be able to violate it."

The Chinese painter did not copy nature either. Su Shi (1036-1101) wrote, "My bamboos do not include sections. What is strange about this? They are bamboos born in my heart and not the bamboos that the eyes content themselves with observing outside."

Before Henri Matisse insisted on the "essential characteristics of the model," Ingres had declared:

"The more the line and forms are simple, the more beauty and strength there is... One should not preoccupy oneself with inessentials; they must be sacrificed to the essential, and the essential is the form, the contour, the modeling of faces... When studying nature, only have eyes for the whole. Question it and question only it. The details are of little importance and must be made to conform to the logic of the work... Beautiful forms are those with firmness and fullness and whose details do not compromise the aspect of the large masses."

And according to Joshua Reynolds,

"The detail of particulars, which does not assist the expression of the main characteristics, is worse than useless, it is mischievous, as it dissipates the attention and draws it from the principal point... It is expressing the general effect of the whole which alone can give to objects their true and touching character... When the general effect only is presented to us by a skillful hand, it appears to express the object represented in a more lively manner than the minutest resemblance would do."

If the East and the West agree on the principles, the manner of applying them differs. In China, painting is closely related to calligraphy and the first characters were pictograms inspired by observing things. *Ren*, human being, was written with five strokes depicting the body, the two arms and two legs, then has been reduced to two. In the same way, *shan*, mountain, was represented by three peaks, then by three strokes. One learns to handle, or rather to maneuver, the brush in by turning it, coordinating one's movements and exploring its speed and slow-

52

Small bird in white onyx. L: 12cm. Casablanca Souk, Morocco, 1987.

ness. According to Su Shi, "There is no established rule about holding a brush. The essential is that the palm of the hand is hollowed and the fingers rigid and firm… Before the point touches the paper, the brush must be held vertically. But once the artist has begun his work, he must allow his brush to bend freely."

There are seven basic strokes whose mastery assures the rest:

1. The horizontal stroke (*heng*) 一 should evoke a cloud formation spreading over a thousand miles and finishing abruptly.
2. The dot (*dian*) 丶 should give the impression of a rock falling with all its force from a high cliff.
3. *Bie* 丿 , a stroke slanting from right to left, has the sharp edge of a saber or resembles a shining rhinoceros horn.
4. *Na* ㇏, the opposite stroke, slanting from left to right, resembles a wave that is breaking suddenly or a flying cloud traversed by the rumbling of thunder.
5. *Zhi* 丨 is a vertical stroke, vine stock that is very old but still firm.
6. *Wan* 亅 is a hook like the joints of a powerful bow.
7. *Ti* ㇀ is less steeply inclined and stiffer than *na*, evoking a pine tree that is leaning although it is firmly rooted. (Chiang, 112-113)

During the Song dynasty, Jiang Kui described calligraphy as an art of gesture:

"The slow gesture produces grace; the rapid gesture produces strength. However, one must possess speed to master slowness because he who limits himself to slowness without having the resources of speed will have writing that lacks life. On the other hand, the characters of he who cultivates only speed will lose face". (Billeter, 110)

During the Tang dynasty, Sun Guoting wrote, "In the work of the great calligraphers, one can see straight characters like hanging needles and round characters like dewdrops. One can also see curved characters like a lighting flash or falling stone blocks and slanting characters like birds taking flight or galloping beasts. Characters resemble dancing phoenixes, slithering snakes, steep rocks and abrupt summits. Some characters are as heavy as thick clouds while others are as light as the wings of a cicada… It seems that all this is a natural creation and not one of human skill" (Alleton, 98).

The graphic qualities of Chinese painting are a direct result of the teaching of writing. Both use the same "four treasures of the literati": brush, paper, ink and stone. The brush dates back to the 11th century B.P. at the latest: we know of the painted motifs on the Neolithic pottery of Yangshao and the painted inscriptions on the divinatory bones of the late Shang dynasty. A wide variety of animal hairs are used according to the expression required. Ink is smoke black and comes in solid sticks that are rubbed on a stone tablet in the water; the oldest sticks are worth their weight in gold as they give the deepest black, especially when they are ground on a good quality stone. The traditional date of the invention of paper is 105. Silk predated it by more than 400 years: the first known painting is a fragment of silk depicting a priestess with a phoenix and a dragon found in a tomb from the 4th or 3rd century B.P. Silk and paper have to prepared like canvas. But, while oil painting allows the artist to work progressively and make corrections and changes until the work is finished, the absorbent nature of the Chinese support implies a mark with no turning back. Thus, it demands both an absolute mastery of the instrument and the concentration of the mind on the image to be realized as the following expression sums up: "The idea comes before the painting." "It means that before commencing a work (or making the tiniest stroke), the painter possesses the idea (*yi*); thus, once the work

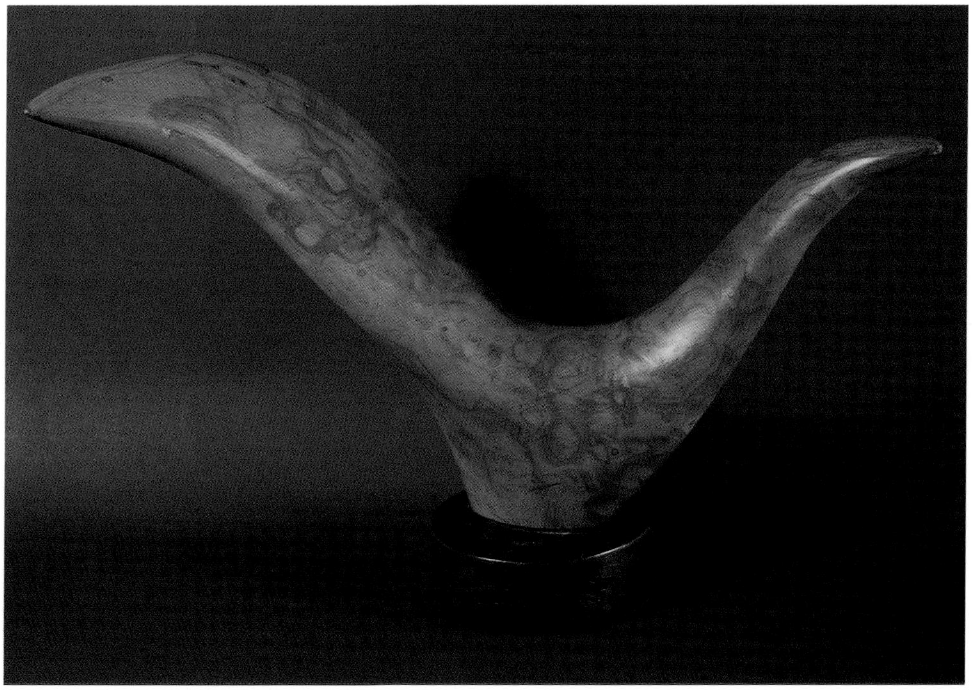

Sadik Sadiki, *Bird*.
Thuya wood. L: 30cm.
Essaouira, Morocco,
1995.

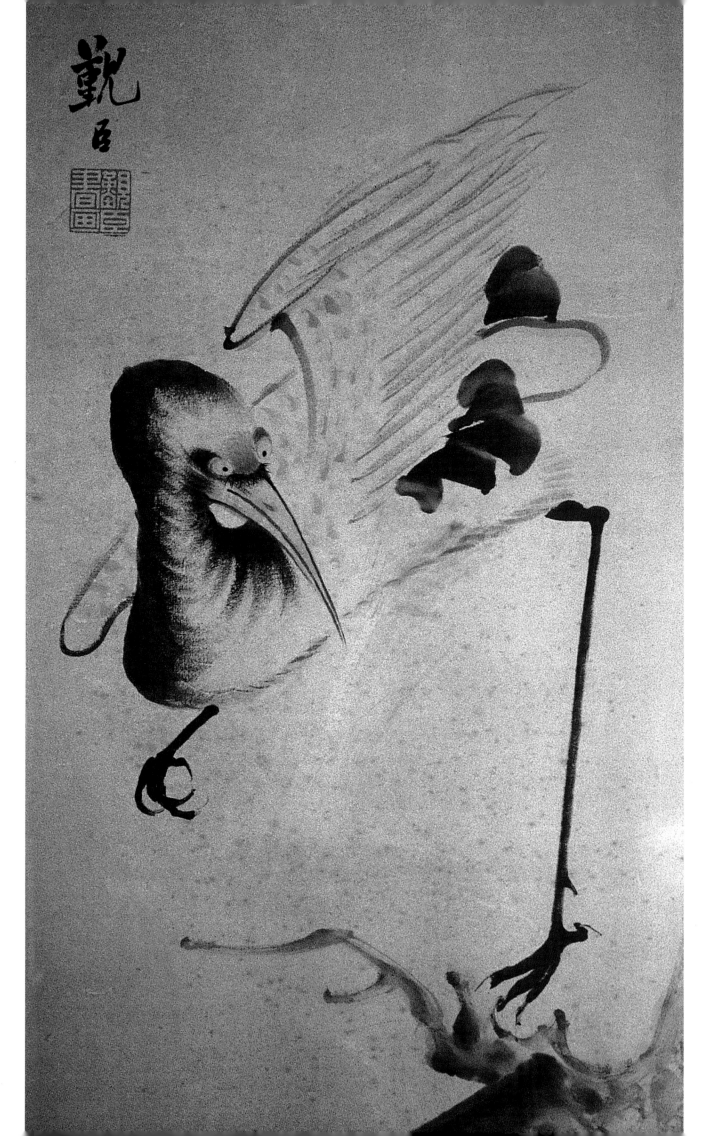

is finished, the *yi* subsists and prolongs it" (Cheng, 1989, 21).

Su Shi wrote,

"Before painting bamboo it has to grow in your heart of hearts already. That is when, brush in hand, the gaze concentrated, the whole precise vision appears before you. Seize this without delay with your brushstrokes like a falcon swoops on a hare ready to leap. An instant of hesitation and the vision will dissolve" (idem., 76).

The word *xie* means both to write and to paint. More specifically, *hua* means to draw and to paint, which demonstrates the importance attached to the brushstroke. In reality, it is neither a stroke nor a line in the Western sense of the term, when the instrument is a pen or analogous instrument. It is a form, a volume, a movement and a rhythm all at once. One learns to paint by being inspired by the brushstrokes used for characters. The first subjects are those whose forms evoked these strokes: bamboo, orchid, prunus and chrysanthemum. They also have symbolic meanings: according to Confucius, man increases his virtue by contemplating nature and thus understanding the raison d'être (*li*) of things.

Bamboo incarnates rectitude because it grows straight and is resistant to wind and rain; it is always green. Its trunk is hollow, its "heart" is "empty", that is, without attachments. It humbly accepts all the accidents of existence equally.

According to Li Rihua, "The orchid, with its long, graceful and slender long leaves and tenderly blossoming flowers is inhabited by joy." The *Manual of the Mustard Seed Garden* adds that orchid leaves have "an airy grace that floats with the wind, moving like an immortal in a rainbow dress".

The prunus flowers at the end of winter and announces the spring. Its small flowers with five petals, red, pink or white, incarnates both resistance to adversity and purity. The Zen monk Huaguang (11th century) had a veritable passion for the prunus:

"Each time the blossoming season came, he transported his couch under the trees and sang poems all day without anyone knowing his secret thoughts. One moonlit night, as he had problems sleeping, he contemplated the play of shadows on his window screen and sought to reproduce this with his brush. At dawn, he looked at his work: the thoughts of the moonlight imbued the whole of it" (Vandier-Nicolas, 184).

In the *Manual of the Mustard Seed Garden*, the chrysanthemum is described as a flower with a "proud character" because it defies the mid-autumn frost. Its straight stem possesses great dignity, even when it is painted bent.

One also learns to paint trees, notably the pine, and rocks to master *cun*, wrinkles, in order to give these stable masses "a presence that is mobile as breath and as fluid as water." They serve as an initiation to landscape painting, a major theme since the 11th century.

The portrait has a less prominent place. The category of "Characters" existed in the classification of the subjects of painting and the portrait appeared very early, during the Han dynasty, to celebrate emperors, generals and the beauties of the court; beginning in the Tang dynasty, Taoist and Buddhist

Kano Yasunobu (1613-1685), *Portrait of a Monk Holding a Fly Swatter.* **Signed Hogen Eishin. Ink on silk. H: 91cm x L: 45cm. Japan.**

monks and the people of central Asia were also depicted. However, after the blossoming of landscape painting during the Song dynasty, man was considered only as an element of "the mountains and waters" and only figured in a painting to demonstrate his smallness. What developed was the funerary portrait used in ancestor worship: men and women were depicted sitting down in a conventional pose, generally expressionless. Painting nonetheless produced a few beautiful portraits. As in Europe, it was thought that the painter had to get hold of the particular features that reflected a man's character. Gu Kaizhi (circa 344-406) said:

"The expression is primarily in the eyes, then in the cheekbones and the chin. I have often looked, by lamplight, at the shadow of my chin on the wall and asked someone to paint me this way without putting in my eyes or eyebrows. Those who saw the result could not stop themselves from laughing because they recognized me. When the eyes, cheekbones and chin are right, the rest follows because the eyebrows, the nose and the mouth may be modified to obtain a resemblance.

Portrait painting and physiognomy make up part of the same art. To discern the character of a man, one must secretly observe him in a crowd. Somewhere in each man resides his distinctive trait. For some, it is in the eyebrows, for others, in the nose or mouth. By adding three hairs to the cheek (of Pei Kai), I gave life to his portrait" (Siren, 60-61 and 12).

One of the most admirable portraits that have been preserved is that of Li Bo by Liang Kai (13th century, Tokyo, Commission for the

Protection of Cultural Heritage): a few lines of more or less black ink suffice to reveal the independence and the pride of the poet's character. It is the way of painting called "spontaneous and free" (*xie yi*) characterized by an economy of means, by suggestion rather than representation and the use of the void rather than the filled space.

In Europe, the technique differs, but not the idea:

"Make the face in such as way as to suffice to show what the person has in his soul; if not, your art will not be worthy of praise." (Leonardo da Vinci)

"In my head, the first thing for an artist to do is to make the eyes speak." (Ingres)

"If the artist only reproduces the superficial traits like photography can do, if he records exactly the various features of a physiognomy without relating them to a character, he does not deserve to be admired. The resemblance he has to obtain is that of the soul; it is the only one of any importance… In a word, all the features need to be expressive, that is, useful in the revelation of a consciousness." (Rodin)

Western art comes from a tradition long dominated by geometry and the study of the human body. It dates back to the Greeks whose motifs for ceramic vases gave the so-called geometric period its name (8th century B.P.). The Classical age (5th century B.P.) saw the apogee of mathematics in architecture (the Parthenon), sculpture (Polyclitus may have been the first to use constant proportions between different parts of the body, the head representing a seventh of the total height), philosophy (Pythagoras thought that numbers were the basis for all things, a theory adopted by Plato: numbers are Ideas that help us discover the essence of things and translate the beautiful). The Renaissance engaged in a methodical search for harmonious proportions in sculpture and architecture: the ideal measurements for a building were calculated based on those of the human body. Luca Pacioli devoted a book to the "divine proportion" (1509) that in 1932 Matila Ghyka would call the "golden number," the inverse of which is 0.618. It is, in a given length divided into two segments, the ratio of the smaller segment (a) to the larger (b) equal to the ratio of the larger to the total length – a/b=b/a+b – or the ratio of the smaller side to the larger side in the "ideal" rectangle, the size of most European paintings. It has since been demonstrated that this is a myth. With "a good dose of bad faith," the adepts of the golden number systematically rounded to 0.618 when painters and architects used the banal proportion of 5/8, or 0.625 (Neveux).

The Greek model explains that, since the Renaissance, the learning of drawing and painting begins with the human body and knowledge of its proportions. "When one is well taught," wrote Leonardo da Vinci, "and one is used to it, it is easy to paint any painting, even without recourse to them." And, according to Albrecht Dürer, "Good measure results in good form, not only in painting, but also in other works of value."

It is essentially a matter of the female nude, a major theme in art since the Greeks, while it did not appear in East Asia before the end of the 19th century (except in erotic art which has no artistic interest) due to the European influence. Woman was the incarnation of

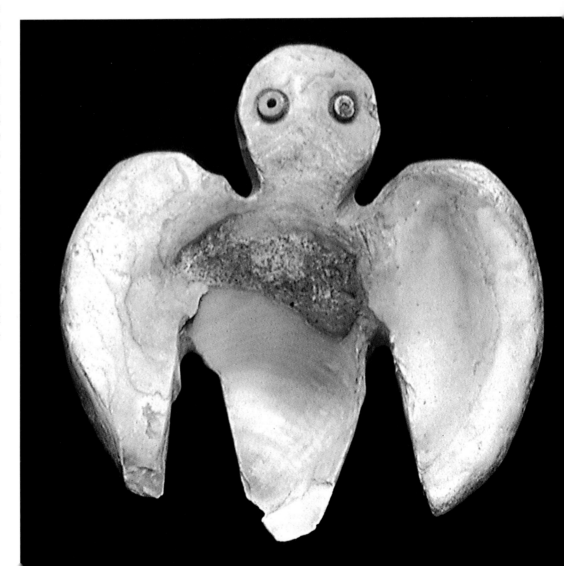

beauty, both that of proportion and that of movement. Rodin spoke of character and expression:

"There is nothing in nature that has more character than the human body. With its strength or its grace, it evokes the most varied images. One moment, it resembles a flower: the flexing of the torso looks like the stem, the smile of the breasts, the head and the shine of the hair matches the blossoming of the corolla. Another moment, it is reminiscent of a supple liana or a bush with a fine and strong curve… Other times, the human body bending backwards is like a spring or a beautiful bow… Yet another time, it is an urn… The human body is above all the mirror of the soul from where its greatest beauty comes… what we adore in the human body, more than its so beautiful form, is the inner flame that seems to illuminate it by transparency".

Conversely, landscape was long considered unimportant. In the beginning, it was only a background for paintings dedicated to biblical, mythological or historical figures or scenes. Despite the forerunners of the 16th century (Bruegel), it only triumphed with the Impressionists Cézanne and Van Gogh. Here too, East and West agree about the principles of composition: first, see the whole, the main lines to which the anecdotic details must subordinate themselves; these may be simply sketched or even left out to bring out the general effect. But, in the West, geometry did not lose its preeminence. The Renaissance elaborated laws of perspective by determining the line of the horizon situated at the observer's eye level; on this line is the vanishing point on which the lines of the drawing converge. Thus, perspective is a system for projecting on a plane three-dimensional objects and their spatial relationships. It was not the only one conceived. Egypt, Mesopotamia and the Aegean world all knew the perspective of registers, India, radiant perspective. In 11th-century China, Guo Xi defined the "three perspectives": of height, when one looks from the foot of a mountain towards the top; of depth, when, from an elevated position, one takes in the entire landscape; and of level, when one looks from a mountain that is close towards one that is farther away.

In Europe, from the Renaissance until the end of the 19th century, geometric perspective was considered as an indispensable starting point, Leonardo da Vinci wrote, "for knowing how to give everything its place and its proper measure according to this place." He added, "Practice must always be founded on a good theory of which perspective is the true guide and the gate because without it, no painting or any of the arts derived from it will be successful" (*Treatise on Painting*).

And, in the same way as the human body, all other subjects are reduced to lines and geometric figures that allowed their essential characteristics to be grasped. Cézanne recommended first studying "the cone, the cube, the cylinder and the sphere. When one knows how to render these things, their form and plane, one can then do everything one wishes." Certainly, one also comes across Chinese allusions to geometry, but they are limited. One example is this rule, which has been more or less accepted in landscape painting: if the mountain measures 3 meters, the trees will be 30 centimeters and man the size of a bean.

Abstraction and representation of nature

The 20th century has beaten exciting new paths in the domain of sculpture. Abstraction, asymmetry and movement spread as common tendencies and dynamic principles encouraged by the availability of new techniques and materials that change the traditional notion of sculpture and bring it sometimes closer to painting (Picasso's *Guitar* hangs from the wall) and sometimes closer to architecture (Tatlin's *Monument to the 3rd International*, supposed to be 440 meters high, remained a model in 1920 – now there are landscape sculptures in cities such as Martin Goeritz' *Five Towers Plaza*, 1957, in Mexico). For some, space which only "surrounded the masses," has become a component of the work, an "active void" where lines possess their own expressive force when they do not move it. Gabo and Pevsner constructed almost transparent geometric structures with the aid of networks of nylon or steel strings going in different directions; Henry Moore and Barbara Hepworth were inspired by the pure forms of nature such as pebbles on beaches to make the carefully polished figures they pierced or in the hollows from which they strung cords: "open closures" that engendered luminous effects and translated the tension between man and the environment, their communication and non-communication. For others, volume remains closed and is associated to the play

Small stele depicting a stylized owl. Volcanic rock. H: 19.5cm x Max. L: 9.5cm. Chorrera, Ecuador, 900 B.P. - 400.

of light and void via the material and polishing.

For me, the most beautiful contemporary sculpture is Brancusi's *Bird in Space*. There are about thirty versions that the artist produced between 1923 and 1941, all differing in one detail or another, ranging from 140 to 190 centimeters in height. Brancusi was both the heir of an age-old Carpathian tradition of woodcarving and a modern tradition influenced by the schools of Paris, Negro art and Indian Gandhara sculpture. In his country, the bird was a subject linked to the theme of liberation that haunted him all his life. He had begun with the figures of the *Maiastra* (1909-1912), which, in a Romanian tale, is a bird that guides across the forest a lover looking for his princess in order to free her. He continued with the *Golden Bird* from which would evolve the *Bird in Space*. The initially rounded shapes became more and more streamlined by getting rid of the wings and the head to end up with an asymmetrical and elongated spindle that shoots like an arrow towards the sky. Thus, the bird translates, according to his own terms, "the joy of the soul liberated from matter," the artist being "the instrument… that helps the cosmic essence of the material to transform itself into an existence that is really visible… The height in itself means nothing. It is the intimate proportions of the object that do everything."

The material participates in the expression. Brancusi tried white, yellow, black, gray-blue marble, alternating it with bronze. Both incite touching and caressing. Polished bronze not only reflects the light in a way that changes as one circles around it, it is itself light. "For

a lifetime, I only sought," declared Brancusi, "the essence of flight… It is not birds that I sculpt but flight." The purity of line manifests the spirit of things, their essence.

In every civilization, representations of the bird may be found. Because of its nature, it symbolized the relationship between earth and sky, although its precise meaning varies from one culture to another. As early as the Neolithic period, the bird appeared with a surprising level of abstraction but, on the whole, explainable in the measure that the primitive artist was preoccupied with the individuality of the object and with the message to be transmitted than with formal likeness. Wilhelm Worringer thought the tendency towards abstraction of these peoples came from their anxiety about the world that they had to repress by stripping things of their

confusion and arbitrariness in order to make necessity and normality emerge.

The oldest images of birds that we have knowledge of are those drawn on their pottery by Iranian nomads in the 4th millennium B.P. We may see an extraordinary goblet from Susa in the Louvre with the bodies of ibexes reduced to two triangles placed side by side, the concave arch of the back prolonged by the immense double curve of the horns. Above them greyhounds stretch lengthwise in contrast with the long vertical necks of the waders surrounding the rim. On other vases, the bird is depicted in flight, the wings reduced to parallel straight lines along the body.

A Chinese jade from the 2nd millennium B.P. from Shansi depicts a bird with wings that are suggested, the eyes and beak simply sketched (Nelson Gallery of Art, Kansas City).

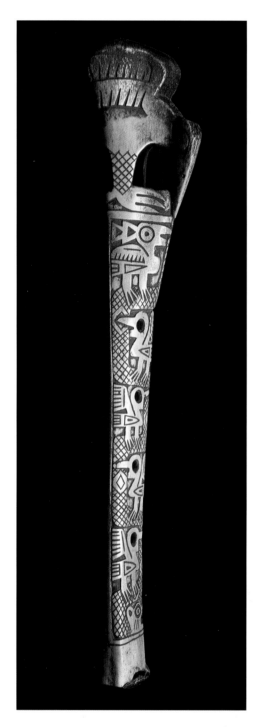

In regard to this jade, William Willets evoked Moore and Brancusi because, although it was produced "probably without metal tools, all the essential characteristics of the animal, doubtless a pigeon, are effectively met, with no trace of effort in the execution and with no loss of vitality" (63-64).

A stone bird from East Timor is remarkably similar to this work although it is three millennia more recent, but also from a Neolithic society. Its eyes and beak are reduced to slits, its wings to lightly sculpted curves. A hole was made in its base to attach it to a pole of the hut so that it would bring the family happiness and prosperity.

On the plateaus of central Viet Nam, the mountain dwellers also sculpt birds that they place beside their tombs and homes. This stylized heron has an admirable rhythm with its spindle-shaped body extended by the neck upward and the feathers and feet downward, the horizontal beak and pedestal balancing these slender vertical forms. Brancusi's bird takes flight into space; here, it is the ancestor soul watching over the living and the dead. It recalls the motif of birds in flight decorating the bronze Dong Son drums (1st millennium B.P.) linked to fertility and rebirth.

Is symbolism always present? At first sight, this little onyx bird, with a very pure line, is only an object to be bought by tourists in the souk of Casablanca, as is this other bird from Essaouira, the sculptor of which has used the veins of the thuya wood to emphasize the beak and exalt the magnificence of the tail. What does it matter if this bird does not exist in nature? But, in both cases, perhaps the unknown artist and Sadik Sadiki unconsciously remembered the verses of the Koran that make the bird a witness to the power of God whom it praises:

I have come to you with a Sign from your Lord:
I will, for you, create from clay the shape of a bird.
I breathe in him and it is a "bird,"
With God's permission. (III, 49)

The bird is a frequently occurring theme in Iranian, Indian and Javanese calligraphy, painting and ceramics. For the Sufis, it is the path that leads to God in whom they seek absorption. In his *The Conference of the Birds,* one

Bone flute with four holes topped with a bird swallowing a snake and five birds and a puma head in bas-relief. H: 22.5cm. Nazca, Peru, 200 B.P.-600.

Pendant in the shape of an eagle with outstretched wings. Golden tumbaga. H: 10cm. Cocle, Panama, 600-800.

of the great mystic poets of Iran, Farid od-Din Attar (d. 1220), describes the initiatory voyage of thirty birds to find their king, the Simorgh, and discover in the end that they themselves are Simorgh (*si* = thirty, *morgh* = birds), that is, the divine mystery in its own self.

"Flowers and birds" (*hua niao*) is one of the categories of Chinese painting. It comes immediately after landscapes and spread to Korea and Japan. Despite its name, it encompasses all beings except large animals (elephants, tigers and horses): small mammals (hares and squirrels), insects (butterflies and dragonflies), fish, aquatic plants (lotus) and shells. Europeans generally painted them with a lot of detail and color: the still life was mostly the product of lesser masters and covered a very limited field as its name indicates, inanimate objects or beings (for example, dead birds brought back from the hunt). The Eastern painter, on the contrary, influenced by Taoism and Buddhism, sees animals and plants as creatures of nature like man, encompassing them in the same sympathy. Some of them have become emblems that are often linked: the rooster and peonies represent the masculine principle (*yang*); the crane and the pine tree represent longevity; the carp going up the Yangzi and jumping over cataracts in order to spawn symbolizes vigor, endurance and success; the falcon (used for hunting) and the eagle, heroism and strength; the phoenix, peace and plenty; wild geese and mandarin ducks, marital fidelity; the magpie, happiness and joy (the five types of happiness – longevity, children, health, wealth and peace – are represented by five magpies).

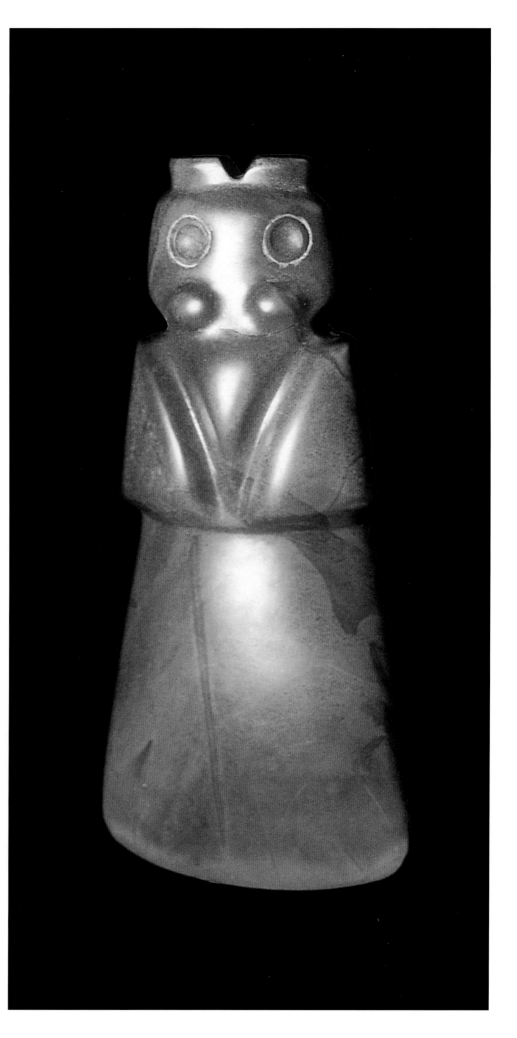

Jade pendant in the shape of a bird god. H: 15cm. Base L: 6.5cm. Nicoya, Guanacaste, Costa Rica, 300 B.P.-600.

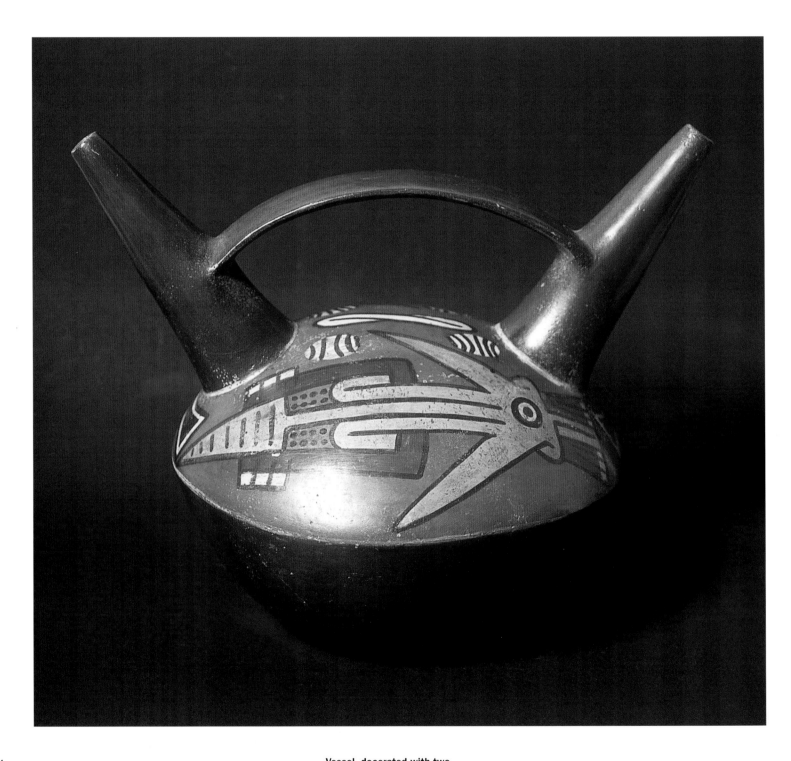

Vessel, decorated with two
stylized birds, with two spouts
linked by a handle. Red and
brown terracotta.
H: 15.5cm x L: 20cm.
Tiahunaku, Peru, -300 + 1100.

The lotus is the Buddhist flower par excellence because it grows in the mud and emerges with its whiteness and fragrance intact.

Contemporary painters continue the tradition by giving it a modern touch. One of the greatest, Qi Baishi (1863-1957), spent years observing "the tens of thousands of creatures" and sketching them. According to him, "a good painted first has to absorb the form of things that he has seen with his own eyes. Only then can he take up his brush with the certitude of being able to render their essence." Qi adopted the free style (*xie yi*) and painted innumerable landscapes, clinging plants, flowers (lotus, chrysanthemums), shrimps, crabs, fish, mice and chicks. A few strokes, a few ink stains accompanied by light colors sufficed to characterize each one and give it a life of its own.

European painting began in the Minoan world where joie de vivre was evident in the colorful wall scenes and the scrolls of vases. Is there any movement more gracious than that of a couple of swallows, open-beaked, playing lovingly in a landscape of rocks and red lilies (fresco from Akrotiri in Santorini-Thira now in the national archeological museum in Athens). This happiness would be lost with the advent of Judeo-Christianity. In the Bible, God created birds and fish before terrestrial animals and man. The dove became the image of the Holy Spirit before symbolizing peace between peoples in the modern era: Picasso used a dove for a political poster reproduced millions of times. For Magritte, the bird was the bearer of hope in a disenchanted world: that is what is expressed by the white clouds in a blue summer sky supporting its immense wings spread in a dark night landscape (*Le retour*, 1940, Musées royaux des beaux-arts de Belgique), blue landscape (*L'oiseau de ciel*, 1966, Sabena Collection) or dissipating the storm clouds (*La grande famille*, 1963, Utsunomiya Museum).

In the Americas, the bird was also associated with divinity. The chief wore feathers, notably of the quetzal with its long green tail, or a jade bird's head to have a part of the god on him always. In Mexico, Quetzalcoatl, the bird-snake or the feathered serpent, was the culture hero, the bird representing the sky and the snake, the earth. We know stone representations of man-birds: the Ecuadorian stele of the owl god (the owl was the symbol of darkness and the underworld) and the pendant axes of the bird god of the Nicoya (Costa Rica). The bird also appears in various forms in the pottery, jewelry and textiles as well as in the famous geoglyphs of the Nazca among the fish, monkeys, spiders, quadrupeds and human beings representing the constellations and the places of worship and feasting in this ceremonial center.

The Canadian arctic has an old visual tradition that dates back to the Dorset culture (7th century B.P.-10th century), which was succeeded by the Thule era (11th-16th centuries). Dorset sculpted animal and human figures in gold, whalebone, walrus tusk and wood to which a magical or religious meaning was attributed, while Thule, from which the Inuit are descended, was especially attached to the decoration of utilitarian objects (combs, needle cases and harpoon counter-

Lock topped by a bird with incised geometric motifs. Furrowed light wood. H: 22.3 x L: 8cm. Dogon, Mali.

Adam Totalik.
Two Flying Geese.
Caribou antler.
H: 19cm x L: 25cm.
Spence Bay, Canada.

Falcon representing the
sun god Horus. Wood.
H: 9cm x L: 12.3cm.
Egypt, 26th Dynasty
(Saïte), 7th – 6th c. B.P.

Parrot head.
Wood and fibers.
H: 21cm x L: 11cm.
Songye,
Congo-Kinshasa.

Loom pulley with
hornbill head.
Wood, fine patina.
H: 16.5cm x L: 8cm.
Senufo, Ivory Coast.

weights). After a long period of inertia due to the European impact, a renaissance took place in the 1950s. Today Inuit art comprises a wide variety of styles ranging from naturalism to abstraction and Surrealism. With these *Birds*, made out of caribou antler, Adam Totalik captured the graceful lightness of a couple of wild geese flying one after the other.

The bird is found all over Africa because it incarnates life and fertility and is often linked to the protection of ancestors for the perpetuation of the family line. In ancient Egypt, the falcon was an attribute of the sky god Horus whose eyes were the sun and the moon. In sub-Saharan Africa, birds figure on the usual objects: locks, pulleys, spoons, canes and ritual sticks. The *opa Osanyin* of the Yoruba is an iron topped with a large bird symbolizing the spirit of medicine, the human life force, surrounded by a lower circle of smaller birds; the soothsayer planted it in the ground to invoke it before making his diagnosis and prescribing his remedy. Certain Akan lost-wax cast gold weights depict single birds or birds in groups symbolizing the solidarity of the family or the lineage; the rooster represents virility and the chief. For the Senufo, the hornbill of the savannahs occupies a prominent place because it incarnates the male fertilizing element and is one of the five main animals of their creation myths along with the chameleon, the tortoise, the snake and the crocodile. Its head often adorned pulleys. Colossal, it has a prominent belly that indicates to the initiate that procreation is man's first duty and a long beak that evokes the male organ. By the same token, the *kpe-*

lie dance mask that personifies the ancestor under a hornbill presides over the Poro initiation rites where the memory, knowledge and techniques of the community are transmitted to the young. Fertility is not only physical, but also spiritual.

The art of Oceania is characterized by its imaginative luxuriance, but it also includes some very pure forms such as the Kanak clubs with a bird's eyes and beak and the white-tailed eagle, wings spread over the founding ancestor on the gable of the men's house in the Sepik villages of New Guinea: it transports the souls of the dead to the other world.

By illustrating a single theme, the bird, with examples taken from every civilization, we have shown both the convergence of symbolism and the diversity of interpretations having purity of line in common. Let us widen the debate. This purity is found in all creations but its expression depends on the culture and different materials are used.

For the Chinese, the perfect shape is the circle because it evokes the sky and the most famous of the jades of imperial worship is the *bi*. According to the *Ritual of the Zhou* (*Zhou li*), which dates from 600 B.P., "the master of ceremonies pays homage to the Heavens with the greenish *bi*; he pays homage to the Earth with the yellow *cong*." The *bi* is round like the sky; its form is that of the ancient character designating the sky, a disk with a hole in the middle. The *cong* is a tube circular on the inside (like the sky) and square on the outside (like the earth). *Bi* and *cong* are of variable size but their colors must be opposites that complement each other

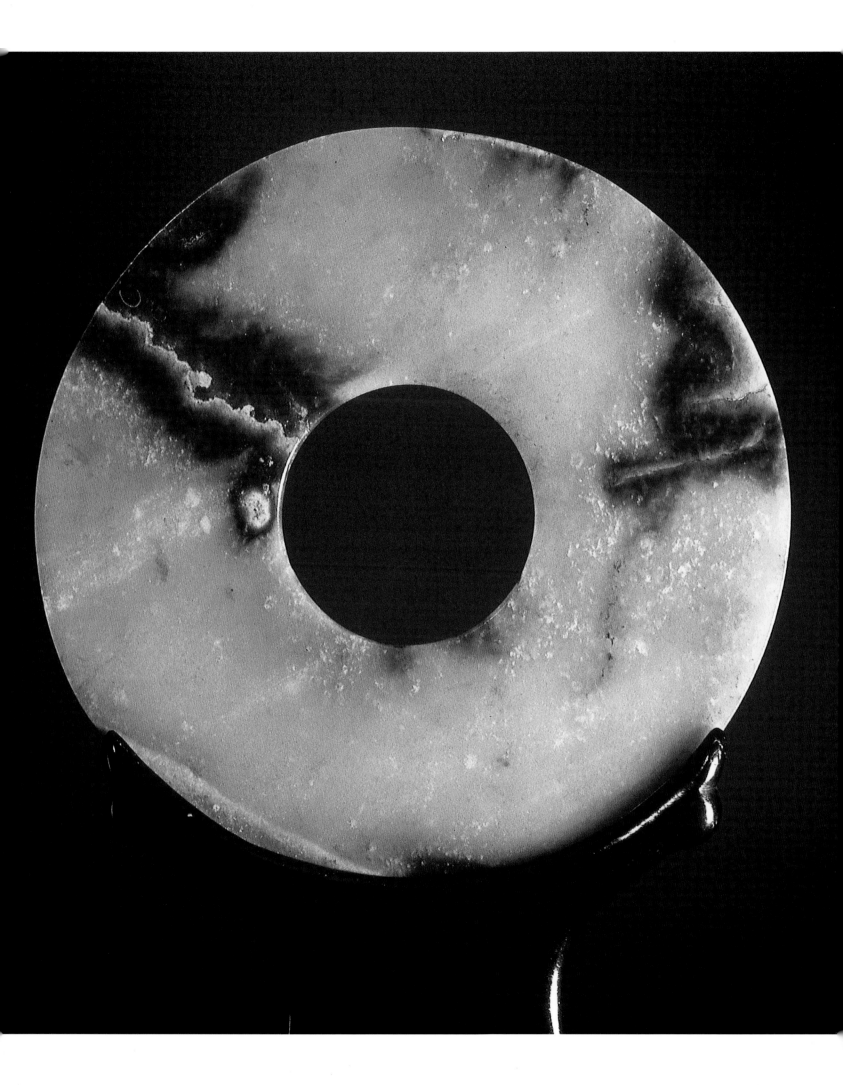

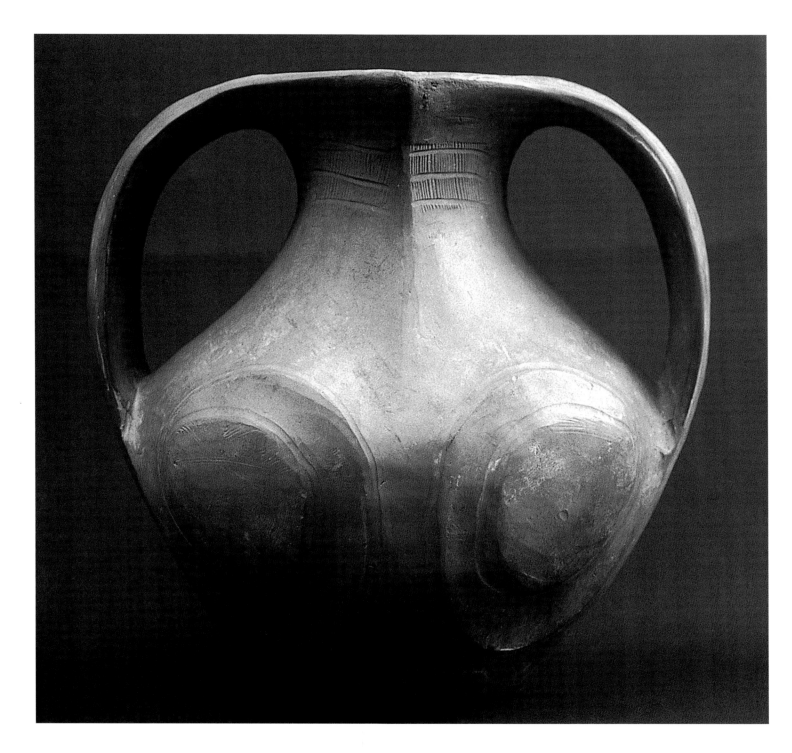

Amphora with two curved
handles joining the neck to the
belly where they end in spirals.
Gray terracotta. H: 19.3cm.
Sichuan, China, Early Han,
2nd – 1st c. B.P.

like yin and yang. Even when jade became purely decorative under the Qing dynasty, some pure forms emerged from the jumble such as these snuff bottles made to look like pebbles. The golden veining of the jade is reminiscent of clouds during sunset; the veining of gray agate is reminiscent of mists on autumnal waters.

Like jade, bronze masterpieces were produced during the archaic Shang (16th-11th centuries B.P.) and Zhou (11th-3rd centuries B.P.) dynasties. These are very finely decorated lost-wax cast ceremonial vases. As with jade, burial in the ground gave them a delicately polished – light green or blue – patina. They were used for sacrifices to ancestors, which comprised offerings of food and wine. Their forms are powerful or elegant: particularly elegant are the *jue* and *gu* drinking vases. The *jue* is a three-legged cup with a spout balanced on the other side by a pointed opening; in the middle are two posts and on the belly there is a small handle. The *gu* is a slender vessel tapering from the base to the lower third before swelling upwards. Its motifs combine geometry with the fantastic *taotie* mask; the *taotie* is a monster with bulging eyes separated by the vertical bridge of the nose (eyes are a universal magical sign). During the Han dynasty, Confucianism became the dominant ideology, philosophical rationalism triumphing over animism and shamanism. Bronze was no longer used for ritual and its use was confined to utilitarian objects (mirrors, urns, basins and incense burners) before the blossoming of Buddhism increased the number of golden statuettes. Ceramics became the great art of everyday life. During its peak during

the Song dynasty (960-1279), it exercised a determining influence on East Asia, the Islamic world and Europe. Its excellence was due to the perfection of form rather than to the brightness of color.

In his *Art and Industry*, Herbert Read distinguished between "rational" and "intuitive" forms. Comparing a Song porcelain to a 6th century B.P. Greek vase, both undecorated, he wrote (21-23):

"Both depend for their appeal on their form alone. The Greek vase is based on exact measurements and its proportions are regular… The Chinese vase does not obey any such exact rules. [On the Greek vase] every trace of the potter's hand has been carefully removed. The Chinese vase is in outline and finish slightly irregular, it still shows traces of the ridges left by the potter's fingers, and the glaze has been allowed to run irregularly down the surface and finish in an uneven surf above the foot. It is superior as a work of art because its form has an appeal which cannot be analyzed, which is not intellectual, but intuitive or unconscious."

Europeans are fond of more or less baroque stoneware with "three colors" (*sancai*) – amber yellow, warm green and Prussian blue – on a creamy white background. East Asians prefer monochrome cups, bowls and vases, whether foiled or not, with pure forms that were more vigorous during the Tang dynasty and finer during the Song dynasty: celadon (named after a character in the novel *L'Astrée* who wore ribbons of this color) whose color ranges from pale green to gray green, reminiscent of jade, crackled or

71

Qingbai bowl, enameled
in bluish white, the
exterior decorated
with a lotus petal frieze.
Diam 18.5cm.
China, Song dynasty,
11th – 12th c.

not – the most beautiful celadon is the imperial pale blue-green *ru;* "snow" white or "bluish white" (*yingqing* or *qingbai*); *jian* (the Japanese *temmoku*) with a black or brown glaze decorated by light-colored ridges that look like "hare fur", "drops of oil" or the imprint of a leaf; and lavender blue *jun* with or without purple, red or violet patches. The splendor of the glaze is sometimes enhanced by splashes. Moreover, we appreciate its translucence, the variations and reflections in its colors, its smoothness and the sound the piece makes when it is gently struck.

Yuan ceramics are characterized by bowls and bottles with a dark brown glaze decorated with ochre floral or cloud motifs as well as blue and white *qinghua*. The Ming dynasty developed porcelain by making use of the properties of kaolin: their famous blue and white range from grayish blue to intense purplish blue. From the 16th century, polychromy dominated – three or five colors – a tendency that became more pronounced during the Qing dynasty at the same time as the movement away from pure forms. Technical perfection killed refined beauty.

Korean ceramics were the only ones the

Chinese thought to be equal to their own. The most well known is the celadon of Koryo which made its appearance in the late 11th century and reached its peak a century later. It was characterized by a magnificent bluish green glaze called "kingfisher color" and painted, incised or, in a specifically Korean technique, inlaid (*sanggam*) with motifs such as cranes, clouds, peonies, chrysanthemums, bamboo, willows and ducks. The most elegant form is that of the *meiping* vase made to contain a single prunus branch. The "iron black" ceramic is decorated with sober and vigorous designs. Used by the people rather than the nobility, the *punch'ong* of the Yi (1392-1910) was esteemed by Japanese masters of the tea ceremony who sought simplicity. It consisted of robust stoneware forms decorated with flowers or animals traced with a firm and free brush in brown or iron black on a grayish white or pale green ground. After the destruction caused by the Hideyoshi invasion (1592-1598) that brought several potters to Japan, *punch'ong* almost completely disappeared, but bluish porcelain decorated with cobalt blue, brown iron oxide and copper red motifs of admirable spontaneity continued to be produced.

This quality is also found in Viet Nam where ceramics, like the other arts (architecture, sculpture and painting) was profoundly influenced by Buddhism during the Ly (11th-12th centuries) and Trân (13th-14th centuries) dynasties: the lotus is omnipresent on bowls, cups, pots and covered jars for rice or wine. Ly pieces often featured cream or celadon glaze, crackled or not, with very pure lines, sometimes decorated on the outside and on

Wine pot in celadon stoneware
with incised lines, lotus flowers
and foliage, with a *makara*
shaped spout. H: 19cm.
Viet Nam, Ly, 11th – 12th c.

the inside with incised or molded floral motifs. During the Trân era, to the ancient forms were added the pot for lime, one of the ingredients, with the areca nut, of the betel chew: this custom, common in Southeast Asia and India, plays an essential role in social relations from the beginning of conversation to the proposal of marriage. During the Lê dynasty (15th-18th centuries), the development of domestic and international trade gave rise to craft guilds and specialized villages. Ceramics diversified its forms, colors and motifs. Blue and white appeared then polychromy. While certain objects are heavy and their decoration elaborate (large altar vases, lamp bases, incense burners), the blue and white or white and iron brown bowls, cups, plates and vases were decorated with floral, animal, calligraphic or abstract motifs using a free and vigorous brush. During the Nguyên period (19th century), Huê blues were porcelain pieces made in China by order of the Vietnamese court which chose the model and the themes sometimes accompanied by verse in *nôm* (Vietnamese characters derived from Chinese):

O, free pleasure of contemplation:
evening mist and clouds.
The prunus is an old friend, the crane
an ancient acquaintance.

The most original Japanese contribution to ceramics is the esthetic of *imperfection*. It originated in Zen Buddhism, which was introduced to the country in the 12th century. Zen emphasizes "seated meditation," attention to the present, the lack of distinction between the "profane" and the "sacred," the "great" and the "small," the atom and the cosmos. It values silence because speech is

an obstacle to thought. This philosophical approach was incorporated into the "way of tea" (*sado* or *chanoyu*) elaborated by monks in the 15th-16th centuries. Tea and Zen were linked because the drink kept one alert and able to concentrate. The rules laid down by Sen no Rikyu (1518-1591) would influence all the arts: architecture, gardening, painting and flower arranging. The notion of *wabi-sabi* emerged as both a way of thinking of the beautiful and an art of living based on simplicity, harmony with nature and the sense of the transience of things. Rikyu often cited this poem by Fujiwara no Teika (1162-1241) in order to describe the spirit of *wabi-sabi*:

All around no flowers in bloom
Nor maple leaves in glory
A solitary fisherman's hut alone
On the twilight shore
Of this autumn eve. (Koren, 55)

Wabi-sabi manifests itself in the construction of the tea pavilion at the bottom of a garden accessed by a path marked by flat stones that symbolize the break with the outside world. After having purified one's hands and

Celadon bowl with an incised motif of elongated petals; interior with stylized clouds. Diam. 11.5cm. Korea, Koryo, 11th – 12th c.

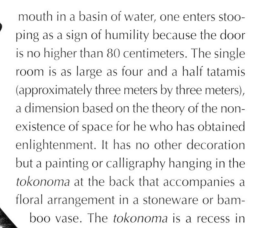

mouth in a basin of water, one enters stooping as a sign of humility because the door is no higher than 80 centimeters. The single room is as large as four and a half tatamis (approximately three meters by three meters), a dimension based on the theory of the non-existence of space for he who has obtained enlightenment. It has no other decoration but a painting or calligraphy hanging in the *tokonoma* at the back that accompanies a floral arrangement in a stoneware or bamboo vase. The *tokonoma* is a recess in the wall, slightly elevated with a lowered ceiling. Its beams are in untreated wood whose only decoration is its own veining. The scroll and the floral arrangement change according to the season, the weather and the guest to be honored. The utensils needed for the ceremony are chosen to harmonize with the rest: the iron kettle, the bamboo spoon, the water pot, the box of tea (*chaire*) and the tea bowl (*chawan*). The bowl is the most important element because it passes from host to guest and enables their communion. Contrary to the luxurious tradition of the court at Kyoto, Japanese monks preferred plain or even rough ceramic with an uneven shape and edges in a dull color in order to highlight the green of the tea, thick enough to retain heat and please the drinker who holds it in his hands.

The first bowls brought back from China were celadon and *temmoku* (from the name of Mount Tianmu "Eyes of the Heavens" in Zhejiang where Japanese monks stayed to

deepen their knowledge of Buddhism). Beginning in the 16th century, tea masters sought out Korean, Vietnamese and Thai bowls which were more sober, rougher and often made by peasants, and thus closer to the nature and the notion of *wabi-sabi*. They encouraged the potters of Kyoto, Seto, Mino, Bizen, Shigaraki, Karatsu and Iga who were, moreover, often of Korean descent. Rikyu liked the *raku* that, fired at a low temperature, were soft to the touch, agreeably transmitting the warmth of the tea whose color changed with the aging of the interior. The glaze, simply red or black, had luminous effects according to variations in the firing. Other tea masters preferred livelier colorful decoration with green, yellow, bluish or purplish drippings and patches, according to exposure to flames, or incised or painted geometric or plant motifs. In the late 16th century, colored enamels that rejected Rikyu's austerity and were more to the taste of the wealthy middle classes made their appearance. The bowls that were appreciated the most bore names, often poetic, such as "Spring Mist" or "Autumn Evening."

In another domain, also influenced by Zen, the perfection of the Japanese sword was not matched anywhere either for sharpness or for purity of line. It was the living soul of the samurai, the emblem of his valor and his pride and also the instrument that affirmed his power over the nobles of the court as well as the people. Thus the samurai had to care for his sword as well as imbue himself with Zen philosophy that emphasized impermanence, the inevitability of death, detachment and self-control. Only the samurai had the right to carry two swords, one long (*katana*) and one short (*waki zashi*). The blade of the katana curves towards the end of the tip, allowing drawing and striking to happen at the same time: it was worn on the left, in the belt, the cutting edge turned upwards. The blacksmith ranked highly among craftsmen. He led a life influenced by Shinto – each operation was conducted like a rite. Great schools flourished in Edo and Osaka in the 17th and 18th centuries. The forge was made out of selected steel and the charcoal used came from a particular type of pine tree. When the blade, heated to incandescence, became the color of a ripe persimmon, it was dipped in water heated to a specific temperature. Sharpening and polishing with stones of various textures took about 50 days. Finally, the sword was tested on corpses or criminals condemned to death. A 17th-century Chinese treatise praised the "steel blades of the Wa barbarians" that "even cut jade." The scabbard was made of wood sumptuously decorated with gold, silver and

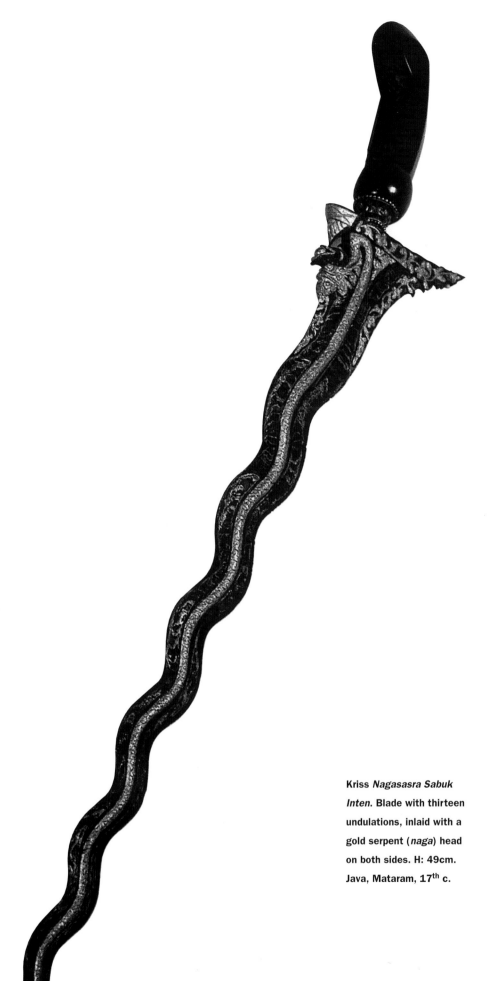

Kriss *Nagasasra Sabuk Inten*. Blade with thirteen undulations, inlaid with a gold serpent (*naga*) head on both sides. H: 49cm. Java, Mataram, 17th c.

75

Three-legged headrest cut out of a forking branch, honey-colored patina.
H: 14cm x L: 33cm.
Shilluk, Sudan.

lacquer, the guard (*tsuba*) was a work of art usually made of iron inlaid with gold or silver and decorated with plant or animal motifs. With the "modernization" of the Meiji period, the wearing of swords during peacetime was forbidden (1876).

In Indonesia, the *kriss* or *keris* (dagger) has even greater significance because it is thought to have a soul. The Javanese call *pusaka* an object that is handed down, making up part of the family heritage and possessing the magic power to protect, heal and avenge. This notion is linked to animist beliefs and ancestor worship that long predated Buddhism and Hinduism. The blacksmith (*empu*) who fashions it performs a sacred act in a carefully detailed ceremony. The blade is straight or wavy, representing a resting or

active *naga* (the mythic serpent). When it is decorated, the motif is most often a snake whose undulations echo the odd-numbered curves: the higher the number of curves, the more precious the arm. The handle is made of gold, ivory or rare honey-colored wood decorated with superb dark patches; it sometimes is shaped like a demon (*raksasa*), set with gemstones, who is supposed to chase away harmful influences. The scabbard, made of wood, gold or silver, is decorated with chiseled floral motifs. But, for the Javanese, beauty resides especially in the *pamor*, the cloudy design the *empu* obtains on the blade using a blend of iron and nickel (the most precious comes from meteorites) because of the notches and small holes, then soaking it in an abrasive solution for several days and cleaning it with lemon juice. Anointed with aromatic oil, it gives off a particular scent. The *kriss*, worn on the belt, is an integral part of Javanese dress. The most beautiful ones have names.

In the Arab world, weapons are signs of tribal membership and of social position as well as ornaments. The most common is the dagger with a handle and scabbard in wood, copper or silver, sometimes ending in a "peacock tail," decorated with foliage, with two rings through which a colored woolen cord

is threaded. In Yemen, the *jambiya* is a symbol of the free man who must always carry it: "We are all born with a dagger at the belly." They are given as gifts for special occasions such as circumcision and marriage. The young circumcised boy shows his courage by holding the blade against his forehead.

In Africa, weapons for hunting and war bear witness to the association of the effective and the beautiful. As soon as they leave the blacksmith's workshop, they are the objects of prayers and sacrifice before being used. They take various forms and, when they are put to prestigious use, have decorated blades and handles of ivory or sculpted wood inlaid with pewter or entwined with brass wires. Perhaps more attractive is the simple throwing knife with several blades that branch off in different directions like a flower or leaves. The Zulu club has the classic shape of a stick with a large round head but the craftsman has chosen the wood with care for its veining, knots and nuances. The same may be said of Australian boomerangs, even when they are made for tourists.

Generally speaking, peoples with a simple economy and simple needs devote all their attention to the beauty of the objects that they use everyday. It is never independent of function. It is sought in the quality of the material and the elegance of the shape rather than in the decoration. When he is inspired by nature, the artist aims less at the likeness and more at the essence. It is this capacity for abstraction due to proximity and close observation that gives his creations their exceptional purity of line like this long and thin

Nuna whistle with triangular arms destined for hunting and war.

Basketry is used to make all sorts of receptacles. The baskets of the mountain people of Viet Nam are noteworthy for their finely woven rushes. In Africa, the boxes with conical covers, baskets and trays of Rwanda and Burundi are well known. They were made by aristocratic Tutsi women who had time for this painstaking work. Zigzag or spiral geometric designs traditionally black or red in color stand out on the pale gold grass background. Since the 1930s, the import of chemical dyes has enlarged the palette to include green, mauve and orange, but the beauty of the work has not been enhanced.

More than pottery and buffalo horn (for drinking), wood is used universally for almost everything. Furniture is not only utilitarian, it is a status symbol. The most elegant stool is undoubtedly the Ashanti one with a concave platform resting on supports decorated with geometric motifs and a large rectangular base. Its shape is derived from the "gold seat" which, since the 18th century, served as an altar for royal ancestors. The stool of the queen mother is covered with silver leaf the color of the moon, which is her emblem. Lobi and Gurunsi chairs are particularly comfortable with their backs tilted 45 degrees; they are carved from a single piece of wood with three legs. The articulated Senufo chair offers additional comfort on an uneven floor.

The most beautiful headrests come from East Africa in conjunction with the elaborate hairstyles of nomadic pastors they are meant to preserve. Young people only have access to them after initiation. They carry them on their shoulders and use them as stools because it is not appropriate to sit directly on the ground. When the headrests are decorated, it is with geometric or animal motifs. The Zulu headrest is the simplest: a rectangular platform with three legs. Somali and Boni headrests are shaped like crescents whose supports blossom like a corolla from the circular base. In Sudan, the Shilluk prune korked branches to produce a skillful asymmetry. A headrest from Congo-Kinshasa reveals a refined simplicity and a subtle balancing of volumes: the platform is not absolutely horizontal and the foot is not exactly central, it divides into four at the base and widens underneath the platform, pierced with a hole to lighten it and to pass a cord through it for transport.

People eat with their right hands. The spoon is used to distribute food and has both a symbolic and prestigious function. The finest is a Zulu spoon (Musée de l'Homme, Paris) depicting a slender female body carved out of a long, slim stem with legs, pubis, buttocks, navel and breasts, the bowl forming the head.

Jewelry and other forms of ornamentation also have very pure forms. They are status symbols, individual and collective, and sometimes talismans against evil spirits: combs decorated with geometric motifs or heads,

Headrest, with slightly inclined platform. Wood H: 14cm x L: 17.5cm Congo-Kinshasa.

pins for hair and clothing and jewelry for men and women. The Zaramo pin is topped by the bust of a woman with lightly sculpted breasts and navel and a triangular hairdo; the bust sits on a rectangular plaque with geometric incisions. The husband gives it to his wife when they move into their home or when they have their first daughter. She wears it at feasts. Ivory takes on magnificent hue in aging. Some jewels are veritable abstract sculptures such as the Lobi *thungbubiel*, a flute-shaped pendant with two holes on each side of the central bride worn to weddings and funerals or the Gurunsi *gungulu* a symbol of prosperity whose central opening allows it to be worn on the arm. In Southeast Asia, mountain dwellers wear a silver torque that the men and women of some peoples never

take off as they are thought to stop the soul from leaving the body. By the same token, the *sanggori*, which depicts a rolled up snake, is attached to the turban of the Toraja warrior in Sulawesi and it follows him to the afterlife to protect him. On the island of Santa Cruz, the *tema* disc is cut out of a tridacne shell and decorated with tortoiseshell motifs depicting frigates; worn as a pendant, it highlights the prestige of a man.

Rituals, games, singing, music and dance determine the rhythms of ordinary life. "If there were no games, we could not live," say the Anyi of the Ivory Coast. Here too, the aesthetic desire manifests itself in objects informed by beliefs and symbolic meanings. For the Beti of south Cameroon, the *abia* (or *abbia*) is played heads or tails with pieces

carved out of a sapotacea almond. On the smooth face, which is rarely longer than two inches, are finely carved human, animal and plant motifs and representations of clothing, tools and musical instruments. The sculptor demonstrates an exceptional mastery of empty and filled space to express on a miniscule surface the life of things.

Representation of the human figure

When one speaks of beauty, one first thinks of the beauty of woman. Its representation varies according to the civilization. During the Neolithic era, representations of woman exalted her fertility by exaggerating her sexual characteristics. But, in a Nubian tomb south of the third cataract dating from the fourth millennium B.P., a strikingly "modern" figure was found: a polished sandstone spindle barely eight inches long widening from the head to the shoulders before narrowing downward; a few incisions suggest the line of the hair and the eyes (National Museum of Khartoum). In the 2nd millennium B.P., naturalism blossomed in Egypt with a timeless masterpiece: the torso of Nefertiti, wife of Akhenaton (circa 1350 B.P., the Louvre). The folds of the veil tightly covering her from the left shoulder to the legs reveal more than they hide all the sensuality of her curves.

However, it was the Greeks who gave a lasting form to their idea of human perfection, which has not ceased haunting the imagination of the West. While, according to the Jews, God made man in his own image, the Greeks thought that man was the measure of all things. The Athenian ideal was the *kalos-*

Headrest decorated
with geometric friezes.
Wood. H: 14cm.
Boni or Somali,
Somalia.

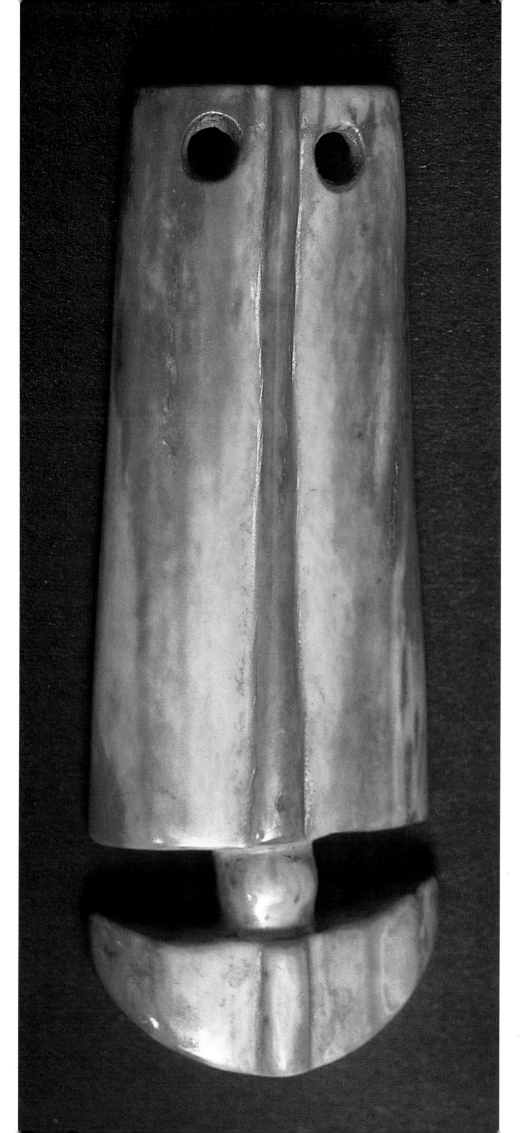

kagathos, the handsome and good man, because physical beauty could not be separated from the beauty of the soul, which was interpreted in a sense of moral and civic duty. That is why education comprised literature, music and gymnastics. Gymnastics were practiced in the nude (*gymnos*) to the sound of an oboe on the palester. "Brilliant and fresh as a flower, you pass your time in the gymnasia," wrote Aristophanes (*The Clouds*).

In the 7th century B.P., under Egyptian influence, the nude adolescent boy (*kouros*), who represented the god in his temple or the deceased on his tomb, was a frontal and expressionless figure. Little by little, movement appeared in the form of a left leg brought forwards. The face wore a malicious half-smile; it would disappear by the Classical period. This period saw the building of the Parthenon (5th century B.P.), a miracle of measure and proportion where the vertical lines are not absolutely vertical and the horizontal lines are not absolutely horizontal in order to correct the optical illusion. It was the incarnation of the Platonic dream of "reason mixed with music." The *Poseidon of Artemision* (the name of the cape where it was discovered) is a masterpiece of Attic bronze sculpture (circa 460 B.P., National Archeological Museum, Athens), capturing the power of the god at the moment he is readying himself to throw his trident from his raised right hand; his left hand is held out in front of him. The breadth of this horizontal axis is counterbalanced by the vertical axis of the body supported by spread legs and lifted feet. A little over a century later, Praxiteles sculpted his Hermes (circa 340 B.P., National Museum, Olympia) with

Thungbubiel, a flute-shaped pendant.
Dyed ivory.
H: 12cm x L: 4 to 5cm.
Lobi, Burkina Faso.

Two pieces of the *abia*
game: bird and deer.
Sapotacea wood.
L: 4cm and 3.6cm.
Beti, Cameroon.

Opposite page:
Paolo Ambrosio
(1945). *Figure* (1998).
Larch wood.
H: 65cm x L: 18-19cm.
Italy.

Gungulu, arm bracelet.
Ivory.
H: 20.5cm x L: 10cm.
Gurunsi, Burkina Faso.

his dreamy gaze and perfect body. He holds the infant Dionysus in his left arm; Dionysus stretches out his arm, probably for a bunch of grapes that Hermes is giving him. The male nude was the norm because it symbolized beauty. In Plato's *Symposium,* in which he spoke of love, it is the love of boys rather than women and it is from the contemplation of their bodies that came the revelation of absolute beauty.

During the Archaic period, the young woman (*kore*) was depicted clothed; the artist

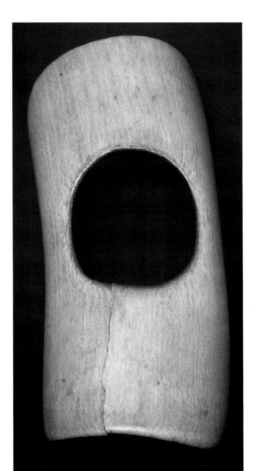

concentrated on the beauty of her face (*Head of Hygia*, National Archeological Museum, Athens). Around 470-460 B.P., the Ludovisi triptych (National Museum, Rome) was exceptional. Its central panel depicted a young woman that two servants are helping to come out of the water; her very thin tunic, wet and clinging to the body, draws attention to her breasts. On the left panel is sculpted a double flute player who is naked and sitting cross-legged. Praxiteles (4th century B.P.) is generally credited with unveiling the female body. One would like to think he was inspired by the beauty of his lover Phryne, even if the "wet drapery" that molded the busts of goddesses prepared the way for this innovation. No original work by Praxiteles in this field has survived. The Hellenistic and Roman replicas possess a grace often close to that of Mannerism. The *Aphrodite of Cnidus* in the Louvre has no head but is superior to that of the Vatican (a little thick) because of her pure lines, flexible hips and rounded breasts, thighs and shoulders. The *Venus de Milo* (2nd century B.P.), also headless, is taller. Placed in the light of a vast room, it attracts more crowds. "Pure like a lightning flash and like a harmony" (Leconte de Lisle), it does not have the sensuality of the *Aphrodite of Cnidus.*

Christianity changed the vision of the world and expelled female beauty from all medieval representations. Eve was the sinner who succumbed to temptation and led Adam astray. The body was considered shameful, the seat of desires that led people to stray from God. The interdiction did not stop either the appearance of some sensual nudes in the images of the *Resurrection of the Dead*

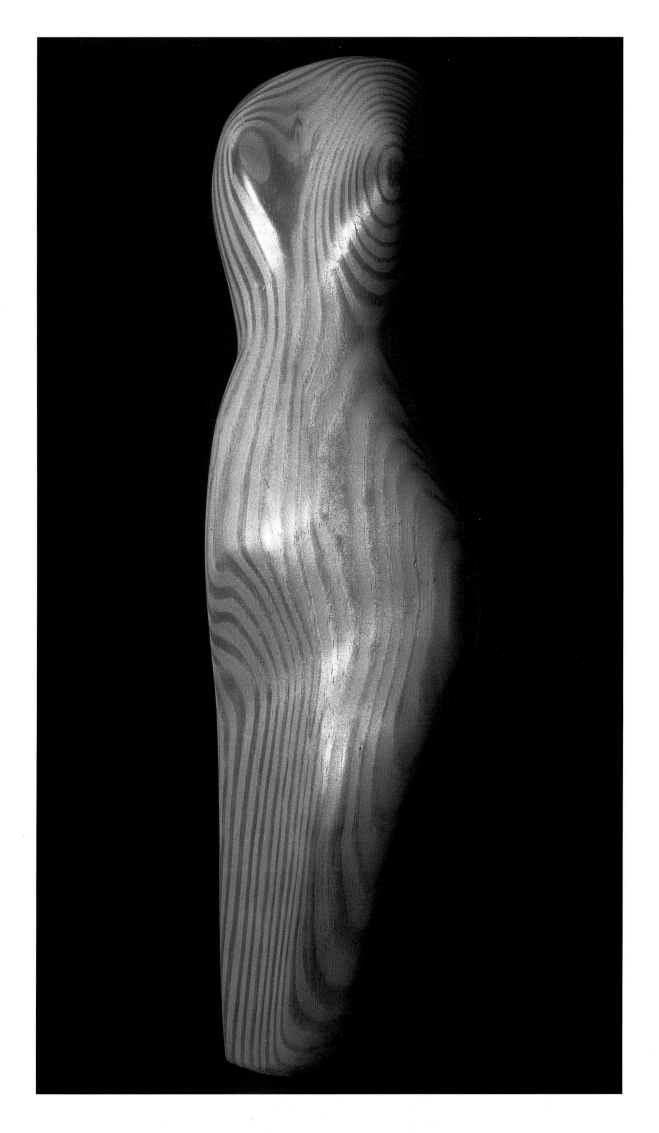

Torso of a young woman in *tribhanga*
wearing jewelry and holding
a mirror in her left hand.
Beige sandstone. H: 50cm. India,
Rajasthan, 11th – 12th c.

Opposite page:
Torso of the goddess Uma, the lower
part of the body cloaked in a sarong
held up by a belt with a flower motif.
Grey sandstone.
H: 68cm x L: 10 to 25cm. Cambodia,
Angkor Thom period, 12th – 13th c.

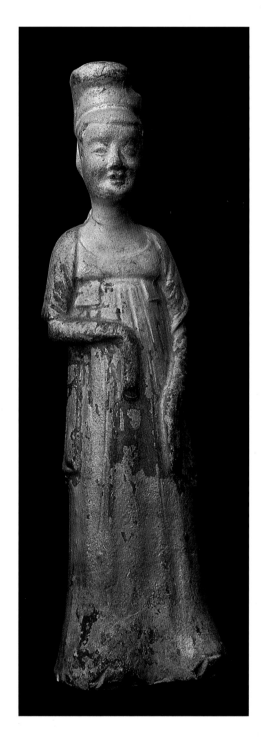

(Bourges Cathedral) or of the *Creation* (Orvieto Cathedral) or the eroticism of images of hell, sin and sorcery.

The Renaissance revived the Greek concept. Circa 1480, Botticelli produced a synthesis of the two aesthetics by putting the face of the Madonna on a Greek body in *The Birth of Venus* (Galleria degli Uffizi, Florence). The dreamy and melancholic air of the face attenuates the sensuality of the body; one breast and the private parts are hidden by the hands and hair. The male nude had reappeared earlier with Donatello's *David* (1440), thinner than ancient models. The *Apollo of the Belvedere*, a Roman copy of a Greek original dating from the 2nd century B.P., discovered in 1479, inspired artists. Michelangelo provoked his contemporaries with his *David* (1501-1504, Accademia, Florence) whose heroic appearance masks other possible meanings for Christians.

The nude and eroticism would imbue Western art whose oil paintings would succeed more than any other technique in exalting the female body. The chiaroscuro modulates the light on a dark background, allowing subtle transitions from one to the other and highlighting the pearly whiteness of flesh. The Venetians, whose city was the only one to obtain pigments from the Orient, were the first (with Corregio) to rediscover Greek sensuality, this time on a flat surface where the play of colors and shades suggested depth. While Botticelli's Venus half-hid her nudity and evoked the Virgin, nothing spiritual showed through the voluptuous bodies of the Venuses of Giorgione (*Sleeping Venus*, Dresden) or Titian (*Venus d'Urbino*,

Venus and Cupid), the Danaës of Corregio or Titian or the Susannahs (*Susannah and the Two Old Men* of Tintoretto). The Eves and Venuses of Lucas Cranach have an ambiguous charm. These mythological and Biblical themes were taken up by Rubens (*The Rape of the Daughters of Leucippus*) and Rembrandt (*Bathsheba in the Bath*) while the School of Fontainebleau audaciously set its subject in the present: *Gabrielle d'Estrées et la duchesse de Villars* are nude in the same bathtub, one pinching the other's nipple (circa 1594). The custom continued in Spain with Velázquez (*The Rokeby Venus*) and Goya (*Maja Desnuda*) while in 18th-century France, Boucher and Fragonard painted charming sex objects that, in the next century, became lascivious odalisques with Ingres and Delacroix which were expressions of Western fantasies. It was Manet who caused a scandal less by his nudes than by their way of looking the viewer in the eye such as the woman in *Le déjeuner sur l'herbe* and especially *Olympia*. Conventions fell by the wayside. The man was no longer the voyeur of the attractive, passive and dominated woman; she looked at him as an equal, peacefully, in a harsh light that accentuated her defiance.

Picasso's *Les demoiselles d'Avignon* broke with the tradition of the beautiful nude. The tradition of the female body offered to male desire has persisted in various forms: available and distant for Modigliani, decorative and troubling for Klimt, dreamlike for Delvaux, fantastic for Max Ernst and immature for Balthus. In sculpture, the abstraction of Hans Arp's white marble torso (1932) or Paolo

Female figure. Beige terracotta. H: 20cm. China, Tang, 7th c.

Ambrosio's veined wooden one accentuates the purity of its curves. Photography and the cinema amplify the process by spreading unveiled images of stars and sexualized advertising everywhere. However, art is not absent in the works of those who know how to capture the moment, playing with light and shade, and use all the capabilities of their equipment: a leg seen by Weston or a mouth captured by Man Ray have more erotic charge than a naked body in an ordinary photo. Black and white tells the essential of the subject better than color, magnifying the contrast of values and forms and highlighting graphic qualities.

Like the Greeks, the Indians gave their deities a human form, but with several heads and multiple arms to symbolize their power. Philosophical concepts also differ. Here, man is not the center of the universe. Under the law of karma – where every act bears its fruit in this world and in the other world – hoping for deliverance (*moksha*) from the cycle of rebirth, he has to practice *dharma*, the duty according to caste that does not exclude universal rules. However, unlike other religions, Hinduism admits that self-interest (*artha*) and pleasure (*kama*) are legitimate goals for believers on the condition that they are subordinated to *moksha* and dharma. Many texts have sublimated the pleasures of the flesh into fusion with the divine and made the sacred syllable *om* the symbol of the union of the sexes. The most widespread image of this vision is the stone lingam, source of life and intellect, associated with the god Shiva, which dates back to the civilization of the Indus (3rd-2nd millennia B.P.): rising from the middle of the

yoni, the female organ, it receives daily offerings. In Tantrism, the original unity is represented by the perfect shape of the stone egg (the lingam) marked with red streaks (the cosmic energy of female nature).

The erotic, as was mentioned, is the first of the aesthetic feelings, the king of the *rasa*. As sensuality constitutes the universe's raison d'être (wasn't it created by ardor and desire, as the most famous hymn of the *Rig Veda* proclaims?) very early on, between the 1st and 4th centuries, the Brahman Vatsyayana wrote the *Kamasutra* to teach men and women how to "enjoy the five senses with the aid of the mind and the soul." Its influence on poetry, theater, painting and sculpture was enormous. The most varied sexual positions that decorate several temples, notably those of Khajuraho and Konarak, seem to have come straight out of the *Kamasutra*. It should be noted that the Hindu temple is not a place for prayer like the Christian church, but a representation of the cosmos and the philosophy that underpins it.

If sensuality gives a sense of the divine, it is also what gives us the strength to renounce the ties that bind us to this world: "Those who seek deliverance (*moksha*) attain it by this detachment that can only come after attachment because the mind of beings is by its nature attracted to the objects of the senses" (*Kamasutra*). The embrace of the male Spirit, immobile and contemplative, tenderly impassive (the gods Shiva or Vishnu), and female Nature, active and dynamic (the goddesses Parvati or Laxmi who passionately embrace him), represents the path of duality to Unity. The sculptor enhances the beauty of the

Female figure. Red terracotta. H: 31cm. China, Han, 1st – 2nd c.

Miniature: young woman, naked
under a transparent veil. Paper.
H: 29.5 x L: 21cm.
India, Mogul School, 19th c.

Page de gauche :
Harunobu (1725-1770).
Two Women in front of a Screen,
one showing the other her calligra-
phy. Book page.
H: 25cm x L: 19.5cm. Japan.

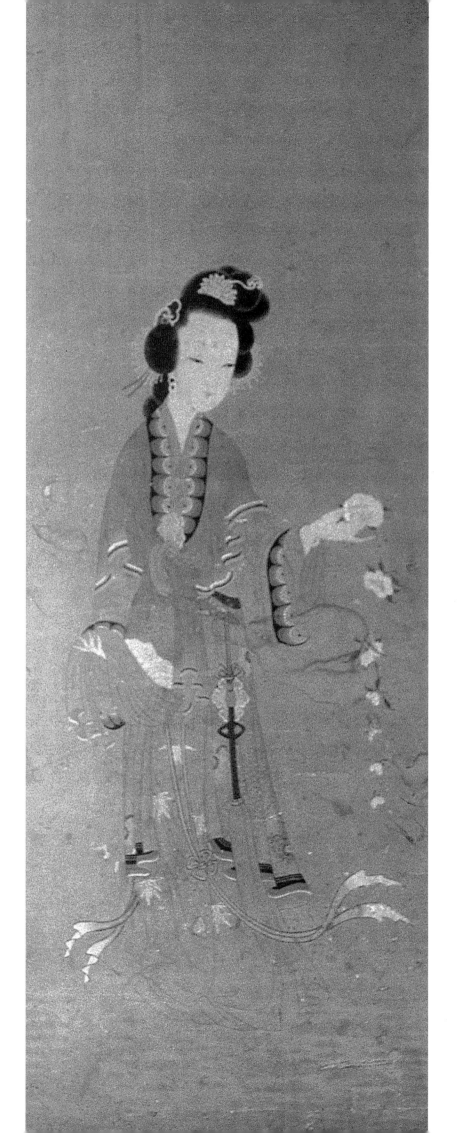

88

Anonymous, *Immortal
with Falling Flowers.*
Paper.
H: 108cm x 28.7cm.
China, late 18th c.

female form with the *tribhanga*, the triple flexing of the neck and shoulders, the chest and the waist and the waist and hips, in accordance to the canons of the theoreticians. In his *Gita Govinda*, "The Ode to the Divine Cowherd," which recounts the loves of Krishna (Vishnu) and Radha (12th century), Jayadeva sings of her "perfect face with water lily features": he compares her eyebrows to bows, her glances to arrows, her mouth to the red flower of the *bimba*, "lure of sensuality," and her hair adorned with flowers to a "voluminous black wave." Her "beautiful swelling breasts distill a charming necklace of pure perspiration." Jewels increase her loveliness: gems sparkle on her breast, the arched small of her back wears a shining belt and rings jingle on her ankles.

Paradoxically, at least in appearance, this sensuality also imbues Buddhist sculpture and painting although the doctrine makes the extinction of desire the path to liberation. The caves of Ajanta that the monks inhabited from the 1st to 7th centuries are decorated with realistic images of the life of Buddha including palace scenes filled with attractive young women with large breasts adorned with jewels who look, swing, caress themselves, dance and make music. There is even a half-naked couple in each other's arms in bed. These images do not come from an idea different from the Hindu one: detachment comes from attachment itself. Didn't Buddha leave his life of pleasure after being put in the presence of sickness, old age and death? The poet Bhartrihari (7th century) became a monk seven times and seven times went back into the world. He ended up thinking that female beauty was the trap that diverted man from his real goal, the search for deliverance:

When I was ignorant in the dark night of passion
I thought the world completely made of women,
But now my eyes are cleansed with the salve of wisdom,
And my clear vision sees only Buddha in everything. (in Randhawa, 3).

In Nepalese and Tibetan Tantrism, the way to initiation is often shown by a woman "bearer of energy": the dancing Dakini or the Tara, seated or standing, making one of Buddha's gestures (*mudra*), their breasts swelling and their bodies adorned with jewels.

Khmer sculpture yields no ground to that of India. This torso from Angkor incarnates the poem of the stele of Pre Rup (10th century) in stoneware:

"Her slim waist, gracious and shining, which perfumes the orients with the scent of the most precious essences, adorned with beautiful and sumptuous jewelry, prevails by its luster over all the beauty of the God with flowered arrows, the God of love, and rejoices the earth like the crescent of the new moon" (in Groslier, 85).

Painting was not left behind. Of all the schools of miniature painting, that of Kangra (a valley in Punjab) glorified most seductively for forty years (circa 1780-1823) female grace, personified by Radha, the cowherd loved by Krishna. In a setting of green hills, the painter lyrically describes the joys and pains of love in the expression of the eyes, the postures, the gestures and the clothing as, for example, when Radha wears white to meet Krishna on the night of the full moon:

"The girl is like the moonlight so as to become invisible, Her maid can follow her only guided by her fragrance"
(in Randhawa).

Radha has delicate features, black hair and a slim waist. The landscapes and colors themselves evoke the lovers' various feelings: desire, hope, doubt, impatience, passion, anger and jealousy. The compositions illustrate not only poems but also musical modes *(ragas)* that change with the hours and the seasons in parallel with the emotions *(rasa)*. Painting, poetry and music are closely linked to the goal of aesthetic exaltation, the path of Indians towards the Absolute.

In East Asia where Confucianism reigned (China, Korea, Japan, Viet Nam), there was no representation of nudity (except in erotic painting) as it was thought to be a mark of the uncivilized. Although official morality rigorously repressed everything that could harm the family, the foundation of society, sex was considered an essential element of life that gave it its flavor and even, for the Taoists, favorable to health and longevity when it is practiced while retaining oneself. The union of yin and yang projects the couple into the harmony of the cosmos (Tao), a concept similar to that of the Indians.

A 2nd-century poem listed the characteristics of the beautiful woman in the following way: tall, with a soft and finely chiselled face, the waist as thin as a roll of silk, the neck long and white, the jet black hair done up in a chignon, so shining that it could serve as a mirror, with a mouche that stresses her

smile; with clear eyes, their moist gaze limpid, with white teeth and red lips and a dazzling white body. (Rawson, 266-7)

Funerary terracotta has preserved gracious hieratic silhouettes draped in a long dress flared at the bottom, hands joined in the wide sleeves under the Han; more sensual, supple and lively under the Tang; musicians, dancers, polo players and ladies-in-waiting endowed with opulent curves for a time after the model of the favorite Yang Guifei whose tragic destiny was sung of by poets (8th century).

The ideal of female beauty was not very different in Japan except for the color of teeth which was black as in Southeast Asia. Artists celebrated this beauty in *ukiyo-e* (or floating world) paintings and prints of the Edo (now Tokyo) period (1600-1868) when the peace established by the Tokugawa led little by little to the decline of the feudal system and the emergence of an urban middle class hungry for pleasure, the path to power being closed to them. The term *ukiyo-e* is Buddhist in origin and was applied to the impermanence of things; it came to mean the world of pleasures symbolized by the red-light district of Yoshiwara. While traditional painting was interested in narrative and landscape, whether peopled or not, the themes of *ukiyo-e* were city life and its inhabitants: courtesans and their lovers, masseuses, theatre people, innkeepers and peasants. The two great masters were Harunobu (1725-1770) and Utamaro (1753-1806). Harunobu was a pioneer of the multicolored "brocade print" depicting attractive figures of the same type: oval face, fine features and a slim waist. As in the Heian scrolls,

feelings are expressed by gestures and colors. Utamaro was the first to depict women in portraits showing the head and bust, and especially to give them an expression, tender, melancholy, in love, worried or jealous. Less famous than Utamaro, Eishi (1756-1829) distanced himself from Utamaro's eroticism and the woodblock print in order to paint refined courtesans in their magnificent costumes on scrolls. These portraits may be compared to Chinese portraits.

The blackening of teeth was a widespread practice in Southeast Asia. The Vietnamese were attached to the practice as it distinguished them from the Chinese as did their long hair, a symbol of filial piety. In a popular song, a young man makes the following declaration to a young woman:

*I love you first for your hair that hangs like
a rooster's tail,
Second for your charming conversation,
Third for the dimples in your cheeks [when
you laugh] that are round as coins,
Fourth for your teeth shinier than jet.*

Contact with the West would lead to profound change. Men would cut their hair to symbolize their break with the archaism that had led to defeat and occupation, teeth whitened and female city dwellers adopted the *áo zài* silk tunic with two tails split on the right side and white trousers (even though white was traditionally the color of mourning). The most important revolution concerned the chest, prescribed flat by Confucian morality so as not to arouse desire: from that point onwards, women wore makeup and lipstick and freed their breasts, but kept their hair long. Contemporary paintings bear wit-

Hairpin topped with female
torso on a rectangular plaque
decorated with geometric
motifs. Wood. H: 21cm.
Zaramo, Tanzania.

ness to these transformations as well as to the differences between cities and the country, which remains more traditional.

In Africa, "classic" beauty is represented by the heads of the Ife. On this Nigerian site, discovered in 1938, there were royal heads in terracotta, bronze and copper, most of them life-sized, dating from the 12th-15th centuries. They are remarkable for their regular features, the parallel ridges covering their faces and the serenity that emanates from them. The art of Benin is derived from Ife. It has been well known since the late 19th century and also depicted royal heads in bronze that were smooth.

During a 1967 conference on Negro Art, H. Memel-Forte stated that, along with the qualities particular to a certain people or other, West Africa was in agreement on the following criteria for beauty: abundant black hair, firm breasts, a slim waist, round buttocks, full calves and a light complexion. But statuary deforms the body to emphasize the most important parts, first the head, seat of spiritual power, the long neck, sign of good health and, in women, the nourishing breasts. Perhaps only the Mumuye of Nigeria sculpt figures with a small head, often topped with a crest, large, stretched ears, very long arms, prominent elbows and notched short legs. These figures were used for divination, medicine and passing judgment. They confer prestige and protection to their owners. The asymmetrical slanting of the arms – quite rare (most are vertical) – makes this one intensely dynamic. The features could be very fine in Baule, Yohure, Guro and Dan work. The body is often highly polished to symbolize healthy

skin. The Guro ideal of female beauty was the following: oval face with a pointy chin, narrow nose, thin mouth, lowered eyelids, striated hair, long neck and arms and pendulous breasts. For the Senufo on the contrary, the face is prognathic and the breasts point forward. In this seated altar or divining figure, there is a double game of balance of curves (concave and convex) and straight lines (vertical and horizontal), the legs acting as two legs of a stool which makes the volume lighter.

There is a great diversity of styles even within a single people. One example of this is the "dolls" given to girls that are not only toys but also serve to inculcate in them the value of fertility as well as to promote it. The Mossi of Burkina Faso produce up to 25 types of more or less stylized *biija* with semi-circular heads and pendulous breasts that symbolize maternity. In contrast, Zaramo and Kwere (Tanzania) dolls sculpted by men have a phallic shape and barely accentuated round breasts and navel. The *akuaba* of the Ashanti of Ghana have a round, oval or rectangular face, but the neck is always long and ringed, which is aesthetically significant. The woman carries it on her back in order to have beautiful children. The heads of the dolls of the neighboring Fanti is more or less rectangular and the arms are not spread like those of Ashanti dolls.

The decoration of the body, particularly scarification and hairstyles adorned with pins and combs, does not aim only to beautify. They are the marks of a civilization that distinguishes between man and animal and indicate social status (young adult, married or not) and collective identity (us and them).

Figure of a man. Wood.
H: 1m. Mumuye,
Nigeria.

Akuaba doll. Blackish brown hardwood. H: 28.8cm. Ashanti, Ghana.

We must not forget their erotic function. According to Faik-Nzuji Madiya (1990), the signs are "in general very salient, for they must be sensitive to the touching hand or the rubbing body and at the erogenous places: belly, side, back, loins, buttocks, inner thighs." Thus a lozenge represents the female genitals for the Luba and Bena Luluwa. On the breasts it is called the "little rat trap" because the male organ has "a rat head." Between the navel and the pubis, it is called *kedjeke-kedjeke mpongo* which means steep slope or ravine, suggesting that the man who enters there can do nothing other than slide to the bottom. *Kedjeke-kedjeke* is onomatopoeic, imitating the sounds produced by bodies making love.

Influenced by the West, modern sculpture has gotten rid of traditional canons. In Kinshasa's market bronze statuettes that capture all the grace of the Black woman going about her daily business may be found.

Haiti is known for its naïve painters. They draw their inspiration from their African roots, the voodoo beliefs that give them their identity and their dreams of freedom and escape from an oppressive reality. The fact that it was the first independent Black republic (1804) is undoubtedly not extraneous to the emergence of a national style of painting, the only one in the Caribbean. Simil named this magnificent painting, which is not strictly speaking "naïve," *Petite allégorie du printemps* in homage to Botticelli – the woman's head is crowned with white flowers and a copper necklace and bracelets encircle the neck and arms – he is celebrating the beauty of a black woman with a pure profile.

The Americas abound in infinitely varied forms and styles with a relationship to beliefs we know practically nothing about. Within a single tradition, naturalism may exist alongside the fantastic. The "mother civilization" of Mesoamerica, the Olmecs (1500-400 B.P.), left colossal heads and masks executed like portraits of leaders with proud or disdainful expressions, adult and child figures in ceramic or jade and gods with half-human, half-animal features (jaguar, bird, dragon). Stylization was pushed to abstraction in Mezcala in Guerrero while naturalism was dominant in Veracruz with its famous "smiling heads." Also eloquent were the seated Qimbaya figures of Colombia, called caciques or orators, characterized by a large rectangular flat face, eyes and mouth reduced to horizontal slits, a nose ring and miniscule arms. In the Andes, the Mochica civilization (100 B.P.-600) most expressively represented the human face (and animal poses) in its terracotta vases.

In Oceania, in the midst of a plethora of fantastic images, emerges the abstract perfection of some works in wood: the paddle-shaped *rapa* dancing bat of the inhabitants of Easter Island one of whose ends represent a human head simply by the bridge of a nose curving into the double arc of the eyebrows to finish on the earlobes while the other represents a penis. The *tino* of Nukuoro (Micronesia) has a geometric body cut off from its featureless face whose small size (14-16 inches), along with it sculptural rigorousness, gives a sense of monumentality (Barbier-Mueller Museum, Geneva; Musée de l'Homme, Paris).

Figure of a seated woman. Wood. H: 22.5cm. Senufo, Ivory Coast.

93

Seated figure of a
cacique or orator, with
nose ring and slit
mouth. Terracotta.
H: 26.5cm. Qimbaya,
Columbia, 1000-1500.

Simil (1944) *Petite allégorie du printemps*: a woman in profile, head crowned with white flowers, arms with copper bracelets. Hardboard. H: 78.5cm x L: 78.5cm. Haiti.

Harmony of Color

According to Georges Seurat, "Art is harmony. Harmony is the analogy of opposites, the analogy of similarities, tones, tints, lines considered by the dominant color and under the influence of lighting, in happy, calm or sad combinations."

Until the 20th century, marked by a revolt against all traditions, harmony was sought out in all the visual and musical arts. Some saw it as a numerical relationship and constructed mathematical theories; others let themselves simply be guided by their sensibility. But harmony is also a cultural phenomenon to which each group adds content. Since the most ancient times, man has attributed magical, religious and social meanings to colors. They varied in space and time as much in life as in the arts.

Societies and significations

Color is a sensation. Man first derived this sensation from his body and from nature. He must have marveled at its wealth and been frightened by its threats. When he constructed his beliefs, he invested color with a function, assigning a meaning to each one. The most elaborate system was that of the five elements combined with the action of yin and yang, which explained the changing order of the cosmos and society in ancient China. To each element – wood, fire, earth, metal and water – corresponded a category of things: the cardinal points (east, south, center, west, north), flavors, odors, musical notes and colors (green, red, yellow, white and black). The relationships wood/green, fire/red, yellow/earth (the loess of the plains of the Huanghe, the Yellow River) and metal/white are obvious. As for the relationship water/black, it probably derived from the fact that water springs from the dark depths of the earth. In medieval Europe, it was thought that the world was formed out of four elements – earth, water, fire and air – each having a color – black, white, red and yellow. In the Indian theory of *rasa*, each feeling was symbolized by a color and a god: love by dark-blue Krishna; happiness by white and the genie companions of Shiva; sadness by gray and the god of death Yama; furor by red and Rudra, god of destruction; heroism by yellow and Indra, the sky god; terror by black and the love god Kamadeva; disgust by blue and Mahakala, the god of time who wears out all things; marvel by gold and Brahma, foremost among the gods; affection, "rosy as the inside of a lotus," by the Mothers of the worlds; and serenity, "milky as jasmine and silvery as the moon," by Vishnu-Narayana who rests on the eternal Ocean in which the universe is dissolved at the end of each cycle of creation. In sub-Saharan Africa, the environment has a limited palette: the ochre of the earth, the red of blood, the black of night "deep and perfidious" and the white of death and the spirits of ancestors. Thus, we see that certain symbolic associations may be found in all civilizations.

Isaac Newton (1671) discovered that white light split into colors including the three primary colors red, blue and yellow. Blended together in pairs they produce the secondary colors: purple (red + blue), orange (red + yellow) and green (blue + yellow). A

Armando Buitron Rojas,
The Traveling Child
(1999). Paper.
H: 33.7cm x L: 23.7cm.
San Antonio de Ibarra,
Ecuador.

secondary color is the complement of the primary color that was not used in its composition: green and red, purple and yellow, and orange and blue are complementary colors. The *shade* is each of the degrees through which a particular color can pass, *intensity* is its brilliance and *value* is its more or less dark character. *Tint* results from blending two or more colors and *tone* is the degree of this mix. Red, purple, orange and yellow are *warm* colors; blue, green and violet are *cool* colors; gray, beige and brown are considered *neutral*. These characteristics are relative because they depend on how colors are accompanied: between the extremes of red-orange and blue-green, a color is warm or cool according to its proximity to a cooler or warmer color. The effect also changes with the quality and size of the patches of color.

In the 19th century, Michel-Eugène Chevreul, director of the Gobelins factory in Paris, studied the consequences of the juxtapositions of colors which would be useful to painters, tapestry-makers and gardeners. He distinguished between two kinds of harmony: analogy and contrast of range (different tones or two very distant tones from the same range), shade, dominant color and complementary color. Orange placed between yellow and red, the two colors that make it up, loses its intensity. Conversely, the association of two complementary colors increases their brilliance; red beside green seems redder. Chevreul stated his *law of the simultaneous contrast of colors*: "In the case when the eye sees two colors at the same time, it sees them as dissimilar as possible as to their optical composition and the degree of their tone. The juxtaposition makes them lose their analogous qualities.

Did Chevreul's book, published in 1839, influence the Impressionists whose first exhibition was held in 1874? In fact, painters intuitively knew the possibilities of their palettes. However, while traditional art was attached to the durable, the Impressionists, sensitive to time and change, sought to isolate each moment according to the vibrations of the light they studied. Depending on the time of day, color changes. Yellow, orange and red become darker, and green and blue lighter at dusk. They do not have the same intensity outside and indoors. Only Seurat attentively read the scientific works and applied the rules of "division" to achieve greater luminousness: using only pure pigments, applying them as dots one beside the other, the impression of the whole coming together in the eye of the viewer (*Sunday Afternoon on the Island of the Grande Jatte*, 1884-1885). The rigidity of this system did not catch on.

In 1895, in front of Claude Monet's *Haystack*, Wassily Kandinsky had an intuition of the "abstract values of colors," an element of expression in itself, not subjected to the theme. While painting his first non-figurative canvases, Kandinsky wrote *The Spiritual in Art* (1910) where he set out his concept of "pure painting" that "begins at the edges of silence… language and music." He summed it up thus:

"Each work possesses its own form and only obeys an internal necessity. Each formal element has its own absolute psychic action.

The builder chooses among these materials in such a way as to transform absolute values into relative values: thus, hot, for example, becomes cold, and the sharp blunt. The simple or complex harmonies that result from these choices offer infinite possibilities."

Piet Mondrian pushed to the limit the liberation from the object. Defining art as the "concretization of logic," the goal of which is "peace of mind," he thought of the "plastic means" as a plane made up of orthogonal lines and primary colors (red, yellow, blue) juxtaposed with non-colors (white, black, gray). The balance of the relationships of these elements, from which symmetry is excluded, "causes the living rhythm." This dogmatism often resulted in lifeless compositions. Works where rhythm is in evidence are rare (*Broadway Boogie-Woogie*, 1942, Museum of Modern Art, New York).

Contrary to the preceding artists, whose works were more influential than their theories, other painters relied on their own instinct. According to Claude Monet, "paintings are not made with doctrines." Henri Matisse wrote: "My choice of colors does not depend on any scientific theory; it is based on observation, feeling and the experience of my sensibility." He highlighted the necessity "of having, from the start, a clear vision of the whole." He added, "The dominant tendency of color should serve expression in the best possible way." The artist does not copy nature, he interprets it. To render a landscape, he begins with the sensation that it inspires in him: "Autumn could be mild

Baya (d. 1998). *Woman and Flowers* (1992).
Paper.
H: 65cm x L: 50cm.
Algeria.

and warm like a prolongation of summer or, on the contrary, chilly with a cold sky and lemon yellow trees that give an impression of cold and already announce winter."

The desired result is only obtained after trial and error:

"If, on a white canvas, I dispense the sensations of blue, green and red, as I add touches, each of the ones I applied previously loses its importance... The various signs that I use must be balanced in such a way that they do not destroy each other. In order to achieve this, I must put my ideas in order: the relationship between the tones will establish itself in such a way as to support them instead of undermining them. There is a necessary proportion of tones that can lead me to modify the form of a figure or transform my composition."

Thus, one color could replace another as the dominant one. "Once all my relationships of tones are found, a living harmony of colors must result, a harmony analogous to that of a musical composition" (Matisse, 46-49).

Matisse is at one with the Chinese painters whose ink expresses color: the green of the leaves of the banana tree or the lotus, the red of rooster feathers or a crab shell. By the same token, white represents the sky or water.

The harmony of color is not only a question of physics. It is first subjective and cultural. Personal taste, symbolic systems and underlying social codes, sometimes for millennia, all interfere with the sensation. The eye perceives millions of colors, tints and tones, but the vocabulary is limited: some

Meal and Music in a Garden.
Manuscript page decorated
with golden foliage and flowers.
Miniature H: 15.4cm x 10.5cm.
Page: H: 30.5cm x L: 19cm. Iran,
Tabriz school, late 16th – early 17th c.

peoples use the same word for blue and green while others borrow the name from the object (orange is the color of the fruit, originally from Asia, that arrived in Europe in the 10th or 11th century); often the distinction is made by using a qualifier (light, dark, bright). Now the rawest colors are used with no thought as to harmony because it is expression that counts. In the Middle Ages, painters took into account the chiaroscuro of the churches of the West and Byzantium in order to harmonize their reredos while in East Asia, it was the gold of lacquered statues that shone in the darkness of Buddhist temples.

Two American anthropologists, Brent Berlin and Paul Kay studied color terms in 98 languages (1969) and found that they all possessed at least two: white and black. When there were three, the third was always red. The fourth was green *or* yellow. The fourth and fifth were green *and* yellow. The sixth was blue and the seventh brown. Purple, pink, orange and gray came after.

The dualism of black and white corresponds to the division between night and day. It was the first natural reality perceived by man. Several religions associated light with goodness and darkness with evil. In China, the yin-yang bipolarity, which imbued all philosophical and social spheres from cosmology to politics and aesthetics to food and sexual relationships, was derived from popular language where yin designated the shady slope of a mountain and consequently the humid and the feminine, while yang designated the sunny slope and consequently the hot and the masculine. The interaction of these forces produce changes in the universe. Opposite and complements, they evolve into each other according to the way of the Tao.

All over the world, man began by decorating his body as a way of identifying himself as a member of a community and indicating his status. During prehistory, he only had ochre and grayish white manganese to paint himself and his caves with, and cover cadavers perhaps believing in an afterlife because red is the color of blood. Nowadays, some of the peoples of Africa, the Americas and Oceania still paint their dead red, sometimes in white and black. However, generally speaking, the magical, religious and social meaning varies according to place and time. Even within a single culture, it can be ambivalent. As industry provides an almost limitless range of colors and manipulates taste through advertising, fashion constantly changes – this means that it is getting lost.

White symbolizes birth, the capacity for generation, ancestral spirits (West Africa), purity (ancient Egypt, Christianity) and mourning (China, Viet Nam). In contemporary interior decorating, white (and all its shades) is the most widely used color because it brightens and enlarges space and serves as a background for all sorts of combinations it shows to their best advantage.

For many peoples, black, the color of night, represents evil or death. On the other hand, in the Arab world, the black veil filters the light and protects from dust. In Europe, the Reformation transformed the medieval sensitivity to colors – during the

Zhang Daqian (1899-1983).
Traveler in his Boat among
Mountains and Water.
Ink and colors on paper.
H: 114.5cm x L: 38cm.
China.

101

Middle Ages, light, thought to come from God, was salvation. Protestantism preferred the black-gray-white axis, especially for clothing, as warm colors were thought immoral. The West still feels this influence as the Protestant ethic has become the capitalist ethic (Pastoureau, 48). In the United States, protesting racism, Blacks launched the slogan "Black is beautiful."

At the top of the rainbow, red, the color of blood and fire, is associated to life everywhere. In the West, it first derived its prestige from its link to purple, the most highly prized color in antiquity: the purple of Tyre (now lost) was extracted from a mollusk, the murex, and used to dye the robes of priests officiating at the mysteries of Eleusis. Roman consuls then emperors adopted it as an incarnation of Jupiter and were later followed by English royalty before red became the emblem of the revolution. Heraldry, which made its appearance in the early 12th century, was military in origin: it was used to

identify a combatant whose face was hidden by his visor. Initially limited to the nobility, it spread to commoners and cities. Heraldry used seven colors, two metals – gold and silver – and five enamels – red, purple, blue (azure), green (sinople) and black (sable). The colors were ambivalent as their existence depended on the way they were used: red represented courage to the point of sacrifice (to give one's blood for one's king or the Church) as well as anger, pride and cruelty. In Iran, red is the color of joy and happiness as it is in East Asia where it shines at weddings and feasts. On the contrary, red is now used for "stop" in traffic signals.

Green is ambiguous because it is both the color of vegetation and life, and the color of rest, illness and decline. In ancient Egypt, green was the color of Osiris, god of the harvest and death. In Europe, it was worn to weddings as a symbol of fertility. In heraldry, it signified plenty (but also disorder and madness).

The color of the earth in China, yellow was adopted as the imperial color because the sovereign received a mandate from heaven to govern the world. Buddhist monks wear yellow or brown because they are the colors of humility and renunciation. In India, during harvest feasts, people wear yellow, color of the ripening stems. In Europe, yellow's fortunes varied. The color of rituals at the end of the Roman Empire, it became less valued in the Middle Ages when it became the symbol of falseness and thus of Jews, Muslims and non-Christians in general. Gold was the exception: with azure, it shone on the coat of arms of the king of France. Today, it has been devalued once more.

This is not the case with blue, which is the favorite color of half the people in Western Europe and North America. This dates back to the 12th and 13th centuries when dyers obtained, instead of the dull blue of work clothes, a bright blue from imported indigo or ordinary woad. Blue became the color of the Virgin Mary, the king of France and the clothing of the aristocracy. Blue was first used by the Egyptians who produced it from cobalt (blue violet) and copper (blue green) for their amulets and beads. Later, Persia became famous for its turquoise whose name came from the semi-precious stone found there; it was called *piruseh* – joy. It was thought to repel the evil eye. It is found everywhere – on the mosaics and tiles that cover the mosques, *madrasah* (schools of higher learning), fountains and palace entrances (Topkapi), rugs (Nain) and ceramics (Nishapur, Isnik).

Turquoise and silver enameled square ceramic plate with iridescent reflections. 25cm x 25cm. Iran, Gurgan, 12th – 13th c.

Milan Rasic.
My Village. **Canvas. H: 44cm x 34cm. Dubrovnik, Yugoslavia, 1986.**

Pictorial colors and monochrome

If the harmony of color makes an object beautiful, we have seen that it is not principally a physiological phenomenon, but a cultural one which varies over space and time. The natural environment plays a part in this: colors do not have the same brightness under the luminous Mediterranean or in the misty air of the North. It is not in the sun, but at dusk that a Chinese or Japanese watercolor should be contemplated because it is the moment that play of the ink reveals all its subtlety.

A profusion of colors, even if they are harmonious, does not guarantee attractiveness. On the contrary, it could lead to the neglect of the essential and the unity of the composition. Leonardo da Vinci wrote: "Too much light results in crudeness; too much shade obscures vision. It is the medium that is good." The great masters are economic with their means: most of the time, a single color dominates. Recently discovered outside his own country, the Danish artist Wilhelm Hammershoi (1864-1916) was able to render, with simple variations of gray or beige crossed by a ray of light, all the strangeness of the familiar universe of interiors and farms with no human presence. Ultimately, the shades of India ink and the blank areas that it arranges in the space of the landscape evoke, with their filled and empty spaces, the rhythm of universal flow.

The first painting was on the human body and the caves where man made a print with his hand coated in ochre or soot and traced on the walls figures in red, white and black

Krishna, Radha and the Cowherds. **Pitchvaï (Ritual painted fabric used in the worship of Krishna). H: 187cm x L: 127cm. India, late 19th c.**

derived from clay, charcoal or easily accessible minerals: ochre, iron oxide and manganese. Of the two first civilizations, Mesopotamia left no paintings other than those on ceramic because they built with clay. This was not the case in Egypt where stone was abundant – we can admire the works that decorate its temples and tombs. The painter's palette was limited: smoke black, chalk or plaster white, gray, ochre yellow, red, brown, green (derived from malachite) and blue (obtained from a mixture of copper and calcium). He had to conform to the norms that guaranteed efficiency and survival: figures are always shown in profile, man was in red ochre, woman in yellow ochre and all colors had to stand out against the background. These conventions were not an obstacle to the lively representations of humans (scenes of daily life in the tomb of Nakht at Gurna north of Thebes) and animals (Meidum's *The Geese*) in beautiful colors. The highpoint of this painting is undoubtedly the *Scene Showing the Official Nebanum Hunting Birds* of the New Empire (British Museum) built around the opposition of vertical and horizontal lines on the right: the barge in the foreground, the columns of hieroglyphics in the background, the hunter brandishing his throwing stick and his standing wife, a bouquet in her hands, and, on the left, the commotion of the birds flying in every direction above the swaying papyrus. Only four colors were used – blue, ochre, white and black – but what harmony.

These colors may also be found in the spontaneous and charming frescoes of

Knossos: scenes of processions, a prince with lilies, a "Parisienne" priestess, women in blue alternating with images of dolphins, partridges, papyrus flowers, bulls, of a cat ready to leap on a bird in the middle of luxuriant vegetation. Crete was the great intermediary between Egypt and Europe.

If Greece was best known for its painted vases, Etruria has left behind moving witness to its love of life and its anxiety about death in the colorful frescoes full of movement of its tombs: banquets, dancers and musicians, hunting, fishing, landscapes, athletic games and couplings. From Pompeii

to Herculaneum, volcanic ashes have preserved the brilliant multicolored wall decorations of the 1st century: mythological, marine, floral, animal and pastoral scenes, portraits and depictions of daily life remarkable for their freshness and imaginativeness.

Byzantium was influenced by the Greco-Roman heritage as well as by Islam, using these influences to serve the Christian faith. The Christian religion and its mysteries were taught by images of Christ, the Virgin Mary and the saints and by narrations from the Scriptures. Byzantine frescoes and mosaics were not surpassed by the Latin West. They

are particularly well adapted to the domes and cupolas whose spherical shape recalls the vault of heaven. Blue and gold predominate – one evokes the sky; the other symbolizes divine majesty, reflecting the light and illuminating the figures and the details, making an unreal brightness reign in the church. The mosaic itself, made of cubes of multicolored glass paste, increases the effects of the chromatic aberration that is still intensified by the architectural design.

Johannes Itten, who taught the art of color at the Bauhaus, describes the "strange luminous atmosphere of colored grays" of the mausoleum of Galla Placidia at Ravenna (6th century):

"It arises from the fact that the blue mosaic walls of the premises are inundated with an orange light coming from the narrow windows fit with orange alabaster and filtering into the room. Orange and blue are complementary and, when they are blended, generate gray. When the visitor of the chapel moves around, he perceives in each point of the premises different quantities of light, with blue or orange predominant, for the walls reflect the colors under unceasingly differing angles. These variations of luminous colors give rise in the visitor to a sensation of wavering colorings" (Itten, 13).

The glass artists of the West used similar methods for their stained-glass windows. The most magnificent ones may be found at Chartres Cathedral (12th-13th centuries): the use of complementary colors (principally blue and red), the application of grisaille which attenuates or reinforces light colors and blown glass whose uneven shape and color enhance the decorative effect. The unequalled luminosity of the blue and copper red used changes according to the time of day and the angle of lighting. The otherworldly beauty of the stained glass contributes to the spiritual elevation of the believer, the goal of art that Suger inscribed above the portal of his abbey-church of Saint-Denis: "The infirm spirit awakens to the (immaterial) truth by material things."

The invention of oil painting in the 15th century offered artists an extremely supple technique with a very rich palette of colors, which became soft and transparent. Their thickness and their long drying time allowed all sorts of corrections and modifications while mathematical relationships, perspective and the play of light and shade suggested the illusion of space and depth and made the painting an "open window on the world." From Giorgio Vasari, the first biographer of artists, to Maurice Denis, the definition of a painting has barely changed: a "flat surface covered with colored zones" according to Vasari (1550) and a "surface covered with colors assembled in a certain order" according to Denis (1890). But the words do not have the same meaning and each creator has his own concept of shapes and colors. At the beginning, the intimist painting of the Flemish reproduced the local color of faces, clothing, furniture and landscapes; there was usually a dominant color which the other colors matched. The painters who followed – Italians, Dutch and Spaniards – were more sensual or profound, playing with the contrast of colors and chiaroscuro that exalted the flesh and accentuated the mystery of everyday objects as well as the drama of genre or historical scenes.

In the late 18th century, the palette was enlarged by artificial pigments and, in the middle of the 19th century, the tube of color became widespread while the large brush and the knife were used alongside the paintbrush. The research of John Constable and J.M.W. Turner, then the discovery of the Japanese woodcut with its flat colors and two-dimensional perspective overthrew the traditional vision: each object does not have only one color, it changes according to the time of day, the position of the sun and the environment. To render these effects, the Impressionists applied patches of pure colors that join together in the viewer's eye. Paul Gauguin used color to express his ideas about the world and Vincent Van Gogh to express his sensibility. For Van Gogh, yellow symbolized friendship or love and "red and green the terrible human passions."

Joan Miró transfigured the real, which he used to create a universe of strange and colorful images full of poetry, humor and imagination. Conversely, Mark Rothko moved from the figurative to "full forms [that] destroy illusion and reveal truth": surfaces filled with colors without contours, more or less luminous, always finely shaded, that succeed each other in bands to evoke, especially in the compositions in red, brown and black, a calm and mysterious beyond. Throughout his life, Pablo Picasso ceaselessly exploited the expressive resources of color, from the meditative blue of the *Portrait of Jaime Sabartes* (1901) to the almost monochrome (white, gray, black) tragic scream of *Guernica* (1937), from the peaceful joy of *Dream* (1932) to the stridency of the cries of *The Crying Woman* (1937). For Matisse, "the feeling is independent of a change in color. If a green is replaced by a red, the painting may have changed in aspect but not in feeling. Colors are forces that must be organized with a view to creating an expressive assemblage." Expression was also the key word for the naïve and abstract painters whose use of color was even more arbitrary than that of Matisse. From figuration, expression became a signifier independent of all reference to the visual. Since representation has been eliminated, color in itself may be enjoyed. John Ruskin felt that any object that gives us pleasure by the contemplation of its external qualities alone without the intellect intervening in a direction and definite fashion, can be called beautiful to a certain degree and in a certain sense. For those still preoccupied with harmony, the contrast between warm and cool, which has a spatial effect, prevails over chiaroscuro.

In some respects, contemporary Western art has points in common with Islamic art. Matisse discovered this during a 1910 exhibition in Munich: "Persian miniatures show me all the possibilities of my feelings. I could find in nature once again how they must come. By its accessories, this art suggests a large space, a veritable plastic space." Elsewhere, he spoke of "haunting dominant blues. The crescendo that goes from the deepest ultramarine to light azure tonalities, with a discreet counterpoint of pinks and

Shosen'in (1823-1880).

Landscape. **Thatched roof cottages among flowering prunus by a river with sailboats, at the foot of the mountains. Silk.**

H: 99cm x L: 40cm.

Kano school, Japan.

107

oranges, acts in these canvases like slow threnodies."

However, in Islam, color and abstraction come from a religious vision. The Koran forbids the worship of idols. It does not forbid the ordinary representation of animate beings, which may be found in the palaces and castles of the first centuries, but not in the mosques. It was conservative theologians who, beginning in the 11th century, wrongly interpreted the Koran, stating that the imitation of the real was an affront to God, the sole Creator. Painters got around the ban by suppressing the individuality of humans and animals and representing concepts and types and getting rid of anything that gives the illusion of life – perspective and modeling, light and shade. Only the Ottomans did not hesitate in having their portraits done, beginning with Mehmet, the conqueror of Constantinople, whom Sinan depicted smelling a rose. In India, the emperor Akbar (1542-1605) declared the exact reproduction of the real impossible: "in drawing any living being, a painter is obliged to admit that he cannot give individuality to his work. He is thus led to think of God, Creator of all life, and thus increases his wisdom." The Mogul rulers followed Akbar, as did the Safavids and Qajars of Iran.

The general non-imitation of nature led to conceptual art with regard to the representations of humans and animals and geometric and abstract with regard to décor. The importance of the color used was stressed, as in modern Western art, for its intrinsic properties independent of form. The prestige of the Koran made the art of the

book a major art: calligraphy and painting ranked highest, as did the binding decorated with arabesques, flowers or figures in gold. The oldest illustrated manuscript is an astronomical treatise from the 10th century. In the 13th century, Arab figurative painting developed with the illustration of the *Book of Kalila and Dimna*, a collection of fables of Indian origin, al-Hariri's *Maqamat*, "sessions" in which the author dissects the society in which he lived, and the *Book of Antidotes* (*Kitab al-diriyaq*). There are Byzantine influences as well as fairly realistic representations of animals and human beings, sometimes half-naked (Adam and Eve in *The Usefulness of Animals*, Maragha). Colors were limited, conventional or arbitrary (a slave and a lord are both dressed in purple and gold) and, in general, rather crude. Colors blossomed in the Persian miniature where artists made use of the rich minerals of their country. To avoid images casting shadows, they used pure colors of the same intensity on their simply juxtaposed surfaces. Papadopoulo wrote:

"The grass is green, but of a green that suited the artist in each miniature, in every place in the autonomous world. Certain artists chose a very dark green so that flowers and robes would stand out more while others chose a lighter shade but, in any case, the color did not depend on the reality, but on the internal needs of the work. Likewise for the flowers and fruits: always imaginary with conceptual colors and shapes, they are painted one by one, in the most distinct manner. It is the pure colors of these conceptual flowers that give the impression of a vision very

close to flowers, fruits and leaves and thus the sentiment of *being immersed in the plant world* – a romantic and pantheistic sentiment at the level of the 'world represented' and its numenal aura". (113)

The genius of painters, especially the Persians, was to execute an exceptional harmony of colors. Does not beauty bear witness to God? The Persians were more concrete and more sensual than the Arabs. After the fall of Baghdad in 1258, painting experienced a renaissance under the Ilkhans who introduced Chinese influences. The principal centers were Tabriz, Shiraz, Herat and Isfahan. In the illustration of the masterpieces of the national literature, Firdowsi's *Shahnameh* (Book of Kings) or other great poems like Nizami's collection of five tales *Khamseh*, or Saadi's *Bustan*, there are scenes of hunting and combat, of palaces and meetings of lovers in magical gardens that evoke paradise (the word is Persian in origin). Representation developed into a succession of tiered paintings viewed from above, a little in the Chinese manner, with sumptuous colors (lots of blue and gold). A few painters have left behind their names: Junayd (Baghdad), Behzad (Herat) and Reza Abbasi (Isfahan).

Iran influenced its neighbors. In Turkey, the first illustrated book was the history of Khosrow and Shirin (famous Persian lovers), dating from 1499. More original was Matraki's *Description of the Stages of the Campaign of Suleiman in the Two Iraqs* (1537), which shows cities and nature in a fresh way. However, the most vigorous art form was that of the portraits of sultans,

Lao Pakou (1947)
Mountain and Clouds.
Ink on paper.
H: 83cm x L: 77cm.
China.

which are evidence of great psychological acuity.

In India, where Islam gained a foothold in Sind in the 8th century, but did not begin to spread until the 11th century, the Mogul emperor Humayun brought painters from Tabriz whose technical contribution combined with indigenous traditions that remained predominant as far as the sensibility, motifs, design and colors were concerned. In addition to the school of Delhi, there were provincial schools with their own individual styles, shapes and arrangements, but the themes were common to all: palace, hunting and feast scenes, women at their toilette, meetings of lovers, grief and jealousy and the loves of Krishna and Radha. The Mogul school of Delhi was distinguished by admirable small paintings of animals while Rajput painting exalted the legend of Krishna and the cowherds who, as with the European mystics, couched in allegorical terms the relationship between man and God. Painting and music were closely linked. As in Europe, the word scale applied to the corresponding flavors (*rasa*), sounds (*raga*) and colors: "the tonic is luminous like lotus petals, the second is of a fawn color, or like a parrot; the third minor is golden; the fourth evokes jasmine; the fifth is Krishna the dark and seduces you; the sixth is yellow and the seventh minor is multicolored" (Rawson, 131). Thus, Krishna and dark blue symbolize love, the first *rasa*. Furthermore, the pentatonic scales are considered masculine while the others are considered feminine (*ragini*). Poets composed "raga garlands" (*ragamala*) that were interpreted by painters and musicians. Miniatures called *raga* or *ragini* illustrate poems describing moods in different seasons and different times of day. Color creates a specific emotional climate.

In China, color plays a lesser role. It is only the fourth of Xie He's principles, coming after the cosmic breath, the vigor of the brushstroke and the correspondence with the object. Here, the ink is enough to render the color of things and has the advantage of concentrating attention on their essence rather than on their exterior resemblance. Contrary to Mondrian's statement, black and white are fully-fledged colors. The white of the background has different nuances according to the quality of the silk or paper, their texture, age and priming. Silk predominated until the 12th century and was used for portraits, court scenes, flowers and birds, fruits and vegetables, and animals and insects, which are usually in watercolor, while paper is better suited to the effects of depth in landscapes, mountains and trees. White differs according to whether it comes from shells or ceruse, which blackens with oxidation. By the same token, black varies according to the mineral or plant material from which it is derived (pine soot produces the most brilliant black), the manufacturing process, the age of the stick (which makes it a treasure), the degree of dilution with water and how much ink is loaded on the brush. Three types of chiaroscuro (yin yang) are obtained by the play of ink and brush: dry-wet, concentrated-diluted and black-white – the first two are also used for color. According to Han Zhuo, a 12th century critic, "The brush gives shape and substance; the ink separates the light from the dark. If the ink is too abundant, the appropriate style is lost and the work of the brush is spoiled and thick. If the ink is too thin, the breath becomes timid and weak. Too much and too little are errors."

A Qing era author specifies:

"Everything under the sun is endowed with shape and color. It is for the brush to draw the shape and for the ink to recreate the color. When one says color, one does not refer so much to green or red, etc., than to a thousand light and dark shades that give things their aura. Skillfully handled, the ink is able to bring out the subtle expression of things, to reconstruct a scene in all its freshness. It is by ink that harmonious breaths most fully manifest themselves.

When painting, the artist must use the ink in successive layers, otherwise it will only result in a black blotch. Applied lightly, ink is as discreet as an evanescent mist; concentrated, it shines like an open eye; dry, it suggests the indescribable state between being and not being; wet, it shimmers. It can be limpid as an autumn lake, luxuriant as a hill in spring, fresh as a flower at dawn and delicate as fragrant grass. It conserves its luminous quality over the centuries when even silk would be threadbare. Because of its radiance, the soul of the painter doe not perish and the viewer experiences infinite pleasure. This is called the transforming power of ink (*mo hua*)" (in Cheng, 1989, 41).

The distance Europeans create from colors (warm colors seem to advance while cool colors seem to retreat), the Chinese obtain by the values of ink. In landscapes, nearby objects are in black and those in the background are in gray due to the dilution of the ink. This is not to say that color is not used. Even ink landscapes are enhanced with light colors. In effect, according to Tang Tai (Qing dynasty), "the color of the mountain varies according to the time of day and the seasons." He adds:

"To paint a mountain in the spring, blue and green is mainly used to highlight the tones of grass sparkling with raindrops or petals strewn along a riverbank; also to represent the boat of fishermen who come and go along the edge of a cliff. These colors inspire a feeling of joy in the viewer. For a mountain in the summer, blue and green are also used, as is mineral ochre notably in the representation of shadowy foliage or large lotus leaves diffusing an exquisite fragrance, or a hill after the rain, all surrounded by luminous mists. These colors inspire a feeling of peace in the viewer. For a mountain in the fall, ochre, red and green are mainly used to bring out the nuances of maple leaves and the deep reflection of a pond or to represent a solitary temple raising itself to the clouds without anyone on the paths that surround it. These colors inspire a feeling of meditation mixed with melancholy in the viewer. As for the mountain in the winter, it demands discreet or dark colors – silver gray, dark brown, etc. With these colors, which inspire a feeling of respect mixed with fear, one can paint icy water trickling down, snowflakes brushing past a balustrade and a bare forest or high peaks enveloped in white. When one understands the spirit of each season, the colors one uses make the ink radiant" (Cheng, 1989, 43).

Paintings of flowers, birds and people are generally in colors whose pigments are derived from plants (cane yellow, indigo blue) and minerals (iron oxide, malachite, azurite). Nowadays, ink is still the preferred material. It has lost none of its force as in this painting by Lao Pakou. Abstract at first sight, one can see the age-old image of the mountain and find the first quality of the tradition: the cosmic breath (*qi*) that goes

Uzbek cotton caftan with a gold and silver brocade floral pattern on a red background. H: 138cm. Uzbekistan, 19th c.

through it. The artist used "splashed ink" (*po mo*) in wide concentrated or diluted black, gray and blue vertical strokes that suggest the volumes and the distances. He used neither wrinkles (*cun*) nor dots (*dian*) to depict the veins or unevenness of rocks: abusing this process made it artificial, stripping the ink of its sculptural power. The dark mass stands out against a white background. Its diagonal is highlighted at the ends by two small patches, one pink, and the other red: the fundamental relationship between yin and yang and empty and full is present. This relationship is not often found in the paintings of, say, Franz Kline or Pierre Soulages.

Chinese painting entered Japan via Korea at the same time as Buddhism in the 6th century: art was first used to teach the religion.

The Japanese soon distinguished themselves from their model in the handling of landscapes (the roofs of houses were not painted to enable the people inside to be seen), the realism of the subjects (Buddhist, Shinto or profane narratives or portraits, especially terrifying gods, the illustration of the *Tale of Genji* where emotions do not show in the faces or the gestures but in the folds and colors of the clothing, the humor and satire of scrolls illustrating the life of the people) and in the colors whose harmony differed from that of the mainland. Thus developed the national *yamato-e* in contrast with the Chinese influenced *kara-e*. The most famous Japanese painters, Sesshu and Sesson, worked in ink while the Tosa school was dedicated to the *yamato* style and the Kano

blended the two tendencies. According to Japanese authors, "Chinese painting is enamored of the real, the true and immutable laws while *yamato*-style painting prefers the immediate, the ephemeral and instantaneous balance" (in Linhartova, 265).

This statement is perhaps not entirely justifiable. However that may be, the characteristic of Japan's own forms of painting – the sliding door, the folding screen and the woodblock print – is the richness of its polychromatism. There are, of course, exceptions like Hasegawa Tohaku's *The Pine Wood* whose variations in ink evoke all the mystery of a misty landscape (National Museum, Tokyo).

The sliding doors (*fusuma*) and mobile screens (*byobu*) are part of Japanese architecture, serving to separate or enlarge rooms. The decoration of these items developed in the Momoyama period (1568-1615) with the construction of castles and the lords' taste for luxury, later imitated by the rising merchant class. Kano Eitoku was the first to use gold leaf as a background for depicting the earth, the clouds and the sky. Sotatsu and Korin brought this art to its peak. Korin's masterpieces are *Irises* (Nezu Museum, Tokyo) and *Plum Trees* (MOA Museum, Atami). With three colors, the two blues of the successive irises and the green of their leaves on a gold ground, Korin created a musical rhythm. *Plum Trees*, also on a gold ground, has a more complex composition: in the middle of the screen is a dark river with undulating waves, on the left, a plum tree with white blossoms above a rock and on the right, a plum tree with red blossoms whose

113

Cushion decoration in silk embroidered with multicolored floral and geometric patterns and two ewers, multicolored fringes on three sides.
57cm x 53cm. Bukhara, 19th c.

branches spread out in all directions. A magnificent decorative ensemble results from the balanced contrast of shapes and colors.

The polychromatism of the woodblock print varied according to the artist, the subject and the era. It only dates back to Harunobu, whose production – using 10 blocks in 1765 and 15 at the end of his life – was so successful that it was called *nishiki-e* because of its brocade effects. In addition to courtesans and actors, landscape won acclaim with Hokusai and Hiroshige. Hokusai became famous with his *Thirty-six Views of Mount Fuji* (1828-1833), really 46, and Hiroshige with his *Fifty-three Stages of the Tokaido* (1833). Hokusai was the "madman of drawing" and Hiroshige was a subtle poet despite or because of his limited palette (gray, blue and black). Both of them influenced French Impressionism by their description of variations in the weather, the seasons, the mist, the snow, light and rain in different views of the same subject (Mount Fuji). Today, the woodcut print remains very lively.

The magic of ornamentation

The ornamentation of the body and the home makes everyday life more beautiful. Weaving is the interlacing of two sets of threads, warp and weft, to make a cloth. Its origins must lie in basketry, evidence of which is preserved in Neolithic pottery. The horizontal warp loom was used in Egypt for weaving linen as early as the predynastic period (5000-3100 B.P.) and the vertical loom around 1900 B.P. The pedal loom, invented in China to weave silk whose range of colors was nearly complete during the Han dynasty (205 B.P.-220), arrived in Europe in the 13th century. The pull loom, then jacquard (1800) were other technical innovations but the beauty of the cloth still depended on the taste of the craftsman as the Peruvian textiles of the 1st millennium B.P., preserved by the dryness of tombs, testify. They contain more than 120 shades from three main pigments: indigo, an unknown brown-yellow colorant and cochineal. Despite rudimentary tools, Amerindians

Gulbadan, **silk woven with gold, silver and colored threads. Sind, India, 18th c.**

made unequalled tapestries, embroideries and brocades.

This is because cloth has several functions. It is not only used to clothe or furnish. It also indicates the social or religious status of a person until his death. Each stage of life – childhood, adolescence, marriage, childbearing and death – may be marked by a change in clothing. Gender and clan are also factors of differentiation as is rank in a hierarchical society: in imperial China, the motifs and colors of the official robes of mandarins varied according to the wearer's rank. In fact, in no society, even the most "democratic," is clothing identical for everyone. Fabrics are also used as money (in China, silk was used to pay or reward officials), taxes (the Incas) and diplomatic gifts.

Weavings, using fibers of animal, plant or synthetic origin, take various forms. The oldest fragments were discovered in Çatal Höyük (Anatolia) and date from the early 6th millenium B.P. Tapestries from the era of Thutmosis IV and Tutankhamen date from 1400-1300 B.P. and those of the Paracas of Peru date from 700 B.P. In both cases, the dryness of the desert preserved them. Elsewhere, ice played the same role: in a Scythian tomb in the valley of Pazyryk in Altaï was a knotted carpet decorated with horsemen, reindeer and geometric motifs dating from 5th-4th centuries B.P. The first known fibers were linen (Egypt, 5000 B.P.), wool (Mesopotamia, 4000 B.P.), silk (China, 2640 B.P.) and cotton (India, 3000 B.P. – the word comes from the Egyptian *goton*, which became *qoton* in Arabic; Amerindians discovered it independently).

The attractiveness of a fabric comes from the finesse and the softness of its threads (which is why silk has been the most highly esteemed since its appearance), the richness of its decoration and the brightness of its colors. It is conditioned by advances in weaving, dyeing and printing techniques either directly by block, roll or serigraphy or by resistance (*batik, plangi, ikat*), particularly widespread in India and Southeast Asia.

Luxury goods that are easily transported, fabrics were soon traded internationally. Remnants of clothing dyed with Tyrian purple found in Ur in the late 3rd millennium B.P. are evidence of this. This trade then spread to Egypt and Iran and increased considerably during the Hellenistic and Roman eras. In the East, Chinese silk was exported as early as 3rd century B.P. to Korea, Mongolia and Xinjiang and later to India and the West via the Silk Road. India and China traded and met in Southeast Asia before the expansion of Islam beginning in the 7th century influenced this part of the world. In the 16th century, European ships began a new era of commercial and cultural exchanges.

This history affected methods of weaving and dyeing as well as themes. China borrowed the motif of animals or birds facing each other in an oval or round frame from Sasanid Iran and the technique of petit point and the word for it (*kesi*) from the Uighurs of Turkmenistan. China exported the dragon – the imperial symbol – to Viet Nam and the "three friends" (pine, prunus, bamboo), the crane (symbol of longevity), the carp (symbol of endurance) and the tortoise (symbol of

Multicolored brocade with vines and bunches of grapes. Hyderabad, India, 19th c.

Detail of a double bro-
cade sash decorated
with predominantly
blue and red flowers
and foliage. Fez,
Morocco, 19th c.

the universe) to Japan. Byzantium set up silk workshops in the 4th century and enlarged them after the introduction of silkworm breeding from China in the 6th century. Imperial silks, dyed with purple from Tyre, and other silks dyed gold, green, blue and red, were decorated with griffons, bulls, lions, elephants, birds, hunting or religious scenes and floral motifs which revealed the Iranian influence. Western churches have conserved superb pieces that, along with Sasanid, Muslim and Chinese cloths, played a major role in the rapid development of the European silk industry. This industry was born in Sicily where the Arabs introduced silkworm breeding in the 9th century (in Andalusia in the 8th century) and spread to Venice, Genoa and Florence which, with their gold lampas, velvets and damasks (from the name of Damascus), made Italy predominant in the 14th and 15th centuries. The 18th century saw the emergence of France, which made Lyons the center for silk. Another luxury good that became well known – tapestry – was successively associated with the cities of Arras, Tournai, Brussels and Paris. Social revolutions and changes in living spaces and tastes led to its decline.

Other fabrics changed less. Destined for the aristocracy and the middle class, motifs remained floral for the most part, varying little, with rather monotonous colors. There is more imagination and gaiety in the magnificent embroidery that decorates headdresses and costumes of the Central and Eastern European countryside. This wealth is explained by the attachment to traditions and the affirmation of cultural identity faced

with foreign domination (by the Austrians, Russians and Ottomans) even if some motifs are borrowed from them (the rose, the tulip and the pomegranate, all Turkish in origin). The beauty of clothing and furnishings are the only luxury that poor country people could give themselves at feasts, the most important of which was marriage. Geometric, plant, animal and human motifs were combined harmoniously in colors that were sometimes bright and contrasting and sometimes in monochrome.

In Japan, silks were initially reserved for the use of the court and Buddhist temples under the control of a weaving office created in 701. During the Heian period (794-1185), a strict etiquette controlled the décor and colors of the costumes of the aristocracy while Chinese themes took on an indigenous allure or were cast aside for more Japanese themes: flowers, birds and butterflies in branches, often enriched with gold and silver powder. Men and women wore several superposed robes whose colors were in harmony with the seasons as shown in illuminations. The monks wore *kesa*, shawls made out of patches supposed to symbolize Buddhist renunciation, but the taste of the aristocracy (to which most of them belonged) transformed these into sumptuous robes. The coming to power of the samurais put the accent on the manufacture of weapons where the talents of the weaver (for the decorative cords and tassels), the lacquerer, the blacksmith and the leatherworker came together. It was only after the peace of the Tokugawa (17th century) that the art of cloth was revived, encouraged by the theatre, the

Detail of a *hinggi* (man's
cape) in *ikat* decorated
with two-headed eagles,
horses, tortoises and crabs
on a blue background.
Cotton. H: 240 cm x 88cm.
Sumba, Indonesia.

Detail of a *susani* wall
hanging decorated with
circles and stylized floral
and plant motifs on a red
background. Central
Asia, 19th c.

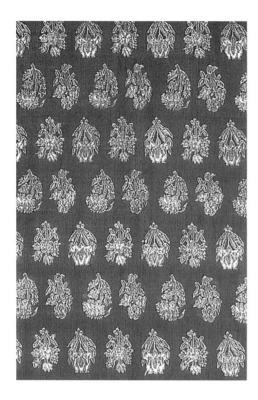

merchant class, the development of plea-sure districts and the growing of cotton. Kyoto became the center of the best known woven fabrics used for the costumes of Noh and kabuki actors as well as those of the geisha. New techniques making use of dye-resistant pastes resulted in more elaborate decorations. Many painters did not hesitate to take part in their design. As demonstrat-ed by the woodblock prints and scrolls of the period, themes and colors were more varied and bold than those used in Chinese fab-rics. Asymmetry and movement were dom-inant whether in the handling of landscapes or in the alternating of geometrical and flo-ral motifs, fans and abstract shapes, bro-cading and resistant dyeing techniques, and soft and bright colors.

Because of the prohibition of idolatry, the magnificence of Islamic textiles comes from their lines and colors. The first fabrics were robes of honor distributed at court that were embroidered with inscriptions in silk thread (the oldest *tiraz* dates from the 8th century). This art reached its peak in Safavid Iran (16th-

18th centuries) whose brocades, lampas, vel-vets and rugs, often adorned with gold and silver thread, were admired by European travelers.

In fact, rug making antedated Islam because the Pazyryk, mentioned above, was attributed to the Scythians who were origi-nally from the north of Iran. When the Arabs took Ctesiphon, the Sasanid capital, in 636, they shared among themselves the carpet known as "Khosrow spring" that was 25 square meters and decorated the main hall of the palace. According to the chroniclers, "the border was marvelous bed of flowers made from blue, red, white, yellow and green gemstones; in the field, the color of earth was imitated with gold; clear stones such as crystal gave the illusion of water; the plants were woven from silk and the fruits formed with colored stones." In the 16th century, the Safavids set up royal work-shops in Kashan and Isfahan whose influ-ence spread through the country to India and Turkey. Cloth and carpets were deco-rated like miniatures with floral, human and

animal motifs, garden, hunting and palace scenes taken from the legend of Leila and Majnin, the *Shahnameh* and *Khamseh*. Some miniaturists, such as Reza Abbasi and his son, worked for the workshops. The rug spe-cific to Islam is the prayer rug the *mihrab* of which the believer turns toward Mecca. The silk rug, made with up to 20 colors, changes in appearance and color according to the lighting and the angle from which it is viewed. To fully appreciate its beauty, one must touch and stroke it.

As it did for miniatures, India brought in from Iran its first carpet makers. However, beginning in the 17th century, it has its own style characterized by a more vigorous ani-mal design, more naturalistic plant motifs and a less cramped surface. In Anatolia, the tradition of rug making is very old. Ibn Battuta praised it in the 14th century. In the 15th cen-tury, carpets arrived in Europe and appeared in paintings, especially those of Hans Holbein and Lorenzo Lotto who gave their names to two types of carpet. Fervent Sunnis, the Turks did not depict scenes with humans or animals, but made splendid variations of geometric and floral (tulips, hyacinths, car-nations) designs in different color combi-nations in which red, green and blue were dominant.

The museums of Europe and the United States have conserved magnificent carpets from the Persian, Turkish and Mogul courts. The most famous is undoubtedly that of Ardebil, which dates from 1540 (Victoria and Albert Museum, London), a huge mosque rug (11.52 m by 5.34 m) in silk and wool, of a density of 5,300 knots per square

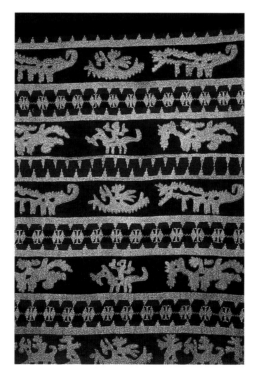

Indian child's *huipil* embroidered with mythical animals. Cotton. Chichicastenango, Guatemala.

decimeter. On a dark-blue background filled with flowers stands out a central medallion made up of a sixteen-pointed star prolonged on the vertical axis by two hanging lamps. Various shades of red and yellow make up a warm harmony. The harmony of the garden carpet of the Museum of Art in Philadelphia (5.39 meters by 5.25 meters) from about the same era is even richer because of its more varied motifs and colors: it features a field covered with cypresses, branches, foliage and stars as well as a border of three bands, the widest of which is in the middle and decorated with interlacing arabesques in alternating blue, yellow and red.

Preferable perhaps to the refinement of the above rugs are the rustic and fresh rugs woven by nomad women or in the villages of Iran, Turkey, the Caucasus and Central Asia whose designs and colors inspired workshops in cities, adapting urban models in turn. Generally speaking, these rugs are characterized by the simplicity (which does not mean a lack of variety) and stability of subjects, the rhythmic repetition of motifs, most often geometric or animal, and the use of a small number of contrasting pure colors (originally derived from nature). Women find their harmony instinctively: red, the color of life, prosperity and fertility, dominates with a little blue, a limited range but quite varied in fact, because of the adjacent different shades.

According to a Persian proverb, "to possess a carpet is to possess a home." Indeed, a carpet placed under a tent gives it warmth and life because of the brilliance of its colors and the softness of its wool. It breaks the monotony of the desert and protects against the cold. The art of rug making is passed on from mother to daughter when she is 6 or 7. The rug plays an important role in the life of the family and of the community. It is given as a gift at weddings and funerals. It makes up part of the bride's trousseau: this is why the woman has to prove her ability to weave it and to make clothing, covers, bags, cushions and wall hangings. Finally, it is a sign of tribal identity: some motifs resemble each other from one group to another, all the while differentiating themselves by a few details such as the well known *gül* (flower) of the Turkmen, octagons or diamonds, whether closed or open. Carpets also include the *kilim* (a flat cloth made of threads without knots or velvet), the *sumak* (a kind of *kilim* in which only the colored weft threads are visible as they cover the warp threads) and the patchwork rug (made of used or new pieces sewn together). The velvet robe embroidered with gold and silver thread

Detail of a funerary cloth decorated with multicolored birds and cervidae on a red background. Cotton. W: 34.5cm. Chancay, Peru, 11th – 15th c.

showed the status of khans and other worthies. The *susani*, a hand-sewn wall hanging embroidered with flowers, is the most precious furnishing textile.

In North Africa, as elsewhere, a distinction must be made between city and country. The country preserves vibrant Berber traditions, especially in Morocco, in materials (usually wool), clothing (women's veils and men's capes), motifs (geometric, animal – serpents, scorpions, etc. – varying from tribe to tribe) and colors (some are reserved for chieftains; for women, colors change for the unmarried, married and elderly). The products of cities include magnificent caftans in silk brocade with floral decoration or in velvet with geometric decoration, often embellished with gold thread trimmings or embroidery, wall hangings, cushions and belts in more subdued harmonies than in rural areas. Rabat is renowned for its embroidered silks whose designs in warm colors of various shades evoke fields of flower petals. Since the 14th century, Fez has produced ceremonial standards decorated with inscriptions, parade horse covers, velvet and silk gold brocade wall hangings and the famous belts that married women wear during feast days on top of their matching caftans. Sometimes single, sometimes double (to be folded in half), they are in brocade geometric and/or floral motifs, often enriched with gold and silver thread with an eight-pointed star and a stylized hand, which guard against the evil eye, on each end. The background is a subtle blend of various shades or colors so that the woman may match the various bands of her belt to her caftans.

In sub-Saharan Africa, the climate reduces the utilitarian function of clothing. It serves above all, with jewelry, to reveal the social status of the wearer and sometimes to accompany him in death. The main material is cotton. Some peoples use raffia, beaten bark and wool. In Ghana and the Ivory Coast, imported silk was reserved for the king and dignitaries. In West Africa, the single pedal loom is associated with woman and the double pedal loom with man; they produce thin strips of cloth that are sewn together to obtain a wider cloth.

At first sight, the colors are restrained. Before the 20th century, the colors were those of mud and plants (blue, red and yellow). The beaten bark of the Pygmies, worn as a loincloth during ceremonies and feasts, was decorated in smoke black geometric or animal motifs whose beauty lay in their rhythm. The same is true of low pile raffia cloth called "Kasai velvet" and the *ntschak* with geometric appliqués for which the Kuba women of Central Africa are famous.

There is more color in the silks of the Akan and the Merina. The *kente* of the Akan are prestige garments worn by their chieftains. Their check decoration plays on the contrast of lines, symbolic motifs and colors – red, yellow, blue and green are predominant. Malagasy *lamba* are shrouds to envelope corpses during the rite of the turning of the dead. The word means red cloth; red is a color associated with power. By using it, the living ensure the protection of the dead. In fact, red is only the dominant color in a series of multicolored vertical bands.

It is undoubtedly in Southeast Asia that

Mola **decorated with appliqué of two fish and two birds on a red background. Cotton. H: 27.5cm x L: 38cm. Kuna woman's work, San Blas Islands, Panama.**

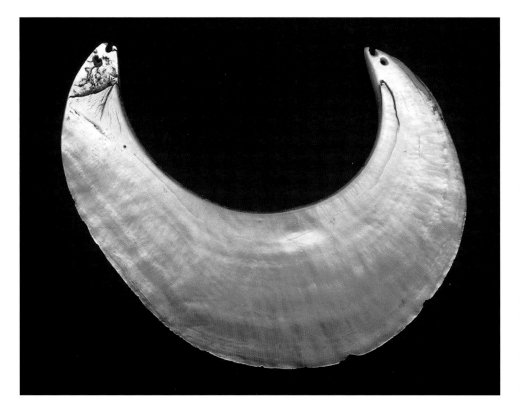

the greatest wealth of colors is found which is explained by the diversity of the peoples and cultures as well as by the variety of the tropical environment and sources of pigment and by its position at the center of international trade since the Bronze Age. After the Dongsonian motifs of Viet origin came the Hindu and Buddhist contributions: the lotus, Mount Meru (or Sumeru), center of the world, the serpent *naga* and the bird *garuda* (Vishnu's mount), themes from the *Mahabharata*, *Ramayana* or *Jataka* (the previous lives of Buddha) and Gujarati double ikat *patola* cloth. The Chinese introduced its silk, clouds, rocks, dragons and phoenixes as well as its embroidery techniques; Islam brought its arabesques and interlacing and Europe certain floral motifs, its synthetic dyes and threads. All these influences were harmoniously integrated, each culture differentiating itself from its neighbors by a certain characteristic such as the choice and placement of motifs or the combination of colors. While cotton and silk are the principal mate-

rials, some peoples, notably in the Philippines, also use pineapple (*pina*) and banana tree fibers. In this part of the world, textiles are a major method of artistic expression (sometimes ahead of architecture and sculpture). They play a major social role during each stage of life as a sign of age and position, a wedding gift, temple banner and shroud.

While the dyeing techniques used were already known elsewhere for a long time (Egypt, Central Asia, Peru, China and India), the fact that many have Malay names bears witness to the renown of the archipelago's fabrics. The indirect and lengthy methods of decoration produce more refined effects than the direct weaving of threads of different colors, embroidery, appliqué work or

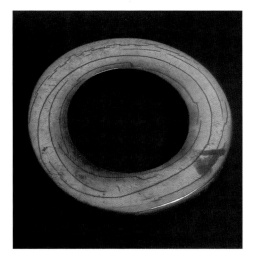

painting. *Plangi* (*shibori* in Japan, *bandhana* in India and *adire* in Yoruba country) is the creation of resistant motifs by tying parts of the cloth with threads before dipping it into the dye. In batik, the design is traced in wax with a *canting* (a small copper pot with one or several spouts) on prepared silk or cotton fabric. The wax is applied on only one side of silk fabric and both sides of cotton fabric; the cloth is then dyed and the wax is removed to be applied to other parts of the cloth. The operation is repeated as many times as there are colors. The resistant pattern may be applied with a *cap*, a copper printing block, introduced in Java around 1850. The result, quicker but rigid, is not comparable to that obtained by hand (*tulis*): it is like comparing a reproduction to a painting. *Ikat* is another resistance dyeing technique before weaving. The warp and weft threads, separately or together, are tied in bundles according to the desired motif and dyed. They are then attached to the loom and woven. The designs appear blurred because colorants seeped into the protected parts.

Batik flourishes in Java more than anywhere else. It decorates cloths for clothing, ceremonies and feasts (rites of passage, offerings to the gods). Motifs are geometric or derived from the society or legends that are more or less stylized. Several of them have a magical signification and some were reserved for the royal family such as the *parang musak* with parallel oblique bands depicting broken dagger blades. Silk was principally used by the court.

Before the introduction of chemical dyes, pigments were natural and sometimes a mor-

Mother-of-pearl
and wicker necklace.
H: 26cm x W: 27cm.
Ifugao, Philippines.

dant was added so they could vary according to region and the plants and minerals found there. The new dyestuffs do not have the same subtleness especially when, after having been used for a long time, the light of day has faded their brightness. Batiks made in central Java for the courts of Jogjakarta and Surakarta make use of three colors: brown from the *soga* tree and blue from indigo on a white or cream ground. Batik is one of the five fine arts of the cultural tradition practiced by the princes and the people; the four others are sculpture, music, dance and poetry. On the north coast, which is open to trade, on the other hand, entrepreneurs were the first to adopt chemical dyes, printing blocks, new motifs and flashier color combinations.

Ceremonial and festival clothing was often decorated with gold leaf or painted according to the design of the motif (Java) or as an independent motif, usually a lotus or a swastika (Bali). A more complex technique, *songket*, consists of weaving supplementary gold, silver or silk weft threads that float over some warp threads to form distinct patterns. In Bali, this cloth was only worn by women of the aristocracy for feasts, dances and the theater (*kain songket*). In the Lampung region (southern Sumatra), the famous *palepai* is decorated with the "boat of the dead" that takes them to the afterworld, a theme already present on the Dongson drums. In fact, they were used for most of the rites of passage linking the ideas of death and rebirth and were associated to other symbols such as the bird (the soul) and the tree of life. Embroidery, appliqué, beads and shell are also used to decorate fab-

rics. Also in Lampung, Paminggir women wear sarongs embroidered with human and animal figures in gold thread on a dark brown ground and geometric motifs in alternate bands. Finally, fabrics may be painted such as the *ma'a* of the Toraja of Sulawesi used as a shroud or as a banner during the inauguration of a house: the central theme is of a water buffalo being led to sacrifice in the middle of geometric, animal and human motifs.

Ikat is predominant in Sumatra, Sumba, Flores, Timor, Bali, Kalimantan and Sulawesi. *Ikat* with cotton warp is the most widespread. The *ulos* of the Batak who live around Lake Toba in Sumatra are decorated with geometric patterns in vertical bands where blue, red or brown are predominant. They are used as gifts by families at weddings and funerals. In Bali, the most well known fabric is the *geringsing* double *ikat*, which is only made in the village of Tenganan Pegeringsingan; its rusty color is obtained from a blend of indigo and red. About twenty patterns, principally floral and geometric, are used to make it; the most prestigious is that of the *wayang* marionettes in beige grouped around a four-branched star depicting a temple on a dark purple ground. Because of the many taboos observed during its making, the *geringsing* is reputedly endowed with the magical power of protection. The island of Sumba is known for its *hinggi*, men's capes whose patterns are the same upright and upside down: horses, horsemen, dragons, dogs, deer, crocodiles, monkeys, birds and trees of life, most often in blue and red.

The fabrics of the mainland are no less

beautiful than those of the islands. Here, silk is as widely used as cotton because the bombyx and the mulberry tree have been grown for a long time. In a single environment and according to different beliefs, certain motifs vary while others are similar. For the Thais, the Laotians and the Khmers, whose cultures share common traits, flowing water (a fundamental resource and symbol of fertility that is rare in northeastern Thailand), pineapples, sugar cane, filaos, bamboo, flowers, water buffaloes, elephants, birds and stars are used alongside Buddhist emblems: the *naga* that protected Buddha from the rain, the lotus and the diamond, symbols of purity, the lozenge depicting the house or the temple and the celestial being in an attitude of devotion. The most beautiful fabrics are those used for women's multicolored skirts and scarves with silk, gold and silver brocade in geometric or animal patterns.

On the other side of the Pacific, the textiles of the Andes were admired as early as the 16th century by the Spanish conquistadors for their incomparable technique and the richness of their colors. In 1518, Cortés sent Charles the Fifth the gifts given to him by Moctezuma including a cape of bright green quetzal feathers that may now be seen in the Vienna's ethnological museum. Albrecht Dürer traveled to Brussels to see them and wrote in his journal, "I also saw things addressed to the king from the New Land of Gold… strange garments, coats and all sorts of objects intended for human use, all so beautiful that they are a marvel and worth 100,000 ducats. Never have I seen anything so fascinating."

126

Multi-lobed pectoral in cotton
covered with cornelian, malachite, turquoise, coral beads
and river pearls. 38cm x 38cm.
Zanskar, India.

Although the destruction of the Indian kingdoms led to a decline in weaving, archeological digs have delivered a large quantity of funerary fabrics conserved by the dryness of the Pacific coast. Cotton, grown since 2500 B.P., is used in five colors: white, cream, tan, mauve gray and brown (the latter is the most highly prized as it dispenses with dye). Wool comes from the camel family – llama, alpaca and vicuna (the finest and reserved for the Inca) – and is used in its natural colors: ivory, pearl gray, beige, sienna and glossy black. The basic pigments are blue (indigo), carmine red (cochineal) and yellow (false pepper plant bark). The first artistic fabrics were made by the Chavin de Huantar (900 B.C.-200 B.C.) and influenced the later cultures of the Paracas, Nazca, Huari, Tiahuanaku, Chimu, Chancay and Incas. During these 1,500 years, religion, centered on the interaction between man, nature, the gods and the spirits of the dead, did not change, so that the iconography has remained more or less constant, although the dominant themes varied according to the culture. Paracas, Chimu and Chancay put the accent on the figurative, whether realistic or fantastic: human and divine beings, head on or in profile, animals of the coast or the interior, fish, seabirds, condors, felines, members of the camel family, dragons, snakes, caimans, monkeys and six- or eight-pointed suns. Nazca, Tiahuanaku and Huari prefer the geometric and the abstract whether reduced to simple bands of colors or evoking landscapes and everyday objects in a stylized manner. The ancient Peruvians knew all the techniques for weaving despite their rudimentary tools

The harmony of color varies according to groups. Analogy is predominant in Paracas, Chimu and Chancay while the Nazca prefer contrasts, the Incas polychromatism and the Huari abstract compositions. Fabrics are often decorated with embroidery, gold and silver ornaments, beads, shells and, above all, marvelous feathers.

The Spanish introduced sheep, the pedal loom and chemical dyestuffs. Despite its prohibition, the Indians have kept their clothing that – while adapting – has kept most of it social significance and traditional motifs. Rural women continue to weave magnificent sleeveless tunics (*huipil*), skirts, scarves, covers and bags. Some of these items are destined for tourists, especially in the Andes, Mexico, Guatemala and Panama. The Kuna of the San Blas archipelago are well known for their *molas*, fabrics with appliqués in different colors whose themes are taken from nature and religious beliefs.

In North America, the Indians wove with their fingers for millennia before the appearance of looms in the 11th century. Here too, cotton was used before wool. Preserved fabrics date back only to the 19th century: the best known are those of the Tlingit in southern Alaska and the Navajo in Arizona and New Mexico. Tlingit *chilkat* covers were worn by chiefs as ceremonial insignia: in yellow, black and blue-green, they depicted stylized bear, eagle and sea monster motifs. The Navajo learned their art from the Pueblo Indians (Hopi, Zuñi): their blankets and rugs are characterized by their geometric designs of lozenges, crosses and zigzags in parallel bands and less common human and animal motifs, some of which have been inspired by the East. In a limited number of colors (yellow, red, black, white and gray), symmetrical, regular, monotonous in expression, one wonders at their being in vogue.

In traditional civilizations, ornamentation is inseparable from clothing. Before they wore clothes and jewelry, men and women decorated their bodies with paint or scarification in order to identify themselves. Ornamentation also signals gender, age and social status. Moreover, precious objects are used as wedding or diplomatic gifts, rewards, magical protection, as a method of hoarding against future hardship and as companions to the dead. All the materials provided by nature in the animal, plant and mineral kingdoms are used to make the shapes and colors that make existence more beautiful. Peoples who are less "developed" in the material sense often reveal more ability and savoir-faire than rich contemporary societies which, in the pursuit of profits and power, have lost the taste for celebration and esthetics (except from a commercial point of view).

The variety of colors is infinite. There are jewels made from a single substance – such as ivory in Africa or mother of pearl in Oceania – whose interest comes from its nuances and, when it ages, from its patina and wrinkles. In other cases, the material itself, such as the jade of Chinese pendants, comes in different colors whose harmony is pleasing to the eye. Two colors are enough to make up a harmony: the *tema* of the men

of Santa Cruz is a prestigious round pectoral ornament made from the patient carving of a tridacne shell, then decorated with turtle-shell motifs depicting stylized frigates.

In three colors or more, jewels become sumptuous. Muslims prefer silver to gold as it is thought to be pure and endowed with beneficial powers. In North Africa, Berber women wear necklaces, bracelets and fibulae (used to hold the veil) in silver, enamel and coral; the necklaces are often endowed with a central amulet, coins or glass paste beads. In Africa, before beads were introduced from Europe, mainly from Venice, agate, chalcedony and cornelian (thought, because of its red color, to coagulate blood) were principally used.

But perhaps the most extraordinary orna-ments were those of the Indians of the Americas who created out of feathers all sorts of shapes and color combinations as illustrated by an exhibition organized in 1985-1986 in Geneva and Paris by the Musée d'Ethnographie in Geneva and the Musée National d'Histoire Naturelle in Paris (*L'art de la plume: Indiens du Brésil*). This art is typical of the Indians as it is nowhere else used for so many ends – cultural, social, artistic and ceremonial – even when the raw material is abundant. It is based on mythic thought: if the bird is defined by its feathers, man is only born man. He only becomes a *kayapo* or *wayana* – "true man" – through the art of the feather: the choice of feathers, their design and techniques. It is art that dif-ferentiates man from bird, Kayapo from Wayana. That is why green is a little appre-ciated color as it is largely represented in Brazilian birds in relation to blue, red, yellow, black or white. A whole range of blues is available to the Urubu while the Kayapo make do with the two tones of light blue and ultramarine. The Urubu like to combine shades of a single color while the Kayapo contrast several basic colors, often strength-ened by the juxtaposition of monochrome elements and blended multicolored elements. The Wayana style is situated halfway between the two. According to Daniel Schoepf, the Brazilian art of the feather is an aesthetic of order because it designates both class and species, man and ethnic group. Together it is the signifier (the support) and the signified (expression) of natural order.

Movement and Rhythm

Colors are a form of expression. Whether they imitate nature or not, they translate feelings and thoughts. Through their position and direction, they contribute, together with the drawing, to render balance, movement and rhythm. An impression of calm comes from Jan Vermeer's *The Music Lesson* (Buckingham Palace, London) because of the horizontal lines of the beams and the harpsichord and the vertical lines of the walls and windows as well as the immobile appearance of the figures. Conversely, Bruegel communicates a movement of successive falls in his painting *The Blind* by making them fall down a slope that goes from the upper left-hand corner to the lower right-hand corner. In his double triptych in Antwerp Cathedral, Peter Paul Rubens uses the diagonal to evoke in a dramatic and moving style *The Raising of the Cross* (from the lower right-hand corner to the upper left-hand corner) and *The Descent from the Cross* (from the upper right hand corner to the lower left hand corner); all the lines of force converge at the white body of Christ whose arms stretch upward on one side and sag on the other. In East Asia, the horizontal scroll introduces a temporal dynamic to contemplation: as the viewer unrolls the scroll from right to left, he views different scenes which he can, moreover, compose himself by isolating one part or another. This Japanese scroll, 11.4 meters long and 26.7 centimeters high, depicts *Eight Views of the Xiao and the Xiang* (two Chinese rivers), a theme frequent since the Song era that each artist treats in the order he wishes:

Wild geese descending on a sand bank
Boat returning to a distant shore

Mountain market in the rising mist
Snow on streams and mountains at dusk
Autumn moon over Lake Dongding
Night rain on the Xiao and the Xiang
Evening bell from a temple in fog
Fishing village in the light of sunset.

Using the gradations of ink, light and dark patches, and the expanse of space, the painter suggests the depth and change of the dissolving shapes. Although there are "eight views," they are not juxtaposed but blend into one another in an immense landscape where unity is provided by the void.

Generally speaking, two types of *movement* are expressed in the visual art: that of the real, which it presents (gardens) or represents (painting, sculpture), and that which comes from the arrangement of its components (calligraphy, abstract painting, Constructivist sculpture and interior decorating).

Rhythm is a more complex notion. The art of space has borrowed it from the art of time – from music and poetry, which was originally sung in Greece as well as in China. Rhythm is defined as the repetition at regular intervals of one or several elements of the composition: line, shape or color. A static work such as a sculpture or a building may suggest movement and contain a rhythm if the artist knows how to give it life.

These characteristics only take on their full value in an organized structure. Whether the work is two- or three-dimensional, it must respect the principles of unity and balance. *Unity* results from the harmony of all the elements when viewed together: diversity is not excluded, on the contrary, as it breaks possible monotony and increases the signifi-

Kiamba, *Fishing Woman*. Gouache on paper.
H: 18cm x L: 22cm.
Kinshasa, Congo, 1994.

131

Detail of a *ntschak*
with yellow and brown
appliqués. Cotton.
W: 72cm. Kuba,
Congo-Kinshasa.

Part of a cotton and
wool poncho depicting
pairs of felines. Huari,
Nazca region, Peru,
200-400.

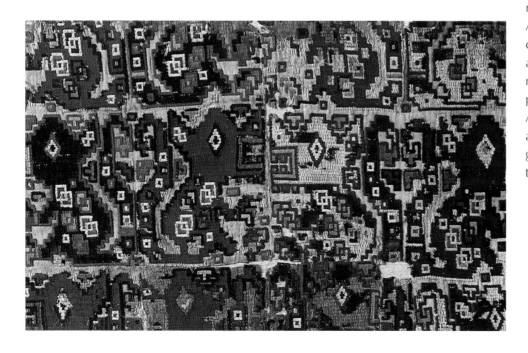

cance of relationships. The Chinese painter Zheng Xie wrote the following about a contrast:

"This whole painting is peopled with orchid leaves representing as many good men. I would, however, add a few thorny bushes, base men. The good men would not be so without the base men; they oblige them to always surpass themselves. Thus, surrounded by thorny bushes, the orchids appear purer and richer!"

Balance is the equilibrium of opposing forces: voids and filled space, large and small, light and dark, warm and cool colors. The simplest form of balance – but not the most aesthetic – comes from symmetry: it is artificial as it does not exist in nature. Asymmetry, less simple, is more resonant when masses, colors, light and shade, horizontals, verticals and diagonals are skillfully distributed. From the ancient Greeks to the 18th century, Europe sought the harmony of plastic structures in mathematical relationships. The current reaction against academicism has blown the rules to bits.

Are movement and rhythm universal principles? They are part of life – a more encompassing notion. Here, we seek to deconstruct the analysis. Life is also rendered by color and immobility…

On a flat or curved surface

In the West, painting is the foremost art. It has not always occupied this position. This does not hold true elsewhere, notably among the American Indians and in Africa. However, rhythm and movement are everywhere.

From prehistory, cavemen expressed rhythm and movement as a result of keen observation of animate beings and with few means. Sometimes, they seized a decisive moment: in battle, the warriors of Khargur-Talch (Libya) lean forwards or kneel to string their bows in a rain of arrows. Sometimes, movement is suggested by a characteristic attitude: the Lascaux artist depicted the gallop of a horse with its front hooves in front and its back hooves in the back, just as in the representation of the gracious Tang female polo players. It is the same position found in Théodore Géricault's *Epsom Derby* (1821). It has been criticized, as it is impossible for all four hooves to be off the ground at the same times, as shown in photos. But the truth of art is truer than physiological truth. From northern Europe to southern Africa to the Andes, troops of cattle depicted in polychrome paints advance across cave walls, attesting to the pastoral life of these communities. These paintings are associated to propitiatory rites: the great white lady of Aouanrhet in Tassili, Algeria, dances, her arms outstretched, one leg lifted, on a background painted with much smaller figures that are also moving. She is probably a priest-

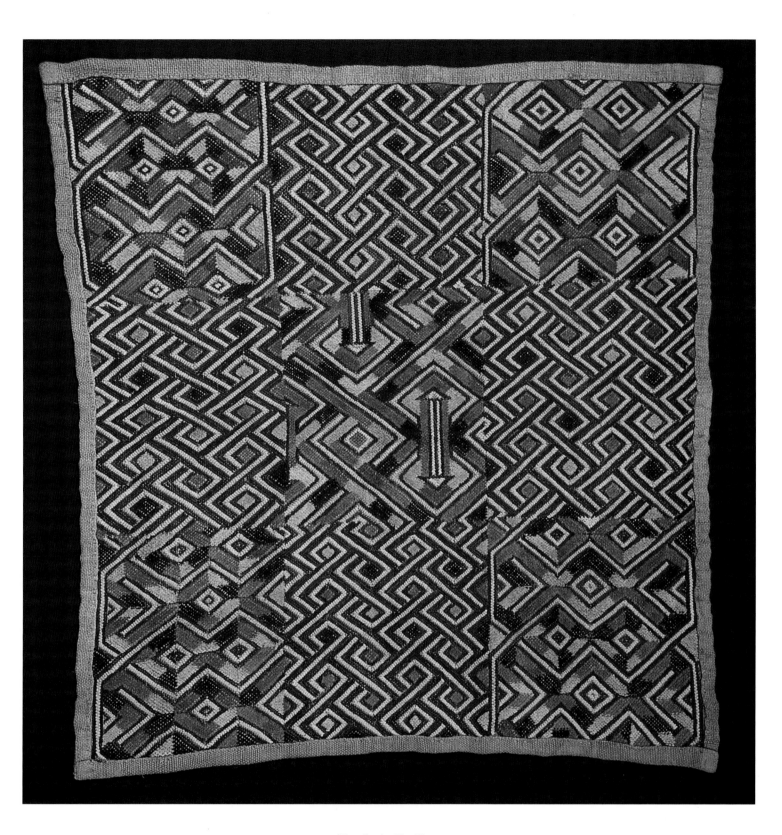

"Kasai velvet" with
geometric design.
Kuba, Congo-Kinshasa.

Roger Druet, *Concerto*.
Calligraphy in the form of
a bird and fluttering notes
on an orange and gray-
green background. Paper.
H: 24.8cm x L: 28.4cm.
Paris.

ess with her headdress with two horns framing a stylized wheat field. Her scarified body is naked except for a loincloth and arm and leg bands whose fringes flap in accordance with the rhythm of her steps. Nowadays, dance is still a primary activity in Africa and the painting of the body as well as scarification and tattoos, which may cover the entire body or only certain parts, reveals its most visual effects during this activity. The body thus becomes a network of colors constantly changing with the glints of the sun or firelight.

Rhythm and movement are also expressed in weavings. The *bogolan* of the Bamana (Bambara), dyed with mud, are decorated with geometric motifs from popular mythology in only two colors: beige and dark brown. The most famous weavings are made by the

Kuba (central Congo). "Kasai velvet" is embroidered with bits of raffia, then shaved with a knife for smoothness. The patterns of black and white lozenges are organized in diagonals that intersect in every direction. Asymmetry and broken lines give each cloth its own dynamic. *Ntschak* are large pieces of cloth up to six meters long which kings and queens wrap themselves in during feasts and dances commemorating Creation. They are decorated with geometric appliqués whose abstraction and rhythm appealed to Paul Klee, some of whose canvases were inspired by them (*Writing*, 1940).

Today, Africans have adopted Western painting techniques while continuing to draw on their own inspiration. For his female dancers and fisherwomen, the Congolese painter Kiamba conserves the profile and

hairstyles of Black women while elongating their arms so that they become lines among other lines, animating his compositions with a rhythm of concave and convex curves sometimes punctuated with squares.

Even more so than in Africa, textiles constitute the veritable pictorial art of the American Indians, the ancient Peruvians in particular. On embroidered or painted tapestries, geometric, human, animal, plant or fantastic motifs are repeated either alternating or in opposition. This may be linked to the notion of reciprocity that dominates the relationships of these peoples: economic exchanges between the coast (fish, salt, cotton, coca, corn), the mountains (wool from the camel family) and the jungle (feathers, dyes) and the mutual obligations of the state (order, peace, public granaries, communications) and the inhabitants (taxes). Thus, there are frequently, beside simple series oriented in the same way, double (two-headed birds), reversible (two creatures head to tail in different colors), opposing (stairs ascending to the right and to the left), mirror (processions of felines), inverted or alternating (columns of birds and humans) images. The most refined decorations are those of Huari tunics. The principal motif is the scepter bearer with a bird's head that may be seen on the Tiahuanaku Gate of the Sun but stylized by changing curves into lines, and repeated with infinite variations so that the whole appears like an abstract composition of shapes and colors.

European painting began in the Minoan world where joie de vivre is evident in the colorful scenes on walls and the volutes of

Detail of the horizontal
scroll *Eight Views of the
Xiao and the Xiang.*
H: 26.7cm. Japan, 18th c.

vases: a particularly charming tableau is that of two children who, looking serious and their bodies arched, exchange blows with their tight fists. The frescoes of Thira (Santorini), now on display at the National Archeological Museum in Athens, bear witness to keen observation of things and a predilection for curves that some attribute to the omnipresence of the sea. Even during the geometric period, Greece did not forget a sense of rhythm in the decoration of craters and amphorae. This love of life is also found in the frescoes of Etruscan tombs and the villas of Pompeii that would be erased by Christianity over a period of time.

From the Renaissance to the 20th century, paintings were often analyzed by tracing diagonal, vertical and horizontal lines and curves in order to make their lines of force come out. However, as Henri Van Lier remarked, "a painting is situated not in the thought, rationalized, abstract space of geometry, but in the lived, proven, concrete space of perception. So that pictorial unity is not mathematic but sensory". It depends on the relationship of lines, colors, lighting and material. Moreover, "the most subtle detail" makes "the network come alive... That is why we can make excellent speculations about proportions and only produce a mediocre painting if one is a mediocre painter." Finally, "the sensorial and attentive progression through the canvas, this test for my eye... makes appear for us the masterpiece as a closed world, but with the closure of the infinite. The unity of the painting is not the tightness of the symmetry; it is the asymmetry attaining balance by becoming inexhaustible." (47-50)

In some civilizations, the rhythm of painting is closely associated to that of calligraphy. In truth, since he invented writing as a support for his thought and even when he only knew how to express his interpretation of the world and his messages to his fellow humans through signs, man has sought to make them things of beauty. The clay tablets that bear the first Uruk pictograms, made more than 5,000 years ago, the hieroglyphic or hieratic inscriptions that appeared soon after in Egypt, later and farther away, the seals of the Indus valley, the divinatory carvings on bones and shells of the Chinese and the glyphs of the Maya stelae of Mesoamerica all bear witness to this. Nowadays, artists have rediscovered the beauty of graphics on paper, canvas and cloth as well as in metallic or textile sculptures. However, European calligraphy is limited by its alphabetic form. Although it can have rhythm and movement, it does not lend itself to all the variations of the Chinese brush to also reflect reality and suggest its shapes. East Asian calligraphy is not only simply decorative as it is in Europe and the Islamic world, it expresses feelings, emotions and a personality. This is why the Chinese consider calligraphy superior to painting; like music, it has the "power to abolish external appearances and blend the objective and the subjective."

More than the Egyptians, the Chinese thought that writing was art. It first appeared in the form of pictograms, representations of beings and objects, carved on bone, tortoiseshell and bronze used for divination and ceremonies during the Shang dynasty (17th-11th centuries B.P.), then on stone to celebrate the kings. This was the seal script (*zhuanshu*), imposed by Qin in order to unify the empire in 221 B.P., thus named because it was used in the engraving of seals. Under the Eastern Han (25-220), the clerical script (*lishu*), with its wide and elongated horizontal traits, became the standard before being replaced by the regular script (*kaishu*) with rectilinear forms in the Tang era (618-907). It would remain the standard until the simplification of writing in 1958. The current script (*xingshu*) is quick and regular with some shortened strokes. Finally, the cursive script (*caoshu*, literally "herbaceous writing") is a form of stenography whose strokes are reduced to the bare essential and linked together; this makes them difficult to make out.

A Chinese character is composed of one or more strokes that always succeed each

other in a predetermined order. One learns to respect the relationship between them in order to have a balanced whole by placing the character in a real (graph paper) or imaginary square. One learns especially by studying and copying the great works. Beginning with imitation, here as elsewhere, is one of the rules of teaching. In the 6th century, Xie He stated the six principles of painting: with the exception of those that apply to likeness and color, they may also be applied to calligraphy. They are the cosmic breath and the movement of life, the vigor of the stroke, the composition and the transmission of models.

The first principle is the most important. It states the essence of the art of writing and painting. In the Chinese expression *qi yun sheng dong*, *qi* is the spirit, the breath and the rhythm of nature, objects and beings, the Tao, *yun* is resonance, vibration, *sheng* is life and *dong* is movement. The last two words are clear for any painter: it is life and movement that signal a work. The first two words are familiar to Taoists. We know the apologues of Zhuangzi (circa 370-300 B.P.) about Prince Hui's cook and the Ying carpenter who carried out the most difficult tasks without apparent effort because they penetrated the secret of the Tao; the "Way of Heaven is not to make an effort, but to know how to overcome." Through the practice of his trade, the cook no longer sees the steer with his eyes, but with his spirit: he instinctively knows the lines to cut. Conserving his energy, his work "nourishes his life." By the same token, by studying the great calligraphers, the beginner is imbued with their qualities and develops his potential. It is through discipline and practice that his own personality will emerge. "Once all the means of expression are mastered, harmony between the mind and hand is established." Like the cook's knife, the brush of the literati expresses itself naturally, spontaneously – a "wonderful state" where beauty is attained without seeking to attain it.

In his drip paintings, Jackson Pollock rediscovered this Taoist approach. From the apparent confusion of his *Autumn Rhythm* (1950, Metropolitan Museum, New York), spring lines of force, rhythms, vibrations of black and white with a density of expression that belies the notions that the work was the product of chance, that it was not brought to fruition after lengthy reflection and guided, when the moment came, by inspiration.

The great man of letters, painter and poet Su Shi (1036-1101) wrote: "Mountain, rock, bamboo, tree, ripples on the water, mists and clouds, none of these things of nature has a fixed shape; on the contrary, they each have a constant internal line. This is what must guide the mind of the painter" (in Cheng, 1979, 44-45).

Calligraphy is a dead thing when the characters are simply well drawn, strictly regular like printed characters and reveal no personality. The current and the cursive are the liveliest writing styles. It is commonplace to compare them to the movements of dance. Zhang Xu (circa 658-748), who was famous in the Tang era for his "crazy cursive" style, stated how much his art progressed after he had seen the beautiful Gongsun perform the dance of the sword. The same thing happened to Wen Tong (1018-1079) after he watched snakes fight. These are expressive moments that the calligrapher who has internalized them renders in his writing. He thus renders the vibration of the world.

The second principle is the vigor of stroke. The Chinese term *gu fa* literally means the bone technique. This reference to the body indicates the importance of gesture (and also the correspondence that exists for the Chinese between writing and the moral and spiritual qualities of its author). In fact, three notions are used for aesthetic appreciation: bone (*gu*), muscle (*jin*) and flesh (*rou*).

According to a text from the Tang period, "Those who have strength in the brush give bones to the characters, those who lack it only give them flesh. Writing that possesses strong bones and little flesh is called 'muscular'" (in Billeter, 203).

Thus, the criterion is force (*li*), a notion that should not be interpreted literally. As the order of the strokes for each character is predetermined, it is a question of balancing speed and restraint, filled and empty space, the proportions of the strokes, wet ink and dry ink, and avoiding the equal dimension for all the characters, symmetry and regularity. These are the same qualities called for in general composition, another of Xie He's principles. The suppleness of calligraphy is such that it allows the expression of the personality in the most varied shapes. Painting follows the same rules: rendering the movement and the rhythm of the world with the maximum economy of means, whether in a landscape or a still life.

Nothing demonstrates the differences in the concept of painting in Europe (until the

Female polo player on a galloping horse. Glazed terracotta.
H: 27.5cm x L: 44cm.
China, Tang, 8th c.

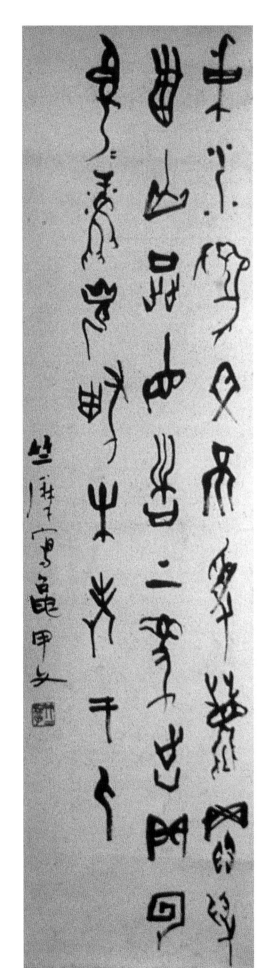

19th century) and China better than still life. European painting minutely renders objects and their colors by concentrating on chiaroscuro effects. Chinese painting – the work of Qi Baishi (1863-1957) for example – neglects details to express essential shapes and colors in a few free strokes, with white providing light. Qi explains Xie He's principle of likeness in the following manner: "Good painters seek the image of the world at the border of the similar and the different. He who paints too realistically falls into banality. But he who paints too unrealistically fools the world." Thorough observation of beings and objects is manifested in the movement and rhythm of his paintings of flowers, birds, chicks, shrimp and mice: who can resist the liveliness of these two mice playing with an egg? Wu Changshuo (1842-1927), an older contemporary of Qi's, painted mainly flowers and fruit, such as this grape vine with remarkable rhythm, that of an arabesque, the black patches of the leaves punctuating the inflexions. In Changchun (northeast China) in 1992, my friends brought me to the home of the painter Li Wei who improvised in front of me: in about ten minutes, his brush made a painting of three squirrels playing in the branches of a tree spring to life which he kindly dedicated to me.

Writing and Chinese culture spread to Japan in the 6th century. It was initially used to transcribe the language which, unlike Chinese, is polysyllabic. Kanji were used, whether phonetically or ideographically, to render Japanese words, which raised difficulties (the same sound can be reproduced by several characters). As the Japanese became more aware of their identity and Tang China went into decline, the Japanese invented the system of *kana* to express their sounds in the early 9th century. Kana are very simplified Chinese characters. *Katakana,* derived from regular *kaishu* script, were used in official and Buddhist documents and to phonetically transcribe Chinese texts; *hiragana* were derived from cursive *caoshu* script. During the Heian period, the aristocrats, keen on Chinese culture, reserved it for themselves, leaving the national literature to

women. Thus, it is women who wrote the first literary masterpieces: Murasaki Shikibu's *Tales of Genji* and Sei Shonagon's *Bedside Notes*. At the same time, a Japanese style of calligraphy developed because of hiragana and the rise of the poem of 31 syllables (*waka* or *tanka*). This style is characterized by fluidity, refinement and freedom, a greater freedom than in Chinese calligraphy because a polysyllabic word may be interrupted at the end of a column to end in the next column, a syllable can be accentuated by the ink to give it more power, columns can begin at variable heights and kanji (Chinese characters) may be blended with kana. All this increases the possibility of visual effects in relation to the sense of the poem to which is added the beauty of the paper itself which exists in several formats and may be dyed, sprinkled with gold and silver or decorated with painted or printed motifs. These are generally small landscapes enveloped in clouds, a riverbank or a pond where reeds are growing: the characters of the poem blend into them because they themselves are reeds, aquatic birds or rocks. The *Anthology of Thirty-six Poets* dedicated to an emperor in 1112 used almost 700 types of decorated colored paper. The illuminated scroll (*emaki*) of the *Tales of Genji* unrolls from right to left the text in kana and the illustrations on paper sprinkled with·gold and silver.

The refinement of the Heian era faded when the aristocracy of Kyoto lost power to the samurais. It was not until the peace of Edo that the kana were revived for a time because of the talent of calligraphers such as Hon'ami Koetsu. A second revival occurred in the 20th century. The activity of authors specializing either in kanji or in kana or combining the two is even greater than in China.

Japanese painting has many of the same qualities as Chinese painting with perhaps a greater sensibility to the ephemeral because of the Buddhist influence. Such as, for example, Suzuki Shonen's (1849-1918) *Haiga Poem and Cuckoo* where the light stretches of clouds and the flying bird, wings spread, contrast with the vertical lines of the verses. In fact, the slanting body and tail of the cuckoo have the same direction as some of the strokes and some of the clouds' contours, which accentuates the flowing of things. In Torin's *Ducks and Reeds*, the slanting from right to left of the reeds, water and frolicking ducks is echoed by the neck and head of the descending bird and in contrast with its outstretched wings.

In Islam as in China, calligraphy is foremost amongst the arts and even those who do not read the language are fascinated by its beauty. However, the origin of this preeminence is different because it is religious. Embodying the word of God transmitted through the Koran, calligraphy is found everywhere, not only in the Scriptures, but also on all monuments and objects, the walls of mosques, *madrasah* and palaces, lamps, carpets, basins, fabrics, ceramics and ivories. Like Chinese calligraphy, Arabic calligraphy plays on the contrast of black and white, full and empty, straight lines and curves, balance and rhythm, and abstraction and meaning. Because of the prejudice against the representation of animate beings, the presence of writing is even more universal than in China.

Wu Changshuo
(1842-1927). *Grapevine.*
Ink on paper.
H: 173cm x L: 44.7cm.
China.

Qi Baishi (1863-1957).
*Two Mice Playing with
an Egg*. Ink and colors
on paper.
H: 26cm x L: 34cm.
China.

Li Wei, *Three Squirrels play-
ing in a Tree*. Ink on paper.
H: 44cm x L: 67.5cm.
Changchun, China,
October 22, 1992.

Two main shapes, one stiff, the other flexible, gave birth to numerous types of script, which may coexist on the same page or panel. The first is *kufi*, from the city of Kufa, south of Baghdad, where it was developed. Angular, hieratic and monumental, it was used during the first centuries of Islam to copy the Koran as well as to decorate architecture, pottery and textiles. There are eight variants: the main ones are geometric *kufi*, foliated *kufi* where the vertical lines end in leaves or half-palmettes and the floral *kufi*, more ornate and dominated by the rosette. The last two forms are of Egyptian origin (9th century). *Naskhi*, on the other hand, is round and supple, even the vertical lines. Its codification is attributed to Ibn Muqla who lived in Baghdad in the 10th century and created *thuluth* or *thulth*, whose forms are even more varied. Other cursive scripts were created in Iran such as the elegant, thin and flowing *nastaliq*, which became the common style in the country in the 15th and 16th centuries. *Maghribi* script (used in Andalusia, North Africa and the Sahel) is characterized by vigorous, accentuated strokes and large curves open at the top or the left. Ottoman Turkey produced *diwani*, a rounded chancellery script, in the 15th century, and the most beautiful of royal signatures, the *tughra* of the sultans, a golden interlacing of straight lines and curves sometimes accompanied with floral motifs. However, since the instrument is a cut reed, or a fortiori a metal nib, the writing has neither the fluidity nor the nuances of ink produced by the Chinese hair brush.

What both types of calligraphy share is the seeking out of life, movement and rhythm. It begins with the mastery of the laws governing script. While the ideogram is inscribed in a square, the Arabic letter is drawn within a circle whose diameter, Ibn Muqla recommended, should be *alif. Alif* is the simplest character of the alphabet, a vertical stroke attesting to divine unicity (the simplest Chinese character is a horizontal stroke that signifies one that also has a metaphysical connotation for the Taoists). The calligrapher has more freedom in Islam than in China because he can shift the letters up or down, superpose them, add small characters or accents, choose between a final form and an initial form (normally the form of a letter differs according to whether it occupies an initial, median or final position in the word), and juxtapose several types of writing in the same composition. Some scripts are themselves endowed with movement (*taliq*) while others (*kufi*) are static and thus require rhythm. Rhythm is obtained through the repetition at regular intervals of the same letters or of letters with similar parts. One plays with the contrast between suppleness and stiffness, between vertical lines, which give an impression of force (*alif* and *lam* are frequently encountered) and horizontal lines, which suggest calm. A phrase usually written on a line may be recomposed in a square or a circle to accentuate the rhythm. The calligrapher establishes an equilibrium between letters and that which surrounds them. To fill the voids or, on the contrary, highlight them, he can move diacriticals or draw simply decorative points (with no meaning). He creates perspective with colors: gold seems closer

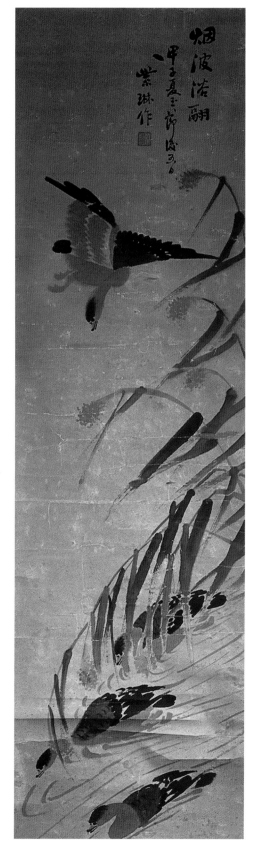

Torin (18ᵗʰ c.) *Ducks and Reeds.* **Ink on paper. H: 141cm x L: 39cm. Japan.**

than black, blue in the background produces depth, which may also be created by the use of smaller and smaller letters. Mirror composition where one of the parts reflects the other (left-right, high-low) is often used by Sufis who aspire to union with God (He is me; I am Him). The geometric lines of *kufi* appear much more beautiful than those of Piet Mondrian not because they have a meaning while the art of the painter is gratuitous, but because of their movement and rhythm, which are absent from most of Mondrian's work. Many Arab calligraphers now seek to enrich their tradition with contributions from Western painting, principally in the drawing of lines and the use of color. The Iraqi Hassan Massoudy, who lives in Paris, is one of the most talented. From European and Muslim proverbs and literary quotations, he constructs landscapes of multicolored curves that evoke the domes and scent of the East.

Alongside calligraphy, the arabesque is the principal motif of Muslim decoration, omnipresent in the arts of the book (illuminations), wood (*minbar*), metal (ewers, cups, trays, basins), glass (lamps, goblets), ceramics and ivory. The arabesque was derived from the stylization of plant motifs. It developed into interlaced curves, simple or double spirals and star-shaped polygons in different dimensions. It is characterized, unlike Roman interlacing, by its endless rolling and unrolling in the image of the One who manifests himself in the Multiple (*al-wahda fil kuthra*), of the infinite which appears in the finite. Muslim art expresses nothing other than the fundamental idea of the religion: "There is no god but God." All

the rest is transitory. Whether it decorates a copper tray, a page of the Koran or the wall of a *qibla*, the arabesque like calligraphy renders in all places and all eras the ideological community of Islam, however various the forms it takes.

Finally, let us look at painting on ceramic, which is an art in its own right. From its origins in the 4th millennium B.P., the potters of Iran revealed in their motifs a keen observation of nature that allowed them to distance themselves from imitating it to conceive the stylization of birds, ibexes, and beasts reduced to horizontal lines (wings), vertical lines (feet and paws), curves (horns, tails) and waves (water), and more or less geometric patches (bodies). With the same sense of rhythm their Muslim descendants decorated their ceramics sometimes with abstract compositions of colors, sometimes with plant, animal (birds, rabbits, beasts, elephants), human or mixed (*minai*) motifs. In this shiny bowl from Sultanabad, the slightly off-center body of the bird and its outspread wings radiate toward the surrounding leaves and flowers whose blue highlights on a white and bistre ground arrange a dancing symphony.

Three-dimensional expressions

Unlike the works we have just discussed, architecture, sculpture and gardens are situated in three-dimensional space; they are themselves spaces. Since sculpture is no longer a closed volume, but penetrable and moving, its border with architecture has tended to dissolve. But has it not been this way from the beginning? The mystery that hovers

around the circle of Stonehenge only adds to the monumentality of the standing stones whose texture, color and shadows vary according to the change in the position of the sun. Conversely, the Maya or Khmer edifice forms a gigantic sculpture with all the high and bas-reliefs that cover it while the structure of the Islamic building disappears underneath its profusion of ornamentation. The most complete art is that of the garden: it combines immobility and movement, and continuously arranges the spectacle according to the steps of the viewer and the rhythm of the seasons.

Sculpture was undoubtedly the earliest art practiced by man as he had to make tools in order to subsist. The two-sided flints from 20,000 years ago called "willow leaves" or "laurel leaves" by archeologists are striking because of the finish of their alterations and their thinness. The polished axes of the Neolithic period ally the perfection of the shape and the beauty of the veining. There was already a seeking of rhythm and movement in the statuettes that appeared in the 5th-4th millennia B.P.: the woman with raised and rounded arms in painted clay from Amratian Egypt (Brooklyn Museum, New York), the marble lyre player from the Cyclades (Louvre, Paris) and the terracotta humped oxen and deer of Marlik (Amlach), votive rhytons found in Iran southwest of the Caspian. The contours of the humped ox are wavy – sometimes convex, sometimes concave – along the animal's body and four almost parallel lines may be distinguished; the triangle of the head formed by the horns and the muzzle is contrasted with the curve of the

Suzuki Shonen
(1849-1918). *Haiga*
Poem and Cuckoo.
Ink on paper.
H: 35cm x L: 55cm.
Japan.

hump and the forequarters. Seen from the front, the massive body is contrasted with the delicate horns and their curves with the vertical lines of the legs. In Han China, funerary sculpture distinguished itself by the powerful representations of animals, particularly horses, which evoked the imperial rides in Central Asia and the relationship with the nomads. While the most stunning example is the bronze *Flying Horse* whose only hoof balances on a swallow with outstretched wings (it was exhibited in Paris in 1973), those in terracotta do not lack liveliness either and are more vigorously expressive than the Tang horses. The figures of shamans and dancers are strikingly abstract.Sculpture differs from painting in the sense that it is a volume around which one must turn to discover all its aspects. As it absorbs light, terracotta has less variety than wood or stone, which react to it perceptibly: according to the direction, brightness and type of lighting, according to the season, according to whether it is looked at head on or in profile, from above or below, the object is modified.

According to Senghor, for an African, rhythm is "the architecture of the being, the internal dynamism that gives it shape, the system of vital waves, waves that it emits towards others, the expression of the vital force... To the extent that it is incarnated in sensuality, rhythm illuminates the spirit."

Nothing demonstrates this better than sculpture, at first sight more static than dance. In this Bembe mask with protruding eyes inscribed in ovals painted white, the symmetry of both sides of the bridge of the nose is only just apparent: neither the ovals, nor

the globes and slits of the eyes are identical. Lower down, the mouth is a cylinder that also protrudes while the cheeks are incised with lozenge-shaped scarifications of which each half is alternately painted white and not painted. Under the mouth is another row of scarifications also alternately painted white and not painted. Even if he is unaware of the symbolism, the viewer feels its plastic beauty, the rhythm of the curves of the eyes and the mouth, the rhythm of the alternately white and black triangles, which are echoed by a larger triangle in the middle of the forehead and in the middle of the face, the narrow triangle of the nose. This mask is a musical abstraction.

Another contrasting type of rhythm is that made familiar by Cubism. The Mossi "doll" is not only a toy for little girls, but also expresses their wish for fertility. Seen in profile, it is a coordinated ensemble of straight lines and curves with two rounded shapes at the base (it has no legs) and, at the top, a flat head simply pierced with three small wholes for the eyes and the mouth; between the head and base is the vertical line of the neck and the armless trunk with pendulous breasts, triangular forms parallel to one of the sides of the base and the back of the head. The doll has great presence despite its small size.

The modern sculptor has lost none of the African sense of movement and rhythm. In this statuette of a tam-tam player, Malanda, from the Congo, has remarkably stylized the pose of the drummer: the arms continue the curve of the body to finish in hands flat on the drum skin; the head is reduced to a smooth shape that looks forward.

In addition to suggested movement, the 20th century introduced real movement. As early as 1920, the Constructivist manifesto of the brothers Naum Gabo and Anton Pevsner set out a few principles that, with their own realizations, exercised a determining influence on their era. The term Constructivism comes from their claim to "build (their) work as the universe builds its own." Space and time must be the foundations of art because they are "the only factors through which life is manifested." Gabo and Pevsner rejected the line for its descriptive quality, but accepted it for its expressive force. They rejected volume as the sole spatial element and replaced it with depth. Space was no longer a void, but a space for communication. Time was not translated by static rhythms as it was in ancient Egypt, but by kinetic (the word was used for the fist time) and dynamic rhythms.

In 1920, Gabo's *Kinetic Sculpture* (Tate Gallery, London) provided an excellent demonstration of this. It is nothing but a fine metal rod made to turn by a motor, but the eye perceives it as a spindle vibrating in space. Ten years later, László Moholy-Nagy developed a *Space-Light Modulator* (Stedelijk Van Abbemuseum, Eindhoven), a device with a motor that makes a wood, metal, celluloid and glass structure with some moving parts turn underneath projectors, projecting a play of light and shade on the walls. Along these lines, wanting to demystify art, Jean Tinguely constructed his "useless machines," heterogeneous assemblages of diverse materials, painted in black and colors or not, sometimes odorous, that move haltingly and sometimes self-destruct. In a

Hassan Massoudy (1944).
"Woman is a ray of the
divine light." Jamal al-Din
Rumi (13th c.).
Colored ink on paper.
H: 71.5cm x L: 49.5cm.
Paris, August 7, 1987.

145

146

Deep bowl, interior decorated
with a bird, wings spread,
among leaves and flowers
in iridescent blue. Ceramic.
Diam: 20.5cm. Sultanabad,
Iran, 14th c.

playful, humorous or ironic way, Tinguely denounced the mechanical civilization that condemns us to always do the same thing and invites us to accept change without fear.

Nicolas Schöffer did not dissociate sculpture from architecture or urban planning. He began with spatio-dynamism conceived as "the constructive and dynamic integration of space in the plastic work" and used electronics and cybernetics for the first time. His 50-meter tower in the park of Saint-Cloud (1954) is thus the first sculpture to include (concrete) music accompanying luminous projections. Light was to take on a greater role in his work through the play of mirrors, reflectors, filters and screens whose moving effects reflect the image of time.

On the contrary, Alexander Calder's mobiles may be compared to paintings moved by breezes in space. The movement of these metallic plates in various shapes and colors, suspended from stems whose bases remain fixed, lead to infinite variations, always bearing a joie de vivre and tenderness that are communicated to the viewer. This became active with Jesús Rafael Soto's *Pénétrables*, ensembles of nylon strings or supple metal stems suspended vertically that open out before him. Marta Pan's *Floating Structure* (1961) drifts wherever the water and wind carry it in the garden of the Kröller-Müller Museum in Otterlo, offering a different view each time to the visitor who feels all its calm harmony.

Architecture, the art of constructing buildings, is closely linked to society, more so than painting or sculpture in which the individual genius expresses himself more freely.

Until more or less recently according to the civilization, architecture had to conform to rules stemming from the functioning of the state itself. In the first empires of Mesopotamia and Egypt, architecture was the work of great dignitaries (Imhotep) and exalted the god and monarch assimilated to him. The temple, which may also be a mausoleum, often took the form of a step pyramid whose successive terraces symbolize the gradual elevation toward the meeting with the deity. In India too, located in sites endowed with magical powers, temples imitated the home of the gods. In China, the capital was built in a square in the image of the earth under the round sky according to a north-south axis which is that of the celestial meridian because the sovereign had a mandate to rule.

Obedience to norms does not exclude the quest for beauty: on the contrary, the temple must be worthy of superior powers. It resulted everywhere in the harmony of filled and empty space, the whole and the parts, inside and outside, taking into account the adaptation to function: that is, its meaning and place in the environment. Rhythm is derived from the repetition of vertical and horizontal lines and openings, varying in number, volume, spacing, continuity or discontinuity, unity or intersecting of styles and ornamentation. Movement is brought by the representation of living scenes on the facades and in the interior, the succession of animated spaces that differ as one moves through the building, whether it is a cave in Ajanta or Ellora, a Gothic or Baroque church, a palace or a garden. The play of light increases these effects. From the East to the West, the great-

est architects used the vibrations of sun and shade: the Ramesseum (13th century B.P.) is oriented according to the sun's trajectory so that, at dawn, its rays alight on the statue of Ramses II. The splendor of the marble of the Taj Mahal (17th century) becomes unearthly in the moonlight.

Symmetry and regularity predominate all over the world. This is not by chance – geometry speaks of order and stability; it is the language of power vis-à-vis the people in all cultures, each giving its own interpretation.

Teotihuacan was the largest city in the Americas. At its peak in the 5th century, it had 150,000 inhabitants who lived on 20,000 km2. A religious and political center, it was built according to a geometric plan divided into four quadrants by a double axis in a cirque of mountains symbolizing water and fertility because they concentrate the clouds during the rainy season. From the fields and springs of the south, the ceremonial way (also called the "avenue of the dead") passes from the citadel and the square to climb progressively toward the Pyramid of the Sun on its right to the Pyramid of the Moon standing out against the sacred Cerro Gordo; it is cut by a secondary axis running east to west toward the constellation of the Pleiades that commemorates the annual renewal of time.

In Egypt, architecture was also linked to religion and royalty. The temple ensured the presence of the gods on earth and their protection; the tomb ensured the survival of the embalmed dead. The two functions were associated in the funerary ensembles of the pharaohs of which the pyramids of Giza (2500 B.P.) are the most famous example.

However, the most beautiful temple is undoubtedly that of Queen Hatshepsut in Deir-el-Bahari (1490 B.P.) whose three successive terraces rise to the foot of the cliff, supported with walls provided with rhythm by porticoes, pillars and the large central access ramps.

Greece refined the Egyptian column by tapering it towards the top and carving fluting into the shaft, creating chiaroscuro effects. Because of its physical relief, Greece paid particular attention to the relationship between monument and landscape as illustrated by the temples that dominated the cities or the sea with its "innumerable smiles" (Aeschylus) and the hillside open-air theaters (Epidaurus, 4th century B.P.). The rhythm of the facades was accentuated by friezes, beginning in Persepolis (6th-5th centuries B.P.) with parades of soldiers, courtiers and tributaries of the great Achaeminian king. The facade of the Parthenon (now "shared"

between the Acropolis Museum and the British Museum) depicts the Panathenaic procession, which took place every four years to present the protecting goddess with her new peplos and a gold crown. Phidias magnificently rendered the festive atmosphere of the procession which he divided into two, ending with the assembly of the Olympian gods: riders on horses in various positions, lyre and flute players, old magistrates, girls carrying vases for libations and censers, and rams and heifers being driven to be sacrificed.

Rome widened the sphere of public works with the arch and the vault (borrowed from the Etruscans) and rubblework cemented with mortar. Thus, new rhythms were introduced into the landscape: street porticoes, aqueducts on arcades (the Pont du Gard) and vaulted thermal baths. The Pantheon (120-124) was both the culmination of Roman technology and the starting point for

an entire tradition of Western architecture because this model would be taken up by the Christian Church. Its dome has a diameter equal to the interior height (43 meters), made up of five stories of caissons supported by walls with niches alternating with columns and semi-hemispheric chapels, which lighten the mass. The Pantheon is dedicated to all the gods (hence its name): its dome represents the vault of heaven and is pierced at the top by a large opening through which penetrates the light which gives the whole its unity.

Byzantium combined the dome with the square plan based on the Greek cross (with branches of the same length). Its masterpiece is Aghia Sophia (6th century), which ensured the transition from the base to the circular plan due to the pendentives (the spherical concave triangles between the arches supporting the dome). The central dome, 30 meters in diameter, is supported by a system of half domes and lateral buttresses. The light entering through the many windows plays with the polychromatism of the paintings, mosaics and marbles shining in the darkness. Ravenna and Venice (San Marco) are other sumptuous interpretations of the same plan while those constructed by converted Slavs (Kiev, Vladimir, Moscow) are more specific as to the verticality and the substitution of onion-shaped domes for domes.

In the West, the Romanesque replaced the Greek cross with the Latin cross, which elongated and shrank the nave. Rhythm was provided by the repetition of transverse arches and bays that continue in the lateral naves as well as by the high windows of the apse and sides. The use of arcades also prevails in

Rhyton in the form of a
humped ox whose muzzle
is a spout. Pink terracotta.
H: 34cm x L: 29cm. Marlik,
Iran, 14th c. – 11th c. B.P.
Profile and frontal view.

the cloister while the facade was decorated with towers and windows. The massive bareness of the walls, favorable to meditation in the darkness, is opposed to the richness of the sculptures of the portal and the capitals (Autun).

Created in the Ile-de-France in the middle of the 12th century, the flying buttress supported the weight of the roof and freed the walls from their bearing role, which allowed the pillars to rise up to the vaults, highlight the verticality of the nave and multiply the windows that would become stained-glass narratives. Thus the impulse toward God was nourished by the teaching of the windows in the light from the heavens and the contemplation of the airy harmony of the vaults scanned by ribs supported on the two sides by the cadence of the columns, bays, arches and windows. This musicality, based on mathematical relationships, is apparent on the facade with towers lightened by multiple arches around a central rose window. In the Iberian peninsula, the Muslim influence inspired ornamental exuberance (Léon Cathedral, the cloister of Batalha) while Venice offers the most beautiful "street" in the world to gondola passengers who constantly discover new facades whose rhythm is provided by their arcades, windows and balconies, the play of light on the water and stone, ending in the apotheosis of Piazza San Marco and the Palace of the Doges with its lacy sculptures.

With the Renaissance, which began in the Quattrocento, sacred elevation gave way to profane representation in which ancient shapes and perspectives were reinterpreted.

Its first theoretician, Leon Battista Alberti, defined beauty as "the harmony and accord between parts." It was the victory of the mathematical analysis of proportion, which Brunellschi demonstrated most brilliantly with the Ospedale degli Innocenti (1419-1444) whose elegant facade is superior to that of the Pazzi Chapel whose geometry is too rigid. The codification of the model led in the 17th century to the Baroque reaction, which entailed a profusion of ornamentation and interior lighting effects while royal authority was incarnated in the solemn majesty of Classicism. In the 19th century, the triumphant middle class sought industrial rationalization rather than artistic creativity. It was not until the Russian Revolution and the Bauhaus, and a few preceding movements (Arts and Crafts, Art Nouveau, Jugendstil, the Chicago School), that modern thinking gained ground, marked by the consciousness that the century had to express its identity with a view to a new humanism that respects the environment and communication, open to all the planetary influences.

Never before has there been such a variety of approaches. The materials and techniques of the twentieth century changed the landscape. Glass and steel gave buildings slender, translucent facades where light and shade vibrate (Ludwig Mies van der Rohe, German Pavilion, Barcelona International Exhibition, 1929) and allow nature to enter the house (Philip C. Johnson's "glass house," New Canaan, Connecticut, 1949). Kenzo Tange manipulated steel with virtuosity to hang from immense pillars the asymmetrical double arches of the roofs curved toward

the ground in his Sports Palace in Tokyo (1964). Concrete renewed the rhythms of interiors and vaults (Pier Luigi Nervi's ceiling, Sports Palace, Rome, 1956-1958) as well as of external forms (the shells of the roof of the Sydney Opera House, designed by Jorn Utzon, 1956, look like sails at sea). When a new metropolis springs from the ground, the architect reveals his creative imagination: from the air, Brasilia resembles a bird with outstretched wings. Along these two axes, Lúcio Costa distributed collective functions and residential zones. Oscar Niemeyer built buildings by contrasting straight lines and curves, horizontals and verticals, the concave dome of the National Assembly and the convex dome of the Senate between which rise the double tower of the civil service and the cathedral evoking a crown of thorns; the glass presidential palace, protected by a protruding roof supported by curved marble-covered concrete, seems to be floating on a basin. However, aesthetics forgot social considerations. When I visited Brasilia in 1986, 26 years after its inauguration, all the inhabitants complained about not having sidewalks along which to walk or convivial meeting places. The quadras grouped occupants according to their income level; the richest lived outside the city.

In Islam, the most characteristic monuments are the mosque, a place for prayer, and the *madrasah,* an institution for learning and study: these are the two poles of the religion. In fact, they were united in the mosque which, even after the creation of the madrasah in the 10th century, continues to serve as a place of learning, a tradition start-

Bembe mask. Wood.
H: 35cm x L: 15.5cm.
Congo-Kinshasa.

ed by the Prophet in his house in Medina. The mosque has also retained its plan: a walled rectangle with a vast courtyard surrounded by rooms. In addition to these elements, there is a minaret from which the muezzin calls the faithful to prayer five times a day; the fountain in which they perform their ablutions before prayer; inside, the *mihrab* faces Mecca, the direction of prayer; and, to its right, the *minbar* from whose height the imam gives the Friday sermon. The *madrasah,* originating in Iran, was developed in the Sunni world to counter Shi'ite propaganda. Like the mosque, the *madrasah* has a central courtyard usually surrounded by four iwan, teaching rooms corresponding to the four recognized theological and legal schools (Hanafi, Maliki, Shafii and Hanbali).

Other buildings mark out the Muslim landscape: palaces, caravanserais on the roads, khans in the cities and hammam baths. All have a central courtyard surrounded by arcades whose columns add rhythm to the facades and interior space. But the alternation of filled and empty space is less important that the ornamentation covering the walls from the entrance, made up of paintings and panels in ceramic decorated with calligraphy and arabesques, which are the distinctive signs of this architecture. Another characteristic with the same effect is the *muqarna.* Called stalactite, alveolar or honeycomb because of its niche shape, it provides a transition between a dome or half dome (in a portal) and its quadrangular base: that is, between a circle and a square. Probably originating in Iran, it spread throughout the Muslim world from the Atlantic (North

Africa, Andalusia) to Afghanistan and India. The accumulation of *muqarna* in brick, stone and plaster sometimes make up domes such as those of Tlemcen's mosque (1135), Fez's Qarawiyyn (1142) and Granada's Alhambra (14th century). Like the arabesque, the *muqarna* is both rhythm and symbol. It links earth (the base) and sky (the dome), space and time (through the rhythmic movement).

Ernst Grube drew attention to the effect of the "dissolution of matter" in Islamic architecture and decoration:

"Solid walls are disguised behind plaster and tile decoration, vaults and arches are covered with floral and epigraphic ornamentation that dissolve their structural strength and functions, domes are filled with radiating designs of infinite patterns, bursting suns, or fantastic floating canopies of a multitude of *muqarna* that banish the solidity of stone and masonry and give them a peculiarly ephemeral quality as if the crystallization of the design were their only reality… The result is a world which is not a reflection of the actual object, but that of the superimposed element that serves to transcend the momentary and limited individual appearance of a work of art, drawing it into the greater and solely valid realm of infinite and continuous being" (11).

Thus, the internal structure of the mosque of Cordoba (8th-10th century) is "dissolved" by a forest of columns with double superposed arches and interlaced foiled arches. However, in sub-Saharan Africa, this characteristic disappears because the material is raw earth, which is particularly adapted to the environment and the climate because it pro-

152   **Mossi doll. Wood.**
H: 22cm. Burkina
Faso.

vides protection from the outside heat and naturally regulates the temperature. The interior is bare, punctuated by a forest of pillars that are more an invitation to prayer than a way of breaking up the space. This vertical rhythm is also found on the outside with the elongated cones of the minarets and the walls punctuated with transversal beams, which consolidate them and serve both as ornamentation and staircases during the annual repair of the coating (the mosques of Djenne, Mopti and Bobodioulasso).

A final characteristic of Islamic architecture – also a part of its rhythm – is its use of light. While the Christian church is an enclosed space so that the believer may concentrate on the thought of God and only perceives the rays of light filtering through the windows, the courtyard of the mosque is open to the sky. Like that of the Prophet's house in Medina where he welcomed the faithful, the mosque courtyard is a community meeting place, especially on Fridays when it is not only a matter of praying, but also a manifestation of the union of the umma, of the community under the direction of the imam, its spiritual guide. While the Christian turns toward heaven, hence the elevation of the church, the Muslim directs his thought toward Mecca: its ritual space is horizontal. The courtyard is bathed in sunlight, but the interior is in darkness. Starting with the Great Mosque of Damascus (715), several marble partitions with geometric motifs in multicolored glass diffuse an enchanted light into the prayer room.

The rhythm of the facades, interior columns and their decoration, the rhythm of

Malanda.
Tomtom Player.
Gray ebony.
H: 44.6cm.
Brazzaville, Congo,
1994.

colors and chiaroscuro – all these characteristics of mosques and madrasah are also found in palace architecture. The most famous are Granada's Alhambra, the Ali Qapu and Shehel Sotun of Isfahan (17th century) and mausoleums such as the Taj Mahal (17th century). "God prescribes beauty in all things," said the Prophet.

Alhambra, built by the Nasrid on a hill overlooking Granada, is made up of several palaces surrounding courtyards. The Courtyard of the Myrtles, dedicated to public ceremonies, is in full sun: its white marble paving stones and long basin lined with greenery and flowers reflect the walls and arcades. The Courtyard of the Lions, named after the lions guarding the central fountain, is smaller and divided into four by waterways: it is the private paradise of the prince who framed it with high arcades marvelously worked to filter the light.

In Iran, Shah Abbas I (1587-1629) made his capital Isfahan "half of the world" with the immense royal square *(medan i-shah)*, 510 meters by 165 meters, lined with double arcades that link its four buildings. To the south, the Royal Mosque with its monumental portal facing the entrance to the bazaar is resplendent: its facades and domes are entirely covered in multicolored ceramics dominated by turquoise, decorated with arabesques and calligraphy. The interior courtyard has a central basin where the two stories of arcades of the four iwan are reflected. To its right, the mosque of Sheikh Lotfollah is smaller, but its dome and interior are even more magnificent than those of the Royal Mosque. To its left is the palace of Ali Qapu, the arcades of its gate and its fine columns mirrored in a pool of water. Not far behind rises the Pavilion of Forty Columns (Shehel Sotun) whose name was derived from the fact that the reflection of its 20 columns in the water doubles their number.

The most famous monument in India is undoubtedly the Taj Mahal. It was built from 1634 to 1648 by Shah Jahan for his beloved wife Mumtaz Mahal, who died prematurely. A large portal of red sandstone, inlaid with white marble arabesques and calligraphy and topped with domed pavilions and flanked with towers, provides access to a garden at the back of which the Taj rises like a marble dream harmoniously enveloped in light. In the garden, there is a long basin between two pathways paved in red sandstone and lined with cypresses. The mausoleum itself stands on a pink sandstone terrace with four minarets in the corners. Each principal facade with high arcades is framed by two stories of smaller arcades and the central onion-shaped dome rises between four domed pavilions on multi-foiled arcades. These arcades, repeated at the four corners by the summits of the minarets and the vertical lines of the cypresses and walls decorated with panels of calligraphy and arabesques in multicolored stones, give their rhythm to the whole, accentuated by their reflection in the water and by the shadows of the niches. The Taj Mahal is the masterpiece of Indian Islamic art and was as successful as the interpenetration of the two forms of music that took place in northern India at the same time.

Like Islamic architecture, Hindu and Buddhist architecture is above all in the service of religion. The temple represents the cosmos and is oriented according to the cardinal axes. However, the shapes vary according to the religion.

The Hindu temple is shaped like a pyramid or a multistory onion-shaped dome because it is the reproduction of the superposed worlds at whose summit the gods reside. The decoration of each step indicates the successive stages of reincarnation that ended in the Absolute. It is so exuberant that it makes the building a sculpture. The temple dedicated to a particular deity is centered on the cella containing his or her image, which only the priest enters to pay daily homage. Surrounding it are an ambulatory in the direction of the course of the sun, rooms for worship and dancing supported by pillars and scattered in a quadrangular courtyard (the earth) surrounded by a fence (mountains) and a moat (the ocean).

The masterpiece of Hindu architecture is Angkor Vat built in the 12th century in the capital of the Khmers who were at the peak of their power. At the end of a causeway, the mountain temple stands on a platform made up of three successive terraces, each surrounded by a vaulted gallery – the first on columns, which allow its magnificent bas-reliefs to be bathed in light. The main tower, surrounded by four secondary towers, rises 65 meters above the plain. It symbolizes Mount Meru, the pivot of the world around which the constellations turn. The towers provide the overall rhythm, supported by the horizontal lines of the galleries and terraces,

The "Moon-facing
Mound" in the
Ginkakuji (Silver
Pavilion) garden,
Kyoto, Japan.

157

Ryoanji garden in
Kyoto, Japan.
Late 15th c.

repeated by the curves of the floral ornamentation, the apsaras dancing along the walls and the arched bodies of the naga serpents, water gods, at the balustrades.

The monument typical of Buddhism is the stupa, a hemispheric funerary mound around which the faithful turn, following the course of the sun. The earliest stupas were built to contain the relics of Buddha that Emperor Ashoka (3rd century B.P.) sent everywhere so that the whole country would be blessed. He built the stupa of Sanchi to which four porticoes at the four cardinal points were added in the 1st century. Scenes of the past lives of Buddha and his preaching are carved on their pillars and crosspieces as are figures from popular mythology; Buddha himself is only represented by symbols such as the bodhi tree underneath which he attained illumination and the Wheel of his doctrine. There is a significant contrast between the richness of these reliefs and the bareness of the stupa, which evokes deliverance by the extinction of desire.

Driven out of India, Buddhism prospered in Central, South and East Asia. It was in Borobudur in Java that the stupa was expressed most splendidly at the summit of a hill surrounded by mountains (9th century). Its plan is that of a mandala: a circle inscribed in a square. Its successive stages symbolize the ascension of the believer from illusion to knowledge. At the base, five square terraces whose walls are decorated with reliefs depicting the world of desire, the lives of Buddha and the saints who attained illumination. Then three circular terraces bear openwork stupas protecting seated statues of Buddha meditating. At the top is the stupa of Nirvana: it contains nothing.

Chinese architecture is characterized by the unity of design that governs all structures: cities, palaces, houses and Confucian, Buddhist and Taoist temples. The fundamental idea is harmony between the cosmic and social order. Sites are chosen in accordance with the rules of feng shui, the geomancy of "winds and water" that determines propitious "breaths" according to the nature of the terrain and the arrangement of trees, rocks and water. Orientation is always along a north-south axis, which is that of the celestial meridian. The emperor's palace corresponds to the North Star from which he governs the world. In fact, cold comes from the north and heat from the south. Order and balance are realized horizontally rather than vertically. Buildings are distributed around a square or rectangular courtyard; the main building is distinguished by its location, dimensions and the quality of its materials and decoration. Rhythm is provided by the parallel lines of the columns of the verandahs and galleries and the tiles and curves of the roof and the whiteness of the walls on which light and shade play. However, especially during the Qing dynasty, harmony was destroyed by the overabundant colors and decoration: scarlet columns, gold, green, blue and white beams and consoles, and multicolored ceilings and coffers. This is the spectacle presented by Beijing's Forbidden City and Summer Palace. On the contrary, the whole of the Temple of Heaven, where the emperor paid homage to the heavens at the winter solstice, is admirable (particularly when seen from the air). Along the length of the north-south axis, lined by hundred year-old trees, are distributed a series of circular marble terraces in the center of which rise altars placed successively in a square (the earth), a circle (the sky) and a rectangle, punctuated by porticoes.

However, it was Japanese architecture that influenced that of the West in the 20th century. The West discovered the absence of a rupture between the interior and the exterior, the contact between man and nature (Johnson's "glass house"), the use of materials in a raw state (wood, bamboo, stone) and the module of living that is the tatami, a fine grass mat whose dimensions are around 36 inches by 72 inches – the sleeping surface for a single person.

The earliest examples of Japanese architecture are the imperial funerary mounds (kofun) in the form of a keyhole and the Shinto sanctuaries of Ise characterized by roofs with thatched gables topped with logs and crossbeams; gravel pathways lead to the entrance portico in the middle of a wood of giant cryptomerias.

This union with nature continued to characterize Japanese architecture when Buddhism arrived in the 6th century with Korean and Chinese influences. While it adopted the console system, the stacked trussing, the curved roofs and the square plan of the capital Kyoto (794), Kyoto "borrowed" its landscape from the valley of Yamato whose old main road became the central artery and developed towards the east, which was less humid and more naturally beautiful than the west, without worrying about the initial plan.

Van Miêu (Temple of Letters, 11ᵗʰ c.) garden in Hanoi, Viet Nam.

Kyoto in the 17ᵗʰ century, Katsura represents the acme of refined simplicity with its Japanese characteristics of asymmetry and functional adaptability. It comprises several tea pavilions and a succession of buildings each assigned a specific function – entertaining guests, private residence or music room. The last building, built especially for an imperial visit, is famous for its sliding doors painted in ink by Kano Tanyu and its shelves in precious wood. Its diagonal layout and elevation on pilotis allow different views of the garden changing with the seasons from the inside.

The garden: the art of space and time

In most civilizations, the garden represents the desire for paradise or the dream of a lost paradise. The dimension is less important than the arrangement of the space, water, plants, rocks and sand so that they will make up a landscape in which empty and filled space alternate and each includes the other in harmony colors in the rhythm of time. The contemplation of a garden provides access to wisdom observing the perpetual flow of things.

The garden was born in Mesopotamia and Egypt as the embodiment of the aspiration of the man of the desert for the coolness of water and palm trees. Considered one of the Seven Wonders of the World, the Hanging Gardens of Babylon (7th century B.P.) decorated terraces where canals drew water from the river. In Egypt, the garden was centered on a basin of lotus and papyrus surrounded by flowering and fruit trees. The

Like the north-south axis, symmetry was not often respected. Asymmetry is particularly striking in one of the most magnificent temples in Japan: Itsukushima. Situated at the foot of a hill, its buildings on pilotis linked together by galleries seem to float on the waves of the Interior Sea at high tide. The gallery, whether covered or not, is also an element of the aristocratic home. It unites the house's various parts and integrates the sur-rounding garden. The interior space was initially divided by screens, then by sliding panels. In the homes of the humblest people, its rhythm is provided by tatamis with their dark borders covering the floor (there is very little furniture), white partitions, translucent paper windows divided into squares and wooden pillars. Outside, the play of vertical and horizontal lines is combined with that of light and shade. A royal villa constructed in

Two rocks on a tray. Taipei flower market, Taiwan.

Persian garden gave its name and myth to the West: *paridaiza,* which means "closed place," became paradise. Planted with tall trees, populated with animals and strewn with pavilions, the Persian garden was a hunting ground. Water was distributed by two large rectangular canals that meet at the center and divide the garden into four sections, an image of the universe. The prince, "God's shadow on earth," ensured its upkeep during the winter and its rebirth in spring. The Greeks spread this design after the victories of Alexander and the first translators of the Bible rendered the Hebrew word *gan-eden,* "garden of delights," by the Greek *paradeisos* from the Persian. As in Iran, the earthly paradise was divided in four equal areas by the four primordial rivers: the Pishon, the Gihon, the Tigris and the Euphrates. Having tasted the fruit of the Tree of Knowledge, Adam and Eve were expelled from Eden. Ever since, the West has dreamed of paradise lost and has sought to recreate it.

The gardens of Roman villas were full of porticoes, pavilions, grottoes and statues that were taken up again by the Italian Renaissance. Most importantly, it introduced what became the main characteristic of the European garden until the 18th century: geometry. It attained its apogee in the French formal garden whose most accomplished example is at Vaux-le-Vicomte (1656-1661). There is the perfect integration of the chateau and the landscape: from the main building may be seen a string of flowerbeds and pools symmetrically laid out on either side of an alley punctuated by a succession of ponds that ends at an arcaded wall beyond which spread

a green carpet dominated by a statue of Hercules. The garden of Versailles (1661-1715) is more theatrical with its Grand Canal, walls of greenery, mirrors of water and marbles and bronzes destined to glorify a monarch whose subjects were dying of hunger during his wars of conquest. The chateau is at its most beautiful in the fall when the mist erases the ostentation and the yellowed leaves scattered over the alleys evoke the vanity of power.

The search for effect – grandiloquent in French Classicism, which was imitated by all European princes, Rococo in the Italian

Baroque – provoked a reaction in favor of a return to nature in England in the 18th century: the house is in a wood with its hills and ponds around which pathways snaked. But at the same time, paradoxically, mythological statues, ancient-style temples or Chinese pagodas – as they were imagined in reading the accounts of missionaries and merchants – were placed in the garden. This so-called English landscape garden spread through Europe and the United States and gave rise to the public garden.

Islam incarnates its vision of paradise in its gardens. Paradise was not lost as it was for

"Moon door" in the garden of the "Master of the Fishing nets." Suzhou, China.

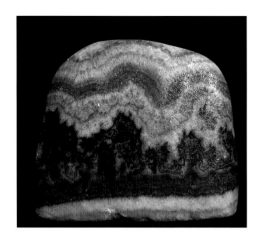

Jews and Christians, but is to come, the Koran announces, to "those men who believe and do good" (it does not mention women):

They will possess gardens where brooks flow.
There, they will find pure spouses
And there will remain immortal. (II, 25)
There, they will wear bracelets of gold and pearls;
Their garments will be of silk. (XXII, 23)
They will recline on carpets trimmed in brocade
And the fruits of the two Gardens will be within their reach.
There, they will meet women whose gazes are chaste
And whom neither man nor jinn has touched before them.
They will be like rubies and coral.
(LV, 54-56)
They will stand among jujube trees without thorns
And carefully aligned acacias.
They will take pleasure in a great expanse of shade,
Of running water,
Of abundant fruits
Neither picked in advance or forbidden.
They will rest on raised beds.
It is we, in truth, who have created the Houris
In a perfect manner.
We have made them virgins,

Loving and equally young
For the companions of the right hand.
(LVI, 28-38)

The emphasis on shade, water and fruit is indicative of their attraction for the people of the desert. Water not only refreshes the eyes and the body, its perpetual murmur accompanies dreams. From the Atlantic to the Indian Ocean, princes created a multitude of palaces and gardens. The most beautiful garden in Granada is the Ria patio in Generalife where the fragrance of all sorts of flowers and birdsong are blended with the sound of fine jets of water that rise and fall on either side of a small canal. When one visits it alone at dusk, one feels all its melancholy imbued with a subtle sensuality. Iran has conserved the composition of the paridaiza divided into quadrants. Some of the surviving paintings at Shehel Sotun show garden scenes in which figures repose or take refreshment. In India, the Taj Mahal was preceded by two "love gardens" (Shalimar) which Shah Jahan designed for his wife Nur Jahan, the first near Srinagar in Kashmir (1619), the second in Lahore (1642). Each comprises black and white marble pavilions on the shaded, flower-covered terraces with stairways, basins and fountains.

In East Asia, the garden is inseparable from the home. Here, it is not a dream of water and greenery as it is for the people of the desert or the desire to master nature as in Europe, but communion with nature. One also finds the dream of paradise symbolized by the mountain surrounded by water where the Immortals reside. This image is linked to Taoism. "Immortal" is written using the pictogram

of man left of that of the mountain. It is the individual who flees the world (civilization) to find refuge in the mountain (nature) where he gathers herbs to make the drug of immortality. The expression "mountains and waters" *(shan shui)* is used to designate the landscape, one of the main subjects of painting, literature and the art of the garden. Li Bo (701-762), one of the great Tang poets, sings about his nostalgia for the Eastern Mountain:

Long have I not seen Dongshan.
How many times have the hollyhocks flowered?
Do the white clouds still disperse?
On what cabin does the moonlight shed its petals?

A little later, Jia Dao (777-843) wrote on the theme of the hermit, which still inspired the painter Fu Baoshi in 1956:

Under the pine trees I question the little servant
The Master has gone to gather simples
Without doubt, he is in these mountains
The deep clouds hide his footsteps.

The Chinese garden tends to recreate a landscape of mountains and water, the two poles of nature *yang* and *yin* through which blows the breath *(qi)* that animates the universe. The mountain is symbolized by rocks raised in the courtyards, sometimes sonorous and perfumed, and by round and rectangular stones whose veining evokes peaks and forests drowned in mist that are hung on the walls, mounted on screens or inserted in the backs of chairs. The passion of the literati for stones is illustrated by the anecdote of Mi Fei (1051-1107) – calligrapher, painter, poet and connoisseur renowned for his extravagance –

who, arriving at his official residence, noticed a rare rock in the garden and bowed low before it, calling it "elder brother."

Water is represented by ponds around which are grouped pavilions linked together by galleries providing different points of view. There are never geometric pools like there are in the West and Islam. Here, water has an untroubled surface and is often dotted with lotus, which inspires contemplation and peace in the soul. Openings in the wall – round,

fan-shaped, rectangular or quadrifoiled – direct the eye towards the most picturesque views. Moreover, the correspondence between painting and the art of the garden was constantly recalled by the calligraphy decorating the halls and columns and praising renowned sites or expressing the sentiments of the master of the house. However, in the imperial gardens of Beijing and the gardens of the literati in Suzhou, Yangzhou or Wuxi, general harmony often disappears in

the multitude of buildings, architectural, decorative and rock forms, in garish colors (especially in the park of Beihai in Beijing). As previously mentioned, the Qing had nouveau riche tastes that, unfortunately, influenced those of their officials.

On the contrary, Japanese gardens pushed simplicity and refinement into abstraction. I think the difference comes from the fact that they were designed by monks whose Zen Buddhism exalted the natural, economy and

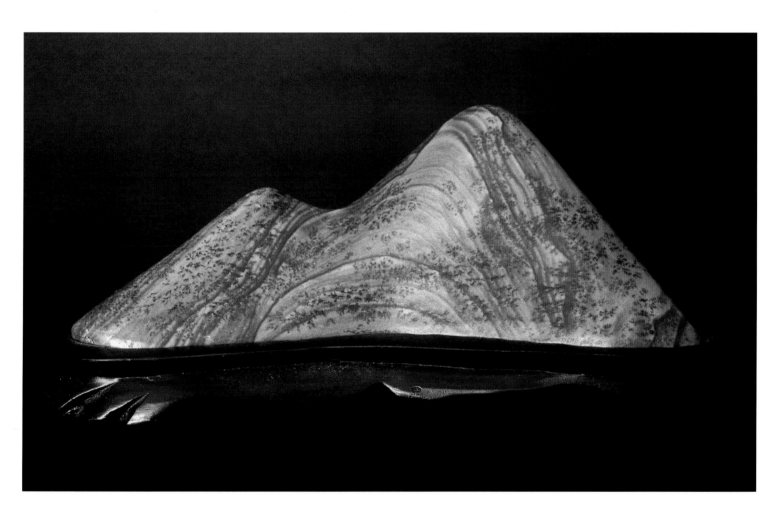

Rock in the shape of
a mountain strewn
with dendrites.
H: 6-9cm x L: 22cm.
Kyongju, Korea.

spirituality. Here, contemplation is not distracted by the gold of the columns, the green of the tiles and the openwork of the balustrades. Architecture is totally integrated into the landscape by the whiteness of the walls and the raw state of materials: thatch roofs, wooden and bamboo pilotis, structures and hedges. The garden is on the human scale and that of everyday banality: in Zen, the smallest space can contain the entire universe and its teaching is "nothing special." Often, it "borrows" an exterior landscape. When the retired Emperor Gumizuno-o designed the Shugaku-in (17th century) northeast of Kyoto, he incorporated the view of a distant mountain chain that may be contemplated from the Rin'un-tei, the "pavilion near the clouds," of the upper garden: from there, a green slope, covered with azaleas and camellias in season, descends towards a lake whose shore follows the wavy line of the mountains.

Water is not always necessary. The Japanese invented the *karesansui*, the "dry landscape" garden, in which sand and gravel represent waterfalls and rivers; rocks are chosen for their evocative shapes – rather than strange or fantastic ones like in China – texture, color and especially their patina: the *sabi* we already encountered in the "way of tea." One of the most famous dry gardens is that of Daisen-in (circa 1513) in the temple of Daitokuji in Kyoto. In a space three meters wide, the architect sought to recreate a mountainous site where a cascade of white gravel falls between high rocks and then becomes a river of raked sand flowing under a stone bridge. Farther along, another rock with two

raised ends resembles a skiff navigating around islands. While this landscape recalls a Chinese painting from the Song dynasty, the garden ends on a genuinely Japanese note: an expanse of white sand surrounded by green hedges in the middle of which rise two mounds of sand, an image of meditation for the monks. By the same token, Ginkaku-ji is renowned fot its truncated "Moon-facing Mound" and its "Sea of Silver Sand."

The most famous garden is undoubtedly that of Ryoanji, also in Kyoto and attributed, like Ginkakuji, to the great painter Soami (late 15th century). Its degree of abstraction is absolute. On a rectangular terrain bounded by walls on three sides, five groups of stones surrounded by moss rise from sand that is raked lengthwise, widthwise and in curves everyday. According to Genryu Kinoshita, the abbot of the monastery, they resemble mountains emerging from the clouds or islands in the sea. What is striking is the play of filled space (the stones) and empty space (the sand) as well as the movement and rhythm that result from it. If, when contemplating the garden from the temple verandah, one traces an imaginary diagonal line from the lower right-hand corner to the upper left-hand corner, the entire left-hand side is occupied by a single large group of five stones. It is in contrast with the four right-hand groups: two of two stones and two of three stones, which are greater in number but smaller than those of the first group. The balance is reinforced by the triangular layout of the groups and, within each group, the size and position of the stones: one large stone balances several smaller ones, a massive tall stone bal-

ances low and elongated stones. In truth, a single stone cannot be moved without ruining the harmony of the whole: harmony of the arrangement, shapes and colors between the dark brown of the stones, the green of the moss and the white of the sand.

The love of nature in East Asia is such that even the poorest people grow plants in pots and decorate their homes with flowers in the New Year, the most important holiday of the year. Some create miniature landscapes in trays or in basins. Techniques and materials vary according to the environment (in Viet Nam, there are no maple trees, but many species of orchid), care is taken everywhere to balance water and rock; the trunk, branches and roots of the shrub and their dimensions if there are many. Colors are chosen according to the season: at New Year, the orange red of small mandarins expresses wishes for happiness and prosperity. The gardens of the literati comprise the "four friends of the wise man" – bamboo, orchids, prunus and chrysanthemums – accompanied by rocks.

Zheng Xie, a famous 18th-century painter and man of letters, thus described his aspirations for a simple life:

"A low hut, a modest courtyard in which fine bamboo grows beside a few raised stones. This does not require much ground or, as a result, much expense. However, one savors the harmonious sounds [of the bamboo] in the wind and rain, and their gracious shadows in the sun or moon. One is never alone at times of leisure or in times of boredom; one is always inspired by drinking wine or composing poetry. I love bamboo and rocks; they know how to love me in turn."

Fu Baoshi (1904-1965).
Scholar in his Garden.
Ink and colors on paper.
H: 78cm x L: 45cm.
China.

The Face of the Invisible

"Painting is a mental thing." Leonardo da Vinci's remark reflects that of the painter and poet Wang Wei who wrote in the 5th century:

"To be accomplished, drawing and painting have to be of the same essence as the symbols of the *Book of Changes*. What is essential to the form is the Breath which, by its movement, informs it and that which, by its dynamism, puts the change into motion is the Spirit. Spiritual energy remains invisible; therefore, what it inhabits appears immobile. The eye has its limits; therefore what it can see is not comprehensive. With the help of a single brush, one can even evoke the body of the great Void, the Tao" (in Vandier-Nicolas, 66-67).

More recently, Paul Klee wrote in his *Theory of Modern Art*:

"In the past, people made representations of the things that they could see on earth, of what they liked or would have liked to see. Today, the relativity of the visible has become obvious, and it is agreed to only see it as a simple individual example in the totality of the universe inhabited by innumerable latent truths. Things reveal an enlarged and much more complex meaning which often appears to invalidate the old rationalism. The accidental tends to pass into the rank of essence."

In his *Journal*, Klee stated, "Art does not reproduce that which is visible: it renders visible."

Rendering the invisible visible is a more general truth that the one affirmed by Klee at the beginning of the first quotation. From the beginning, art has been a symbolic system and not a naturalistic one because every society is made up of people who communicate and communication is above all the exchange of meaningful messages. The very first man sought to understand the world in order to act upon it. Like language, art is an instrument for learning and transmitting knowledge. The two are autonomous – that is, not subordinated to each other – and interdependent because they have the same goal: representation combined with words and actions to increase the effectiveness of communication. That is why the art of oral societies implies a wider domain than that of literate societies, as illustrated by the wealth and complexity of their decoration of the body and their clothing and jewelry. Moreover, the natural object, whether painted or refashioned by hand or not, but always invested with a symbolic weight, has a place in it. From North to South and from East to West, in prehistory, stones were chosen for their shapes and textures in order to raise altars; later, literate East Asia collected roots and rocks whose knottiness and veining evoke the quintessence of the energies of yin and yang. According to Joseph von Eichendorff, "There is a sleeping song in all things that endlessly dream and the world will start singing if you find the key word." The shape and meaning of an object are inseparable; each is able to take on several levels of meaning. Many peoples think of the artist as a mediator for invisible powers because his work reproduces that of the cosmos. In Africa, the blacksmith takes part in the mystery of fire and in the transformation of matter and the weaver participates in the mythical language made of interwoven questions and answers that weaves links of con-

Sarcophagus mask representing a white female face with eyes and brows lined in black. Stucco, wood and pigments. H: 19.5cm. Egypt, New Empire (1590-1050 B.P.).

167

Man's mask. Sheet
bronze with green and
red ochre patina.
H: 21.5cm.
China, Liao dynasty
(900-1000)

Looking and silence

According to Louis-Vincent Thomas, "Every culture transcends death because man cannot live without having accepted, integrated or interpreted it. Death is not what foils culture, it is what made culture surge as a failure for failure, as an affirmation of life despite death, against death" (*Encylopaedia Universalis*, 1984, volume 12, 659).

Religion was created to deliver answers. However, certainty comes only from faith. As for science, it remained silent before it had the effect of disenchanting the world. For millennia, it was in art that the human spirit was sublimated, making the invisible visible. Spokesman for the group and himself, the artist fashions effigies that reflect the feelings and expectations; in front of them, across time and space, the viewer brings them to life. For the fundamental is one and, at a determined moment, is recognized. What is immediately compelling is the look. The look man directs at the divinity, whatever its name: the look returned by the divinity. The magical charge and the prodigious presence produced by the earliest civilizations that emerged in West Asia will not be surpassed. Who else could conceive these "idols with eyes" from the 4th millennium B.P., these abstract shapes that live through their eyes, through two holes that allow light and dark to pass through? Six hundred years later, statues were reduced to a gesture of prayer or offering accompanied by a distraught look in their huge eyes, which are sometimes empty and sometimes have dilated pupils. Later, a smile flickered on some female faces (Museum of Baghdad). One also

dreams in front of the Cycladic marble head in the Louvre (circa 2300 B.P.). The oval face is bare except for the bridge of the nose. It has no eyes; however, it looks. Its looks beyond the real.

Egypt is better known. Egyptians believed in life after death to which one acceded, for eternal happiness, after one lived a moral life on earth. Mummification and embalming preserved the body so that it could continue to live in the tomb, which contained all its needs: furniture, food, women, servants, dancers and musicians, either painted on the walls or sculpted. The right to resurrection, available to all beginning around 2000 B.P., was initially reserved to the sovereign. The son of Ra, he was reunited with his father through the pyramid that represents the ray of the sun god. But, because of its bulk, the pyramid also symbolized royal authority imposing itself on nature and the people. The Sphinx guarding the tombs at Giza is a representation of the pharaoh with a lion's body whose head is turned towards the Nile and the rising sun where life is reborn every day. Its expression changes according to the orientation and brightness of the light and the shadows of its relief. Wind and sand have eroded its face, accentuating the emptiness of its gaze withdrawn into eternity. Faith in immortality gave princes a peaceful face and even the hint of a smile to Queen Ahhotep, Thutmosis III and Amenophis III. The only exception is Sesotris III whose drawn features and falling eyelids and mouth reveal weariness and disillusionment after endless expeditions. Notable among private individuals is the moving face of the majordomo Sa-Kaherka. Generally

tinuity between past, present and future generations. In Japan, the forging of swords was an operating placed under the Shinto sign of purity of the soul.

Very early on as well, man expressed in his productions his anxiety about his mortality and his desire to perpetuate himself. Biologically speaking, fertility is the means. On the spiritual level, religion and philosophy propose their responses. Art too is a path to the absolute. In various ways, with different accents, all cultures express their passionate need to attain the eternal through their works. Beyond the divergences in designs and forms, beauty builds a bridge between human beings because it bears witness to aesthetic and spiritual correspondences that resonate in the core of one's being and because it is the same fundamental interrogation on the meaning of life and death.

Fenestrated axe. Bronze.
H: 10.2cm x L: 5cm.
Iran, 1st millennium B.P.

speaking, while the pharaoh dominated all the other figures, men and women were represented in the same size. Whether they are seated or standing, the woman affectionately places her hand on her husband's shoulder or links arms with him.

Serenity in the face of death does not preclude the enjoyment of the present. This was exhorted by the *Harpist's Song* (Middle Kingdom):

"Nobles and illustrious men are buried in their tombs. They built houses whose location no longer exists. What has become of them?... No one comes from there to announce what is the matter, what they need or to appease our hearts until we approach the place where they have gone. For this reason, appease your heart. Let oblivion be profitable to you. Follow your heart for as long as you live... do not tire your heart until the day when the funerary lament is sung for you... This is why you must make your day happy and do not become weary... Look, no one who has gone has come back" (after F. Daumas).

The portraits of Fayyum were the last stage of the Egyptian funerary mask. Painted in encaustic on wood panels, they covered the mummy's face. After Egypt was conquered by Alexander, then by Rome, the ancestral religion slowly disappeared. Serenity vanished. The eyes have a serious expression that is almost grave and often apprehensive.

On the shores of the Red Sea, the southern Arabian civilization flourished for 1,200 years due to writing, irrigation and trade in myrrh, incense and products from India and Africa (700 B.P.-500). "Stelae with eyes" –

square limestone blocks into which a schematic face (sometimes just eyes which take up a third of the face) is carved – remain. Did they guard tombs from being profaned or simply the memory of the deceased for those close to him? Marvelous alabaster funerary heads also remain including the famous Myriam of Tamna, the capital of Qataban, with her large lapis lazuli eyes and tranquil smile. The inlay has disappeared from other faces, which makes their bewitching gaze even more striking.

Around the world, many peoples used the mortuary mask, which may exist alongside the sculpted head. In fact, the mortuary mask represents the majority of masks discovered during archeological digs. Placed on the face of the deceased or by his side, did it serve to protect him from the dangers of the afterlife? Or was it a double destined to survive when the flesh had turned to dust? The gaze varies according to the culture. While, as we have seen, it was serene in Egypt, it is worried and worrying on this Liao – a dynasty with proto-Mongol origins that occupied northern China for almost 200 years (937-1125) – mask. Jomon, the first Japanese civilization (10500-300 B.P.), had masks with empty eyes or "snow goggles" curiously similar to those of Taino statuettes of spirits.

In the Americas, Teotihuacan was famous for its masks with almond-shaped eyes with a great nobility of expression. Also famous is the half-bat, half-man mask with terrible eyes of Monte Alban II, a jade pectoral found on a dead man (100-200). In the Maya Temple of Inscriptions at Palenque, the face of the priest-king Pacal, who was buried in 694,

Munkala. *Mask of Anguish.*
Gray ebony.
H: 45cm x L: 18.3cm.
Brazzaville, Congo, 1994.

Bailer.
H: 30cm x L: 13cm.
Trobriand Islands.

was covered in a green jade mosaic mask, which symbolizes eternally young corn. It was in effect out of corn that the gods created man by molding it with water to make flesh and blood. On the cover of the sarcophagus, the king is dressed in a corn god costume; from his body rises the tree of the world topped with the first bird to indicate that death gave him another life. The way of thinking was not very different in the Andes where gold, stone, wood and ceramic masks have been found, which also served as mediators between man and the supernatural.

However, masks are also worn by the living. Thus, it has multiple functions. First, it conceals: this is its raison d'être. It hides and changes the wearer into a living or dead character, an animal, a plant, a hybrid being, a spirit, an object, a myth or idea. It ensures the communication between the group and the afterlife to be reconciled with it or protected from it, facilitates social order, encourages the fertility of the earth and of women, presides over rites of exorcism or of the passage of the seasons or ages, and sublimates historical events; in order to channel licentiousness, it appropriates the qualities of wild or imaginary animals.

Japanese Noh theater is one of the most fascinating spectacles in the world, where the bareness of the stage, the hieratic slowness of the movements, the codified masks of the actors and the contrast of musical time signatures (one flute and three drums) abolish the border between the real and the unreal. In front of a simple backdrop decorated by a large pine tree whose green color represents the eternity of nature, Noh only has two principal characters: the hero – warrior, lady, god or demon – who may make several appearances (either living or as a ghost) and the medium, often an itinerant monk who evokes his spirit and appeases it. In a dreamlike ambiance where shamanist, Shinto and Buddhist beliefs mingle, Noh plunges the spectator into the most secret depths of his soul.

Balinese theater is based on another dialectic. Here, the Barong, a mythical creature, incarnates good, and Rangda, a witch, represents evil. The two fight, but neither wins: good cannot exist without evil.

The arts of Oceania and Africa are very different although the civilizations have several similarities: animism, the worship of ancestors and spirits, the value given to fertility and fecundity, the authority of the spoken word and of age, the importance of rites, secret societies and initiation and the correspondence between man and the cosmos, and the sacred and the profane. These characteristics are a product of the lack of advanced technology and science which, in addition to the absence of writing, does not permit adequate control of nature or the explanation of natural phenomena: consequently, the spirits that inhabit this world, the culture heroes and the founding ancestors of the community who continue to live another life after death must be propitiated. Art mediating between the visible and the invisible must be effective to carry out its spiritual functions: it obeyed rules for design and the method of production handed down from generation to generation, which have proven themselves.

In Oceania, people believe in *mana*, a force inherited or acquired by ritual behavior, victory at war or luck, which ensures the success of both artists and chieftains. Melanesia offers the most varied, complex and fantastic tableau, which inspired the enthusiasm of the Surrealists. Does it not come from the imaginary, the unconscious and dreams during which the wandering soul may visit the land of the dead and of the gods? While Africans, who also dream, are more or less naturalistic despite stylization or distortion, Melanesians repudiate any imitation of the human figure of which they only keep the intensity of the eyes whatever their shape: pointed circles, slits, protrusions or round, semicircular and almond-shaped holes. A sense of strangeness is accentuated by the use of all sorts of materials – human hair, animal teeth, tree fern, basketry and shells – assembled in a way that seems eccentric to someone who does not know its symbolism. A given individual is not depicted, but a god, ancestor or spirit as understood by tradition. A concept defined by the criteria of the style, including serene, inquisitive, menacing or happy gazes, is substituted for the portrait. The exception to this rule (there are always exceptions) is the overmodeled skull of some peoples such as the Iatmul of New Guinea: the skull of the deceased, once clean and dry, is recovered with his own face sculpted in clay. The *yipwon* sculptures of the Yiman (who live south of the Iatmul) are remarkably abstract. They are made to be seen in profile and almost disappear when they are viewed head on. The *yipwon* are protective spirits of hunting and war. Only

Girl's head. Alabaster.
H: 18cm. Tamna,
Qataban, Yemen.
2nd c. B.P.-1st c.

their heads, with their fierce eyes, and a single leg are depicted; the body is reduced to an ensemble of hooks (the ribs) placed on either side of a striated cone (the heart). Conversely, the *malangan* of New Ireland form complex structures linked to initiation and burial rites. They include poles, statues, masks and multicolored openwork bas-relief panels. The poles are a confused tangle of figures and animals (snakes, fish, birds), lines, curves, volumes, voids and contrasting surfaces and colors which only allow the piercing gaze of the principal face to stand out. Funerary rites give rise to festivities during which sculptures are exhibited and dances performed by people wearing masks with large crests painted red, black and white, which evoke the triumph of life over death.

Objects produced in Micronesia are not abundant but of a great purity of line, whether they are everyday objects (plates from the islands of Maty and Aua), ornaments (*kap kap*) or figures of divinities or ancestors. Those of the Nukuoro (Caroline Islands) already discussed are striking because of their powerful abstraction: the absence of features on the faces makes them more fascinating. The only mask of the region comes from Mortlock (Caroline Islands). It is white with red eyebrows and lips, its eyes reduced to slits with a meditative gaze. Incarnating the spirit of the ancestors, it is worn during ceremonial dances to protect the harvest of the breadfruit tree from storms and cyclones (Meyer, II, 607).

Compared to Melanesia and Micronesia, Polynesia is characterized by its relative stylistic unity. Whether simple (Cook Islands,

Southern Islands) or highly decorated with motifs that resemble tattoos (the Maori of New Zealand), in wood or basketry covered with feathers (Hawaii), figures of gods and ancestors with huge eyes show the dignity or power that confer their spiritual force (*mana*), thought to reside in the head. The design of the *u'u* club of the Marquesas Islands condenses their concept of the relationship between man and the cosmos. Twelve eyes carved into the two sides look in every direction. In their usual place, they represent sight; at the top, consciousness; on the nose, the soul of odors, that is, the languages of nature; on the mouth, the soul of taste, which interprets, judges and classifies; at the base or on the chin, they symbolize matter available for transformation by the spirit. The beginning and the end coincide in harmony (Gabus, 1963). However, the most famous sculptures in this part of the world are the monumental heads of Easter Island carved out of the volcanic tuff which, raised on stone platforms, contemplate the sea: like the Mezcala of Mexico, the shadow of their hollow eye sockets adds to their mystery.

Africa has a sculptural heritage whose wealth, inventiveness and forceful expression are prodigious. Unfortunately, we have little information about it. According to a proverb: "Whoever does not know the origin of a mask, the myths, songs and dance steps that go with it as well as the way in which it is propitiated, knows nothing of this mask." This is often the case. This art is characterized by the secrecy that surrounds it. Many statues and masks are forbidden to be seen by women and children as well as by

uninitiated or low-ranking men. On the other hand, it is very rare to find a smile. The African "gaiety" praised by so many authors is only superficial and fleeting. The profound reality is the existential angst that has come from a long past of powerlessness, caused by a low level of technology, when faced with the forces of nature which must be endlessly appeased by prayers and rites. Man lives with the constant sentiment of the invisible, of the presence of ancestors and spirits, and the relationship between things whose meaning must be deciphered. The fear of sorcery so typical of such societies bears witness to this. Sorcery is the ultimate evil because it directly attacks the supreme value, life. While in Europe sorcery was essentially female and linked to sexuality and sin, in Africa it reveals social conflicts, every individual being a potential sorcerer since he can feel resentment, jealousy and hate towards another person, which makes him try all sorts of ways of hurting this person. Opposing him is the magician, both healer and soothsayer, who has acquired the knowledge of illnesses and remedies, the power to interpret observable signs in objects and people and, as a result, to detect sorcerers and their malevolent practices. However, more profoundly, aren't the sorcerer and the magician both "initiates," complementary poles of the same social reality, contradictory by nature, a reflection of the dialectic of disorder necessary for order and of death as rebirth?

By their beauty – that is, the power of life that they manifest – statues and masks contribute to the effectiveness of rites that continually remind the community of the truth

Dance mask with tubular
eyes and big nose framed by
the forehead, eyes and upper
lip, all protruding.
Painted wood. H: 34cm.
Kran, Ivory Coast.

and value of the beliefs on which it is founded and the individual of his place and duties to perpetuate it by following the way of the ancestors. The essential element of these sculptures is the gaze while the mouth is sometimes absent (on certain Bamana and Kwele masks). The eyes are represented in a wide variety of manners. Whether full, globular, tubular, empty, round, square, rectangular, crescent-shaped, diamond-shaped, slits or sometimes in multiple pairs (Grebo), they are distinguished by their dissymmetry and the intensity of the feelings expressed that this dissymmetry reinforces – expectations, fears, desires, anguish and appeasement.

Figures of ancestors and spirits that are placed on domestic and village altars and are honored by giving them offerings evoke the myths of cosmogony, culture acts and genealogies. During the feasts when the figures are carried around, they transmit their strength to the members of the community, favoring the fertility of the fields and the fecundity of women and punishing those who have transgressed the customary norms. Individual figures or couples are frontal, vertical, hieratic and dignified. Many have cavities into which magical substances are placed, some have eyes in polished metal destined to blind malevolent forces (Fang), while others are spiked with knife blades and nails that are planted to activate their power (Kongo, Vili). As in Oceania, they are not generally portraits. The most famous African effigies, those of the Bushongo kings of Kuba – 17 examples of which have come to be known since the 17th century – have

Anthropomorphic mask representing an antelope with a long muzzle previously covered in brass. Wood. H: 40cm. Marka, Segou region, Mali.

more or less the same face, eyes lowered in an expression of distant majesty; each is identified only by the emblem engraved on its pedestal. The correspondence that we note here between content and form (which expresses royal grandeur) is a general principle of beauty: we have earlier given examples of convergences (health, scarifications, abundant hair) and divergences (firm or pendulous breasts, the ringed or bare neck). The ancestral statues of the Hemba, who lived in eastern upper Zaire, are perhaps a little more individualized. However, almost all of them have a serene expression and half-closed eyes.

Masks offer the greatest variety of types, shapes and styles. Most are worn on the face, others on the forehead, head or shoulders and miniature masks in pendant form worn as amulets. Some are large horizontal (Bwa "butterfly" masks), rectangular (Toussian) or vertical (Mossi "antelope" masks) boards. Themes and motifs are human, animal, hybrid or geometric and always endowed with one or more symbolic significations in relation to the groups who possess them and the activities to which they are associated (rites of passage, seasonal holidays, religious ceremonies). In effect, they have multiple functions ranging from education to entertainment via the working out of differences, participation in work and mourning, and the maintenance of collective order and well-being.

The mask never acts alone. It is an integral part of the fiber costume that envelopes its wearer and inseparable from the singing, music and dancing that accompany it. Identifying with the mask, the wearer becomes a spirit, ancestor or animal whose movements he imitates: at the paroxysm of the action, he goes into a trance. The Ijo who live near the Niger delta venerate aquatic genies in whose honor they organize a celebration to beseech their favors at the beginning of the year or at the time of the floods. Their masks, worn horizontally in the water, are characterized by their abstraction. This mask represents a crocodile with tubular eyes and a large, protruding snout. It is topped with a protuberance rising out of geometric motifs evoking scales that is echoed by the diamond-shaped plank that forms the animal's mouth. The Bamana *tyiwara* headdress represents the antelope sent by God to men to teach them agriculture. Dancing couples wear on their heads stylized male and female figures associated with the sun and earth during celebrations that precede the rainy season with a view to increasing the fer-

Crocodile mask with
protruding eyes and
diamond-shaped snout.
Wood. L: 78cm.
Ijo, Nigeria.

Monkey mask.
Wood, bronze patina.
H: 26cm. Baule, Ivory
Coast.

tility of the fields. The Marka, who live north of the Bamana, hold analogous celebrations, which also involve masks, of a completely different style – "anthropozoomorphic" – a long, thin face topped with two or four small horns. This ancient example, with its meditative eyes, has lost its brass plating. Made by the Baule, this rare monkey mask is powerfully abstract, its empty eyes reflecting all the mystery of the forests of the Ivory Coast.

Tyiwara is the name of one of the six Bamana initiation societies. Almost all African peoples have initiation societies that involve mainly young men, rarely women, such as those of the Mende of Sierra Leone or the Bidyogo of Guinea-Bissau. However, initiation as an institution exists everywhere as it prepares young people for their adult responsibilities. Isolated in a sacred wood, they receive the necessary knowledge and skills, under the direction of the masks, through a physical and moral training to endure fatigue, danger and suffering in a climate of secrecy and emotional feverishness that aims to place the neophyte in contact with the world of ancestors and spirits and make the age group more cohesive. At the end of the tests, the individual loses his former identity to be reborn as a new person with another name. He has learned the meaning of signs and the dialectic of the sacred and the profane.

The highest-ranking Bamana initiation society, the *koré*, aims to lead the initiate, via the symbolism of masks, to mystical union with God. The hyena incarnates limited human knowledge, which must be killed to gain access to divine wisdom. The mask that represents the hyena has the animal's pointed ears, but a wild-eyed human face with a prominent forehead (that is where the spirit lives); its mouth is only visible in profile as half-open. Among the Senufo, the *poro* organizes the initiation in three seven-year cycles. Although it is for men, elderly women may be admitted because Senufo society is matrilineal, the supreme deity is a woman and elderly women are mediators with the other world. The *kpeliye* mask is used in fertility rites as well as during burials so that the spirit of the deceased leaves the house and does not trouble the living. The typical mask has a female face with eyes reduced to slits that watch the invisible, scarified cheeks and forehead topped with a hornbill and ram's horns, symbols of fertility; the "legs" may recall the side locks of the hairstyle of a woman who has borne children.

In addition to initiation societies which, as well as teaching, play a role in social control, there are even more secret societies whose essential function is to ensure the power of their leaders by intimidation, fear and sorcery. One example is the *kifwebe* of the Songye who live east of Congo-Kinshasa (Hersak, 1985). The mask, worn atop a long raffia costume, represents a supernatural being and aims to frighten. One imagines this powerful creation at night, dancing in the firelight, all angles with its crest, empty eyes, triangular nose and protruding cubic mouth. The whole is covered with parallel, vertical, horizontal, oblique and curved stripes painted in alternating colors: red (blood, strength, danger), black (night, evil) and a bit of white. The female *kifwebe*, which has no crest but a black band dividing the forehead in two,

Koré mask. Wood.
H: 49cm.
Bamana, Mali.

179

has rounder shapes, more widely spaced stripes; white, the color of day, purity and health, predominates. The nose and mouth are less protruding and the eyes are arch-shaped. Its dance calls on benevolent spirits (white magic). Combining menace and gentleness is a universal way of governing. Only appearances differ.

If initiation is an essential moment because it prepares young people for their role in the perpetuation of the community, the funeral is another, equally crucial, because it transforms the deceased into a protective ancestor; moreover, as death is not a natural and individual phenomenon but the sign of a rupture that affects the entire village, masks are used to purify the village and restore balance, proclaiming the continuity of life. In West Africa, white is also the color of death.

In Ivory Coast, the Dan and Yohure idealize the female faces of their masks, which are oval and highly polished, a sign of health, with slits for eyes. The "classic" Dan mask has a slightly bulging high forehead, prominent cheekbones, diamond-shaped open lips and a protruding chin. This more elaborate Yohure mask is dark brown with white highlights. The hieratic traits come out of a frame topped by three hornbills. Under a headdress carved with triangles in three semi-circles, a sign of wealth and power, the eyes are half-closed. The straight, thin nose supports the double arch of the eyebrows and the crescent-shaped eye sockets, and the closed mouth is pouting. Because of its harmonious design, purity of line and inward-looking gaze, this mask is a masterpiece of sensibility.

Farther south, the Punu of Gabon are famous for their white masks with their enigmatic pouts. They depict the dead – men and women (the latter with scarifications on their foreheads and temples) – that the dancers on stilts wearing them honor by their cries and acrobatics during funeral ceremonies. The white of the face is in contrast with the black of three-shelled headdress; the center shell rises higher than the other two. The double arch of the eyebrows is simply traced and the eyes are long slits closed to the world to open to the other world.

Europe has a more tragic approach to death, probably because of Christianity and individualism. No one has expressed this with more force than Francisco Goya whose *Tres de Mayo* makes an instant of war an appeal to the universal conscience. In 1808, Napoleon invaded Spain. The people rose up. On May 2, French troops quashed the demonstration at the Puerta del Sol. On May 3, a group of partisans was executed. In the light of a lantern on the ground, a faceless firing squad aims their shining rifles. In front of them, out of the obscure mass of the condemned, a man stands out in a white shirt, arms spread above his head in a gesture of defiance, his eyes full of hate. Goya has not only painted a scene of execution; he passionately denounces the horror of war. It is still contemporary: the 20th century was the most murderous of all.

We experience the individual anguish of being in the world in front of the inordinately stretched figures of Alberto Giacometti: standing, hieratic women, their arms close to their bodies, and men walking without looking

in limitless space. Georges de la Tour provides a response to this solitude, the "secret wound of all beings and even of all things," in his *Newborn* (Musée de Rennes), a better title, because it is universal, than Nativity with its Christian connotation. In the light of a candle sheltered by a woman's hand, the baby in his swaddling clothes, his mouth open, sleeps in the arms of his mother who watches over him, her eyes lowered. La Tour does not depict their happiness, but their grave tenderness in the face of the new life beginning in this "vale of tears." Through the play of light and shade, and silence and stillness, La Tour makes all the mystery of destiny emerge.

In the Buddhist world, the tragic is absent because the impermanence of all things is assumed.

Let us briefly recall the teachings of Buddha (circa 560-480 B.P.). Gautama, born in the royal clan of the Shakya near the border between India and Nepal, discovered illness, old age and death when he went out of the palace shortly after his marriage. He left home to lead a vagabond life seeking the meaning of life. One night, under a pipal tree, he found illumination, the answer to the problem of suffering that was haunting him. He gave his first sermon in a deer park north of Benares and the five men who listened to him became his disciples and made up the community (*Sangha*). They began their wandering to teach the doctrine (Dharma), but the peasants criticized them because, during the rainy season, "they trod down seedlings, impeding their growth and destroyed many small living beings." As a consequence, Buddha decided that the monks would go on retreat during this period, first in caves, then in monasteries that were neither too close nor too far from towns in order to maintain contact with the faithful. Early on, around the middle of the 4th century B.P., Buddhism split into two currents: Theravada, the "doctrine of the ancients," that claimed to be more faithful to the words of Buddha, took root in Sri Lanka and spread to Burma, Thailand, Cambodia and Laos, and Mahayana which considered itself as the "great way" substituting for the ideal of the *arhant* seeking deliverance in the monastic life that of the bodhisattva who, having attained illumination, renounced Nirvana in order to help others enter it. This is the religion practiced in China, Korea, Japan and Viet Nam. A form of Mahayana called "Tantric" predominates in Tibet, Nepal and Mongolia.

However, all schools recognize the Three Jewels – Buddha, Law (Dharma) and Community (*Sangha*) – and the core of the doctrine: "I teach," said Buddha, "only two things: the reality of suffering and the possibility of escaping it." These are the Four Noble Truths that are not dogmas but come from scientific observations announced for the first time in history. Any perceptible phenomenon is a cause that is itself the effect of an earlier cause (the law of causality or of conditioned production). Everything changes; nothing is immutable (the law of impermanence). Conscience and personality do not have their own existence independent of the body and the sense. The self is an illusion as it is nothing but an ensemble of phenomena

Male *kifwebe* mask.
Wood. H: 60cm.
Songye,
Congo-Kinshasa.

in perpetual flux – matter, sensations, perceptions, thoughts and knowledge combining and interconnecting in a relationship of cause and effect (the law of insubstantiality). It is because all is empty of "self" that all is transformed and it is because all is transformed that all is pain.

This is the first Truth. Existence is suffering: birth, old age, illness, death, union with what one does not love, separation from what one loves and the non-possession of what one desires. Suffering is linked to impermanence.

The second Truth identifies the origin of suffering in "thirst," that is, the desire for pleasure. It leads to the three "roots of evil": covetousness, hate and error. Any act (karma) produces a "fruit" that brings corresponding retribution or punishment.

The third Truth is the end of suffering by the extinction of thirst and thus the three roots of evil. It is equivalent to Nirvana which is the unconditioned state because all the productions causing karma and, as a result, further rebirth are suppressed.

The fourth Truth shows the ways that lead to deliverance, the "middle way" that avoids the two extremes of excessive asceticism and the pleasure of the senses. It comprises eight branches, none of which should be neglected in favor of the others: right understanding (knowledge of the Truths), right thinking (whose goal is deliverance), right speech, right conduct, right livelihood, right effort, right mindfulness and right meditation. The first two paths constitute wisdom, the three following paths constitute ethics and the last three mental conduct.

A practical realist, Buddha dismissed use-

Mask with half-open eyes topped with three hornbills. Polished wood. H: 56cm. Yohure, Ivory Coast.

less questions – especially metaphysical ones (Is the universe eternal? What is Nirvana?) – which determine no progress on the path to deliverance or which risk sowing confusion in people's mind. Underlining the fact that he was simply showing the way, Buddha compared his teaching to a raft, which is made to cross a river, but not to be carried on one's back. Whether the traveler crosses to the other side does not depend on him. The first condition is personal effort. Each person is responsible for his own destiny; there is no God to punish or save. Man is his own master, "his own refuge" as Buddha said. He put the accent not on faith, but on reason and the critical mind: do not let yourself be guided by tradition, the authority of texts and masters, including himself, inference, appearances, verisimilitudes and miracles. Even the four Truths have to be tested like the iron in the fire before accepting them. The critical sense that Buddha encouraged is accompanied by a remarkable tolerance of other opinions: "Man has faith if he says 'This is my faith'; until then, he supports the Truth. But, he cannot advance to the absolute conclusion this way: "This is the only Truth and everything else is false."

For many centuries after his death, the respect of the Master forbade all representations of his person, which was simply evoked by attributes such as his footprints, the tree of Enlightenment, the Wheel of Law, the *stupa* containing his ashes and the lotus of transcendence, as on the Sanchi reliefs (1st century B.P.). However, the desire to respond to the devotion of the faithful led to the abandonment of these conventions in the first

half of the 2nd century, and the appearance of the image of Buddha, which occurred at almost the same time in Mathura (south of Delhi) and Gandhara (northwest India). These two regions were part of the Kushan Empire at the crossroads of an important network of economic and cultural exchanges between China, India and the West. In Gandhara, the Greco-Roman influence resulted in an "Apollonian" face whose closed smile and closed or half-closed eyes remained "Asian." The *usnisha*, the cranial protuberance symbolizing wisdom, is covered with hair whereas the Buddha's head must be shaved. Sometimes, it is changed into a Greek chignon or has an Iranian hairstyle. From Gandhara, the figure of Buddha followed the Silk Road and influenced the art of Central Asia, then that of China, Korea, Japan and Viet Nam. Mathura, more deeply rooted in Indian tradition, sculpted the Buddha in the style of local divinities. A third center developed in southern India at Amaravati, which exported to Sri Lanka, Burma, Cambodia, Laos and Thailand. While Buddhism disappeared in India after its absorption by Hinduism and destructions by Islam, it blossomed in the rest of Asia. Each people gave Buddhism its own artistic interpretation whose manifestations eclipsed Indian models. There were indeed constants, notably a codified language of postures – standing, seated, lying down (when he reached Nirvana) – and gestures (*mudra*) – concentration, meditation, preaching, appeasement, giving, arguing and taking the earth as a witness. However, in Asia as elsewhere, the rules have never stopped creators from leav-

ing their mark. As Sukracarya, a 5th-century Indian theoretician remarked, what are essential are not canonic prescriptions, but the meditation of the artist before undertaking his work. "In order for the shape of an image to be fully and clearly represented in his mind, the image-maker must meditate; his success will be proportional to his meditation. No other way, not even the contemplation of the object, will allow him to accomplish his design" (quoted in Boisselier, 38).

According to the culture, the style and the gaze varied. Although always endowed with spirituality and dominated by serenity, the face of Buddha has open, closed or half-closed eyes; he meditates and has a ghost

of a smile, imbued with the peace of Nirvana, detached yet full of humanity. His eyes and smile express compassion (*karuna*), one of the four "sublime dwellings" of the faith along with benevolence (*metta*), joy in the success of others (*mudita*) and equanimity (*upekha*). Compassion is indeed an inadequate term for translating *karuna*: it is not only participation in the suffering of others, but actively helping them even to one's own detriment without hoping for anything in exchange. *Karuna* is disinterested, with no attachments. Buddha asked his disciples to travel the world "for the salvation of the many, for the happiness of the many, out of compassion for all beings." These beings are not only human. A *jataka* relates how, in a previous life, Buddha sacrificed himself to feed a tigress and her hungry cubs.

On the Silk Road, Dunhuang was the first stage of Buddhism's penetration of China (1st century). From the 4th to the 14th centuries, monks decorated their caves with paintings and statues intended to educate the faithful; these have kept the freshness of their colors.

Sculpture attained the highest peak of spirituality under the Northern Wei in Yungang and Longmen (5th-6th centuries) while the face became fatter during the Tang and Song dynasties. The Korean masterpiece is the Miroku (Maitreya, the Buddha to come) sitting in meditation, his right foot resting on his left knee, right hand raised and two fingers touching his cheek. The graceful lines of the admirable gilded bronze of the Duksoo Palace in Seoul (7th century) inspired numerous sculptors in Korea and Japan. In Cambodia, sculpture reached its apogee during the middle of the Angkor period (late 12th-early 13th centuries) with the Buddha protected by the *Naga* of Prea Khan. He meditates, eyes lowered, an ineffable smile floating on his lips, an interior smile of infinite compassion for all beings (Musée Guimet). Thailand's contribution was the walking Buddha whose movement is particularly elegant and fluid, one leg in front of the other, arms swinging in a supple manner and one hand raised in the gesture of argumentation (Sukhothai, 15th century). Because they had less sandstone than the Khmer, Thais chose to cast their masterpieces – with serene faces, lowered eyes and slightly smiling mouth – in bronze. The forms differ, but the serenity and smile remain in the statues of the Vietnamese and Burmese who preferred wood.

The history of Christian iconography was not very different from that of Buddhism. In the first two centuries, there was no representation of Christ because of the ban inherited from Judaism and, as in India, it was the pressure of popular piety that led to its lift-

ing. The "handsome Christ" with curly hair and gentle-looking features appeared in the middle of the 4th century. Byzantium, the theocratic monarchy where the Church was subject to the emperor, exalted the Pantocrator, who was the all-powerful sovereign of the Kingdom of Heaven as the emperor was of the terrestrial kingdom. The bearded Christ, whose wide-open eyes stare at believers, stands out, hieratic and severe, from a gold background that reflects His glory in the unreal atmosphere created by the multicolored mosaics that evoke the intelligible world. In the West, there is a greater variety of representations, each people giving, as in Buddhism, its own interpretation according to environment and era. The teaching Christ of the south portal of Chartres Cathedral (1205-1215), eyes half-closed, right hand raised, left hand holding the Bible, is close to Buddha; the Christ of suffering, collapsed on the Cross, with a tortured expression on his face, is very far from Buddha. The fundamental difference between the two doctrines of salvation is that Buddha was a man who attained Enlightenment, while Christ said – and Christians believe – He was the Son of God who came to suffer for the redemption of all people. The two religions have a rather similar figure: the Virgin Mary, full of grace, for Christians, and the bodhisattva Avalokiteshvara or Guanyin (China), Kanseum (Korea), Kannon (Japan) or Quan-âm (Viet Nam), whom popular piety feminized in East Asia – he or she who lowers his or her gaze on the distress of the world in order to relieve them.

Spirituality similar to that of the Mahayana

Buddha's head. Bronze
with yellow patina.
H: 25cm. Thailand,
U Thong C,
14th – 15th c.

may be found in the most beautiful icons,
notably those by Andrei Rublev: his *Trinity*
(circa 1410, Tretyakov Gallery, Moscow) was
inspired by a passage from Genesis, which
relates how Abraham was visited by Yahweh
in the guise of three men whom he invited
to rest and take refreshment underneath his
oak. A great mellowness – a little mysterious
– emanates from the panel because of the delicate harmony of the colors and the gentle
curves of the figures who make up a circle
with their haloes and the bending of the
branches of the tree.

Impulses of life and death

In Mexico on November 2, children make
skeletons dance on strings while adults eat
candy skulls. It is the day when the entire
country is transformed into *calaveras*, from
engaged couples to shop windows to mari-
achi bands. This appropriation of life by
death is an old tradition. The great civilizations from before the European conquest do
not disassociate the two: death was not an
annihilation, but necessary for rebirth. No
people has expressed its familiarity with
death more powerfully than the Aztecs. Some
authors have remarked upon the "passive
fatalism of the Indian," their "fanatical religion," their "bloodthirsty gods" and their
taste "for the monstrous and the macabre."
Indeed, their statues do not smile and terrifying shapes abound. The most striking is
the immense statue of Coatlicue, the goddess of the earth and death – "She who has
a skirt of snakes" – a monolith 2.57 meters
high weighing 12 tons representing a decap-

Bodhisattva Chenrezig
(Avalokiteshvara) with a
thousand eyes and arms.
Cotton tanka.
H: 59.5cm x L: 38.5cm.
Tibet, 19th c.

Manjushri seated in *padmasana* on a lotus pedestal holding the book of wisdom and the sword that cuts illusion. Gilt bronze inlaid with turquoise.
H: 12.5cm. Nepal, 18th c.

itated woman from whose neck two snake mouths spurt forth like gushes of blood; her body is a tangle of snakes, cut-off hands and ripped-out hearts with a bare skull in the center and eagle talons for feet (Museo Nacional de Antropología, Mexico City). Tlaloc, the rain god, always looks terrifying as on the vase with his effigy from the Templo Mayor (Museo Nacional de Antropología, Mexico City) – empty-eyed with two fangs; children were sacrificed to him. Xipe Totec, the Flayed One, god of spring and the goldsmith's craft, wears the skin of someone sacrificed, from which hands and feet hang, that leaves only his eyes and mouth visible: it was the skin worn by the priest after having ripped the heart out of the victim (Museum für Völkerkunde, Basel). Even Xochipilli, sitting with his legs tucked under him, empty eyes raised to the sky, does not at all evoke youth, beauty, flowers and music, of which he is the god. All the religious centers of Mesoamerica had playing fields for ball games, which attest to their ritual function, the ball probably representing the sun and the game a combat between darkness and light,

life and death, an opposition that disappeared with the movement of the ball. It ended with the sacrifice of the captain of the beaten team as illustrated by a bas-relief from El Tajin (Veracruz).

However, language and literature illustrate better than art man's worldview. The first Spanish chroniclers translated by "god" the Nahua word *teotl*, which does not correspond to the European sense, but is closer to the Polynesian *mana*, the Chinese *qi* or the *nyama* of some African peoples. According to A.J. Labbé,

"It signifies (at least in part) an impersonal, vital or life-giving energy which is diffused throughout the universe, but which is concentrated in certain persons, places or things... *Teotl* imbues them with power. It has no moral significance with regards to good or evil, being morally neutral in this respect" (36).

Coatlicue, the Earth, is both fertile (the snake symbolizes the life force) and destructive (volcanoes, earthquakes, desert). The rain makes crops grow, but may be lacking, thus leading to food shortage.

"Things were what they were. It was incumbent up on man to take cognizance of the facts of his environment and the uni-

verse, and regulate his life accordingly... Mesoamerican man viewed himself not as being in conflict with nature, but as part of nature. The sculptures placed in temples and shrines [were not] viewed by the educated as "gods." Although these images were meant to represent certain forces of nature, they were not confused with the force of nature itself. They were employed as visible links between the individual and the particular force represented. The blood libations smeared upon [them] did increase their *teotl*... bringing to successful issue the design of the owner. It is for this reason that such temple sculpture was "captured" by inimical armies, the temples razed and the books of knowledge destroyed. Such actions cut an enemy off from his source of beneficent energy (the temple), his esoteric communications media and the knowledge needed to use [them], i.e., the sacred books" (Labbé, 36).

The Aztecs thought of themselves as the sun's chosen people, responsible for feeding it to ensure its course. The food required was the "precious water," blood, and the Aztecs waged "flowered war" in order to obtain large numbers of prisoners for sacrifices. They themselves were prepared for sacrifice from birth. When the midwife cut the baby boy's umbilical cord, she said:

"My beloved son... know that the house in which you were born is not your dwelling: you are a warrior, you are the *quecholli* bird, and the house where you have come to the world is only a nest, an inn where you have alighted... Your real fatherland is elsewhere, you are promised to other places. You belong

190

Yamantaka, the "Conqueror of Death" embracing his *shakti*. Gilt bronze
H: 19cm x L: 15.5cm. Tibet, 18th c.

Green Tara seated in royal relaxation pose (*lalita asana*), hands in argumentation gesture (*vitarka mudra*).
Black bronze inlaid with turquoise.
H: 67cm x L: 45cm x D: 35cm.
Nepal, 19th c.

to the open country where battles begin, it is for them that you were sent, your profession and your science is war; your duty is to make the sun drink the enemies' blood and nourish the earth with their bodies. Your fatherland, heritage and felicity, you will find in the sky in the palace of the sun" (after Sahagun, 439-440).

The child, compared to a gemstone and a luxuriant feather, was warned that he had not come to this world of suffering in order to find contentment, but to work until he was tired and to be afflicted. During the baptism, the midwife, after having purified him with water, lifted him four times to the heavens while imploring the sun to make him a brave warrior "so that he may one day enter your palace of delights where the valiant who died in combat rest and rejoice."

The very consciousness of the precariousness of the world and of the need to establish a harmony between man and the universe, explains the moral rigor imposed in this society:

Can we really say that we live on earth?
A little, for nothing lasts forever,
Even jade shatters,

Even gold crumbles,
Even the plumage of the quetzal tears:
A little, on earth, for nothing lasts forever.
(In Léon-Portilla, 127)

Some concluded that life must be enjoyed while others on the contrary thought that it was a question of "forming faces and hearts" to escape fatalism.

While the portrayal of the gods was terrifying, that of humans is realistic as illustrated by the statues of nobles and the common people (the *machehualli* of the Musée de l'Homme, Paris), women and the elderly. The mask of gray-green stone in Basel's Museum für Völkerkunde is of a pensive beauty that corresponds exactly to Nezahualcoyotl's poem on the brevity of existence cited above.

In truth, the Aztec way of thinking was not an exception in Mesoamerica or in the whole of the Americas. As far as we know, man was considered an integral part of nature, and art and architecture means of communicating with the invisible. The universe was space and time caught in a cyclical movement in which creation and destruction follow each other, linked by a

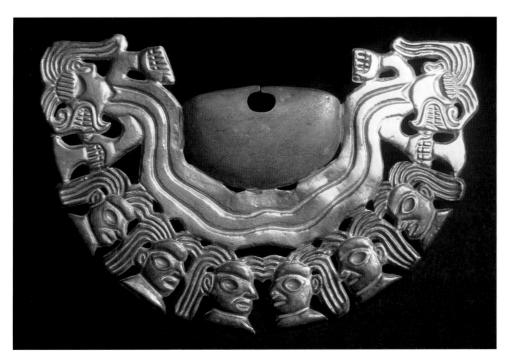

193

primordial need, hence the importance of astronomical observations and the calendar (a way of thinking that was not very different from that of the Indians of Asia). This unitary dualism was found in a Tlatilco terracotta mask from the 1st millennium B.P. – half of the face, with its enormous empty eye, represents death, while the other half represents life. In Teotihuacan (200 B.P-900), the "place where men become gods," the god of death is represented in relief on the square of the Pyramid of the Sun. On Zapotec funerary urns, which have been called baroque because of their ornamental profusion, the figures wearing multicolored feathered headdresses look serene. The Mixtecs who followed them enjoyed sculpted skulls. In the oldest Mesoamerican culture, that of the Olmecs, which reached its peak in 1200-600 B.P., monumental heads have a dignified, severe, authoritarian or even contemptuous expression and stand beside figures with "baby" and "jaguar" features, and human or supernatural masks. Working in hard basalt or even harder jade with simple stone tools, the artist managed to individualize the physiognomies each time. On the central coast of the Gulf of Mexico, effigies of more "classic" beauty have been found: the regular features of a Totonac girl (Museo de la Universidad de Veracruz, Jalapa), the nude Huaxtec adolescent of Tamuin (Museo Nacional de Antropología, Mexico City) and especially the famous "smiling heads" of Veracruz which top bodies whose arms are often raised. These are perhaps the only smiles that may be found in the art of the Indians of the Americas. Were they divinities of play,

dance or music or is the smile only a stylized version of the wide-open mouth of the dead? However, scenes of sacrificial throat slitting are not far away. The Maya stone stelae and wall frescoes of Bonampak represent kings and priests who look noble and dignified, masks of demons, scenes of torture and human sacrifice to the gods, and the mortifications of princes who pierce their tongues with maguey thorns or incise their earlobes.

The proximity of life and death appears no less intense in the Andes. It was manifested in the culture of the Mochicas many of whose ceramics celebrate the pleasures of love while others depict scenes of war and the immolation of prisoners with bulging eyes. In addition to the figures of demons and fantastic animals on mortuary cloths, stone bas-reliefs, pottery and metalwork, a frequent motif is the trophy heads linked to the belief that the valiance of the enemy passed to the conqueror with his severed head.

However, the consciousness of the integration of man and the universe is expressed first in the architecture of cities and temples, designed as places for communication between the earth, the sky and the underworld. The Art Institute of Chicago exhibition "The Ancient Americas: Art from Sacred Landscapes" (1992-1993) illustrated how these civilizations interacted with their environment instead of destroying it like an economic system obsessed with profits and power has been doing for two centuries (Townsend, ed., 1992). We discussed above Teotihuacan, the "City of the Gods" of the Aztecs, the largest nation of Mesoamerica from 150 B.P. to 750, whose serene masks

evoke a style of government and life in harmony with nature. The Nahua *teotl* corresponded to the Quechua *huaca*, which applied in the Andes to all sacred places endowed with a supernatural aura. The local architecture was also dictated by the concept of space and time. The localization and orientation of buildings and monuments, and the design of towns and temples took into account the character of the sites, of the movement of the stars, especially of the course of the sun, and alternating of the dry and rainy seasons that ruled agricultural activities and celebrations, while decoration took its motifs from the fauna which, as an intercessor between man and the cosmos, symbolized royal, shamanist and religious power: eagles, condors, jaguars, coyotes, snakes and caimans. Thus the visual arts complemented the oral tradition in the preservation and transmission of myths, history and scientific and technological knowledge. While renewing the pact between the living, the dead and the gods, periodic celebrations reminded the princes, priests and people of the community's norms.

Chavin de Huantar was the first cultural center (900-200 B.P.) to have a lasting influence. The temple was constructed at the junction of two rivers and two roads crossing the Cordillera: that is, a crossroads of opposing forces between which it served as mediator via its truncated pyramids and U-shaped squares and the themes of decoration involving the elements of the coast, sea and forest. The mountain in front of which ceremonies took place is associated to celestial phenomena and was at the same time the

194

196

Landscape.
Part of a screen attributed to Sesshu
(1420-1506). Ink on paper, six panels.
H: 172cm x L: 370cm. Japan.

power that transferred the underground water coming from the sea to sky via the Milky Way and returned it to the fields in the form of rain and then back to the sea. Around 400 B.P., this symbolic system spread to a vast region comprising plateaus and coasts, to which the motifs of the pottery, jewelry and textiles bear witness (Burger in Townsend, 265-278). The magnificent funerary fabrics of the Paracas (700 B.P.-200) are embroidered with dancers disguised as birds (condors, falcons, eagles), felines (pampas cats, jaguars), fish, snakes, plants and composite beings (bird-feline-snake, shark-falcon). The chieftains who wore these costumes represented natural forces that they propitiated through rites. They were the intermediaries between their communities and the universe. In the same way, the famous figures drawn in the Nazca desert – animal, human or abstract: so large that they could only really be seen from the air and which were also found on painted ceramic vases – were interpreted as being related to a fertility cult, their scale was the result of the desire to attract the attention of the sky and mountain gods so that they would give regular rainfalls.

South of Lake Titicaca, the mythical place where the world was created according to the Quechua, Tiahuanaku is now only a site visited by locals on feast days. For centuries, it was a political and spiritual center exercising power from the Andes to the Pacific. Conceived as the axis of the world, the city was a cosmogram whose center, where temples and the royal palace stood, was surrounded by a wide moat that made it a sacred island in the lake. The royalty thus claimed

the right to intercede with supernatural powers to maintain order and harmony in the universe and in society. To the principle of concentric gradation (the sacred diminishing in intensity from the center to the periphery) was added the principle of the alignment of buildings in accordance with the sun's movement from east to west. At its intersection with the heart of the city, which represents the union of the earth, the sky and the underworld, rises the image of the sacred mountain, dispenser of agricultural prosperity, that is the Akapana step pyramid. Only from its summit can one see both Mount Illimani to the east where the sun rises and Lake Titicaca to the west where it sets. Cutting through this axis, another line (north-south) divides the city into quadrants, a layout that may be found in all the imperial cities from Teotihuacan to Cuzco, the Inca capital from which the four main roads led to the provinces.

The symbolic system was also found in fabrics, the most admirable of which were those of the Huari (500-800) whose patterns and color harmonies have not been surpassed by contemporary non-figurative painting. The tapestry tunics worn by dignitaries and buried with them are elaborate ensembles of what initially appear to be geometric motifs, but which are in fact abstractions of animals and figures recalling the reliefs of the Gate of the Sun in Tiahuanaku. They are repeated by inverting themselves over four to eight columns, but the formal regularity is broken from time to time by variations in color and shape. These voluntary anomalies may reflect the creativity of the artist whose imagination broke the monotony, as well as the conception of the role of the state as the intercessor between the population and a hostile environment (drought, frost, earthquakes, storms), controlling natural chaos through social order.

In India, we enter a completely different continent although there too is found the integration of man and the cosmos. What is

197

striking to the traveler in India is the intimacy of the people with its religion, which is less a relationship with transcendence than a way of living, thinking and feeling. All that he has read about the caste system, the cycle of reincarnation and the law of karma seems to be contradicted by the joy of seasonal holidays when men and women, young and old, rich people and beggars celebrate together: Holi in the honor of Krishna in spring, Diwali, the festival of lights when the houses are lit by small oil lamps and Puja in the honor of the goddess Durga at the end of the monsoon season in Calcutta. Art is closely linked to everyday life. The great epics, the *Mahabharata* and the *Ramayana*, are echoed in the sculptures of the temples and in the recitations of wandering singers as well as in dance, theater, *Kathakali* drama and the cinema. This is because for two millennia the people have lived with the more or less confused hope inspired by the Upanishads: the belief that it is possible for everyone, regardless of birth or gender to attain salvation through personal devotion (*bhakti*) to his or her god.

In a well-known apologue, the *Shandogya Upanishad* stated the identification between the individual self (atman) and the universal self (brahman):

At his father's request, the Brahman Shvetaketu brings him a fruit and opens it.
"What do you see?"
"A number of small seeds, my lord."
"Well, divide one of these seeds. What do you see?"
"Nothing, my lord."
"This subtle essence that escapes our per-

ception," said the father, "is what makes this tree grow, whatever its height. Believe, my friend. This subtle essence animates everything. It is the only reality. It is the atman. You yourself Shvetaketu, you are this."*

Brahman is the Absolute that is everywhere, but it can only be known through its manifestations. It is said that there are 33 million divinities in India. They are dominated by the trinity of Brahma, Vishnu and Shiva meant as a whole comprising the principles of the creation, maintenance and destruction of the universe. But Brahma, often confused with brahman, is neglected and has very few sanctuaries. Vishnu and Shiva are complementary rather than antithetical, the first being associated to the course of the sun and the space through which he travels, and the second to time which preserves and destroys. Each of them is the supreme god for his believers and has a wife who is also honored: Sri or Laxmi, abundance, for Vishnu, and for Shiva the two aspects of his energy (shakti), sometimes benevolent (Uma-Parvati), sometimes terrifying (Durga-Kali).

In fact, Shiva is a complex figure. He is the yogi who reduces the god of love to ashes by the fire of his third eye because he tried to distract him from his meditation. He is also the one who holds a book or a lute and transmits knowledge to humanity. His most common representation is as the stone lingam rising from the center of the disk of the yoni, the female genitals, where the water, oil and milk with which it is sprinkled during worship flow. His most famous image is that of

Natarajah, the "king of the dance," that was magisterially interpreted in Chola bronzes (10th-13th centuries) from south India. Eyes open or half-closed, sometimes surrounded by a circle of flames, the god dances, left leg lifted and right leg trampling the demon of ignorance. His upper right hand holds a tambourine evoking sound, the first element of creation, and a tongue of fire, the agent of the destruction of the world, springs from his upper left hand. His two other hands, one raised, the other hanging, represent appeasement. According to Ananda Coomaraswany, the dance of Shiva has a triple meaning. Its rhythm evokes the source of cosmic destiny. It liberates souls from the illusion that masks reality. It takes place in our heart, which is the heart of the universe.

Rodin expressed his emotion in front of the bronze:

Blossoming in life, the river of life, the air, the sun, the sentiment of the being is an overflowing.
This swollen, protruding mouth, abundant in its sensual expressions…
The tenderness of the mouth and the eye are in harmony.
These lips like a lake of pleasure bordered by such noble palpitating nostrils.
The mouth undulates, sinuous as a snake, in the humid delights; the closed swollen eyes, closed by a seam of eyelashes.
The closed eyes are the sweetness of past times.
Mouth, a den for the sweetest thoughts, but a volcano for the furors.
The materiality of the soul that may be imprisoned in this bronze, enthrals for

Hiroshige (1797-1858),
*River Ferryman in the
Rain.* Paper. Woodblock
print.
H: 36.5cm x L: 12cm.
Japan.

*several centuries; desires of eternity on
this mouth; eyes who are going to see and
speak.*

*For eternity, life enters and leaves by the
mouth, like the bees return and go out
continually; sweet, fragrant breath.*

Vishnu is a simpler figure than Shiva. Like
his consort Laxmi, goddess of wealth – Kali
is the goddess of war and Durga the killer of
demons – he is usually benevolent. The two
most well known incarnations of Vishnu,
constantly depicted in painting, sculpture,
theater and dance, are Rama and Krishna.
Rama, the hero of the *Ramayana,* is endowed
with every virtue. His skill in archery earns
him Sita's hand. She is abducted by the
demon Ravana who imprisons her on his
island Lanka. With the help of Hanuman,
the king of the monkeys, he rescues her. Trial
by fire attests to her purity. In the
Mahabharata, which recounts the battle of
the Pandava and the Kaurava, Vishnu appears
as Krishna, the driver of the hero Arjuna's
chariot. In the *Bhagavad-Gita,* which makes
up part of the epic, he reveals that devotion
(bhakti) is the way to deliverance for men
and women of all castes on the condition
that they do their duty (dharma) without any
hope of reward, "without attaching themselves to the fruit of the act."

Above all, Krishna is the lover of cowgirls
(gopi) whom he drives wild with his flute, a
relationship interpreted by mystics as the
passionate quest of souls for unity with the
Absolute. The *Bhagavata Purana* (after the
10th century) exalts this abandonment to the
divine in terms that are found everywhere.
Krishna is described as a dark-skinned ado-

lescent whose beauty leads women astray.
When they hear his bamboo flute, they cannot resist its strains and abandon their homes
to search for him, burning with a fire that
only "the ambrosia of his lips" can extin-
guish. "Although he carries his pleasure
within himself and is thus inaccessible to
desire," the god shows his benevolence by
dancing with them in the moonlight and
multiplying himself by the power of his magic
so that each of them embraces him or
believes she has. Thus, this dance is a divine
"game" *(lila)* that manifests the grace of the
Lord for his believers and allows them to
unite with him. A thousand years before the
Bhagavata Purana, the *Brihadaranyaka
Upanishad* stated:

"As a man in the arms of a beloved
woman no longer knows anything of outside or inside, the person embraced by the
atman no longer knows anything of outside
or inside. For him is the happy condition in
which all desire is fulfilled, in which he only
desires the atman, in which he has no desire."

India is not the only country that brought
together mysticism and eroticism. It is said
that the European Baroque was the "union
of the spiritual and the sexual" and nothing
illustrates this better than some of
Gianlorenzo Bernini's ambiguous marble
sculptures. The face of the saint in his *The
Ecstasy of Saint Theresa* (1644-1651), in the
Cornaro Chapel of Santa Maria della Vittoria
in Rome, underneath the angel's arrow
(unconscious symbolism?), her dress in dis-
array, mouth open, eyes closed, exhibits all
the signs of orgasm and the same is true of
the *Blessed Ludovica Albertoni* in the church

of San Francesco a Ripa (1671-1674), swooning on her deathbed, clutching her breast.

The most intense eroticism is that accompanied by the sentiment of death. Utamaro achieved this in one of the prints from his album *The Poem of the Pillow* (1788), depicting a couple lying beside a balustrade on the other side of which a tree spreads the green leaves of its branches. Their legs are entangled underneath the transparent muslin of the robe of the woman who is seen from behind. She caresses the chin of her lover with her hand; he grips her right shoulder. We do not see their faces, only the man's pointed gaze. These verses dance on his fan:

This autumn evening
Its beak seized between the valves of the clam
The snipe cannot escape.

How much is the tenderness of the man intensified by his consciousness of the transience of the moment.

While Indian mystics transfigure the loves of Krishna and the gopi, Tantrism does not bother with such a veil. In Radha it sees the omnipotence of the desire felt by all women that they are prepared to satisfy outside the bounds of ordinary morality. It thus contradicts Brahman orthodoxy, which subordinates deliverance to the respect of dharma. It is also opposed to classic Buddhism, which recommends the extinguishing of thirst. Tantrism advocates the experiencing of the totality of being. No doctrine has pushed the association of the spiritual quest and carnal impulses further; making the union of opposites and systematic transgression a means of reaching the absolute. And; contrary to the

tradition according to which the Absolute is one, Tantrism affirms its male and female duality, according supremacy not to the male, the Spirit, but to the female, Nature *(prakriti)* or Energy *(shakti)* in Hinduism and Wisdom *(prajna)* in Buddhism. It is the Great Goddess who plays an active role in her relationship with the male god: supreme happiness is born out of their union. This is why so many deities are represented as embracing couples. The consumption of meat, alcohol and drugs, and sex "beyond rules" are practiced as rites at night, preferably in sites of cremation so that meditation on death provokes a psychic shock – "violence necessary to put the individual in a position to undertake the difficult work that will finally lead him to Deliverance" (Varenne, 8-9).

Both Hindu and Buddhist Tantrism have existed for a long time in Nepal. In Tibet, Buddhism is predominant. It is Mahayana, which arrived in the 7th century and was blended with indigenous beliefs. The adept, guided by a qualified master *(guru),* is initiated in the secret phrases *(mantra)* and meditation on a *mandala* or a *yantra*. A *mantra,* monosyllabic or polysyllabic, is considered

concentrated energy. The most well known is *Om mani padme hum. Om,* which dates from the Vedic era, evokes the original cosmic vibration; *mani* means the jewel, diamond or male organ; *padme* "in the lotus", emblem of Buddhism and the female genitals; and *hum* the force of Enlightenment. *Mani* is synonymous with *vajra* (*dordje* in Tibetan), which symbolizes the energy of the Void in which opposites are reconciled. *Vajrayana,* the "way of the diamond," designates the Tantric Buddhism of Tibet. *Vajra* is also the name of an instrument that is used in most ceremonies, the male pole, while the bell represents the female pole, wisdom. Used together, they symbolize the union of the two complementary principles. *Om mani padme hum* is constantly recited by the Tibetans every day. They hear in it all the voices of the world. It is carved on the stones that line the paths or on prayer wheels and written on the banners that float above sacred sites.

A diagram or an image of the chosen deity may aid meditation.

There are two types of diagrams: *yantras* and *mandalas*. *Yantras* are composed of

Shoshu (18th c.)

Landscape with Mount Fuji.

Ink on paper.

H: 73.6cm x L: 122.5cm.

Japan.

J.-L. Senatus (1949),
Rêve d'amour. **Canvas.**
H: 40cm x L: 50cm. Haiti.

purely geometric shapes: squares, triangles and circles. The most important is the *shri-yantra.* Around the center, which is "all happiness," is a series of triangles: five points below (the female), four points above (the male) which are interlinked (sexual fusion); in addition to the nine basic triangles, there are 34 others which come from the intersection of lines, which brings the total to 43 triangles, inscribed in a lotus with eight petals which is placed in a lotus with 16 petals. This is surrounded by a triple circle inside a triple square pierced with four doors at the four cardinal points. The master trains the disciple to visualize the diagram as a relief whose center is Mount Meru, seat of the supreme energy *(shakti):* from the outside gates, he gradually gains access to final Enlightenment.

The mandala, "circle," is more complex because images of deities are added to the circles and squares. One of the best known in the mandala of Kalachakra, or the "wheel of time," which has been used many times by the current Dalai Lama in his teaching in Tibet, India and Europe. Tibetan monks went to Paris in 1995 to draw it with colored powders at the Parc de la Villette then scattered it over the Canal d'Ourcq. This mandala is a square palace with five stories surrounded by the six large circles of the universe. The adept enters by the east door and, turning clockwise, successively climbs the gradations from the ordinary state to that of the Buddha. They symbolize the body and words of Buddha, the spirit (the Four Truths and Three Vehicles – Theravada, Mahayana and Vajrayana), the primordial consciousness

and, finally, supreme happiness. A lotus flower with eight petals is inscribed in the center of the mandala. At its heart, Kalachakra, represented by a blue (a color that evokes the immutability beyond space and time) *vajra* holding in his arms his consort Vishvamata, incarnated by a yellow-orange dot. Their embrace personifies the union of compassion and wisdom. "The initiation of the Kalachakra," the Dalai Lama has declared, "takes everything into account: the human body and spirit, and the total exterior aspect, both cosmic and astrological. By practicing it completely, it is possible to attain Enlightenment in a single life. We firmly believe in its power to reduce tension. We feel that it is capable of creating peace, peace of the spirit and consequently peace in the world."

To be effective, the mandala must be drawn according to rigorous rules. That is why its production requires a minimum three-year apprenticeship. "The most accomplished ritual requires that a Kalachakra be realized in colored powders so that it may be finally dispersed on the worshipper and mixed with the earth." The Dalai Lama has pointed out that its comprehension is not purely intellectual. A compassionate attitude is also needed: that is, "an availability to others, a desire to alleviate their suffering, help all living beings and respect them" (Crossman and Barou, 33-37).

Another aid to meditation is the painted, sculpted or lost-wax cast image of a deity. It could be of a bodhisattva, notably of Avalokiteshvara, "Lord of infinite compassion," "he who hears prayers" or "he who

Sosen (1749-1821)
Mother Monkey and Her
Young on a Rocky
Headland. **Ink on silk.**
H: 126cm x L: 53cm.
Japan.

203

lowers his gaze on the world's distress," protector of Tibet under the name of Chenrezig. He appears in various forms the most widespread of which is that of the "thousand-handed," each hand endowed with an eye to see all the suffering in the world and relieve them. With the same intention, he has been given a triple crown of three heads each to look in all directions; three express compassion, three wrath when faced with evil and three the joy brought by good. It is topped with a demon's head and at the summit by the face of Amitabha, the Buddha of which Avalokiteshvara is an emanation. According to another interpretation, the whole depicts the ten stages completed by the bodhisattva before arriving at the Buddha state.

Tara, "she who facilitates the crossing [of the river]," personifies the female aspect of Avalokiteshvara. It is represented in two main forms: white and green, incarnated in the two wives, Chinese and Nepalese, of King Songtsen Gampo who introduced Buddhism, elaborated a writing system and built the capital Lhassa in the 7th century; he was recognized as one of the manifestations of Avalokiteshvara. The green Tara opposite is seated on a lotus pedestal, in the royal pose of relaxation *(lalita asana),* her hands in the position of argumentation *(vitarka mudra).*

Another bodhisattva who is often depicted is Manjushri. He symbolizes knowledge and ethical perfection through his two attributes: the *Prajnaparamita* that sets out the concepts of Mahayana and the sword that cuts the veil of illusion.

There are serene and terrifying divinities. The latter, warriors, are the protectors of the

Rosetsu (1754-1799),
Deer in Snow.
Ink on paper.
H: 109cm x L: 43cm.
Japan

religion, such as the guardians of the four cardinal points. The one represented most often is that of the south, Yamantaka with a water buffalo's head and enormous belly. His body is bluish black, decorated with severed heads, and he dances while embracing his sow-headed consort. He holds a skull filled with blood. Cadavers lie under his feet. Yamantaka is called the "conqueror of death" because meditation in front of him rids the mind of the duality maintained by the love of pleasant shapes and liberates it from the desires and chimeras that come from ignorance. Yamantaka is another aspect of Manjushri, the god of wisdom, because all phenomena have two faces. Death is both end and beginning, destruction and rebirth. Deities take shape in the mind of the adept and he must become conscious of this. According to one text, "the form of the gods is only a visible manifestation, a gleaming of the void. In reality, it is its own substantial nature." This consciousness of the void is the "perfection of sapience" that, complemented by active compassion, allows the attainment of Enlightenment, the ultimate, non-dual reality (Padoux in Silburn, 298-299).

The ephemeral and the eternal

There are civilizations that build for eternity such as Egypt whose pyramids, erected 5,000 years ago, we still contemplate; they are embodiments in stone of the ascension of royal souls to their father Ra, the sun. There are others who follow the law of nature according to which things blossom and die to be reborn. The oldest and most sacred Japanese sanctuary is Ise, dedicated to Amaterasu, goddess of the sun, protector of the country, ancestor of the imperial family, and to Toyuke-Hime, goddess of fertility; it is the archetype of the Shinto temple and is rebuilt identically every 20 years. In both cases, there is the same human aspiration of leaving one's mark on this earth.

There are still civilizations where art is deliberately ephemeral, only for the beauty of the moment. In communitarian societies, paintings on the body transform it into a cultural element during celebrations of births, marriages, funerals, hunting and war. Navajo paintings on sand take part of the healing of the sick. The Navajo think of life as a "way of beauty" for which everyone should feel responsible. Thus, health, *hozho,* is not an individual problem but concerns the whole group: the word *hozho* also means harmony and equilibrium. "Illness," wrote Crossman and Barou, "results initially from a separation with the sacred part that everyone carries within himself; microbes and viruses rush in afterwards." The medicine man draws figures of heroes, sacred plants and animals with magical significations on the ground by filtering natural powdered pigments between his index finger and thumb. He chants invocations at the same time, such as that of pollen, symbol of fecundation and fertility:

Let the pollen stop your feet,
Let the pollen still your hands,
Let the pollen lower your head!
Then, your feet will become pollen,
Your hands, pollen
Your body, pollen

Your mind, pollen
Your voice, pollen.
The path is beautiful,
Be peaceful.

The patient sits in the middle of the work. The medicine man pours colored sand from various figures over his body in order to purify him.

With joy, I am cured
With joy, coolness penetrates me
With joy, my eyes have regained their power
With joy, coolness penetrates my head.

The painting is erased after the ceremony. So that the tradition is not lost and to make it known to those outside the community, since the 1950s, medicine men have transposed the sand painting onto tapestry or wood and artists have expanded their scope so that the viewers of their works feel better when looking at them. Joe Ben Junior, who has exhibited his work in Europe, declared: "A painting should not be made to please the eye or, rather, the pleasing of the eye should also have a function. They eye is the instrument through which healing occurs. And, for me, the healing process is the most important aspect of my work. I want it to be able to work for everybody" (Barou, 66).

This attitude is similar to that of the Tibetan lamas who also paint their mandalas on the sand: "We believe that our art, which is full of energy, can change negative to positive and bring peace to the people looking at it" (Crossman and Barou, 170). This gaze, which progresses from the entrance to the center of the mandala, is gradually liberated from its "negative ego" to find unity with the Absolute there. Like Navajo painting, the sand mandala is erased after having been shown and dispersed in nature to offer protection and well being.

In many civilizations, women play an important role in the production of beauty. In western and southern Africa, they decorate the walls of their dwellings with their hands after having coated them in a mixture of earth and cow dung and polishing them. They draw geometric patterns and stylized animals inspired by proverbs and tales in natural pigments. The painting is repeated every year after the harvest to celebrate or announce an event, thus providing an opportunity for women to participate in communal or social activities (Courtney-Clarke, 1990). In India, women paint the entrance, facade or ground in front of the house with propitiatory, floral or animal symbols in the honor of Laxmi, goddess of prosperity who protects the household. In certain regions (eastern Rajasthan), they also paint during religious and family festivals: birth, puberty, engagement and marriage. Elsewhere, such as Tamil Nadu, they decorate their doorstep every day before sunrise with drawings that will be erased by passers-by. Everywhere, each household creates it own designs. White is the preferred color because it is considered pure and sacred (Huyler, 1990).

In Africa and the Americas, masks and other ceremonial objects are not always kept after they have been used; some are destroyed in the fire in homage to the chieftain for whom they were made. A "work of art" to the foreign collector, the object is only important to the indigenous people for its meaning and role in the celebration. The object is temporal, but the idea of it is permanent, at least as long as the tradition and the memory of it last in an oral civilization.

The ephemeral burst onto the Western art scene. Since the 1950s, a multitude of movements have called into question current concepts and invented new forms with all the materials that technology and nature have put at their disposition including the most incongruous such as industrial and household waste (junk and funk). One of these tendencies is the integration of the temporal dimension into the work, expressed differently according to the group. Its precursors were Marcel Duchamp, Dada and the Surrealists, and it is influenced by primary arts and Zen. It objects to the museum and the gallery as places where art is authenticated and criticizes mercantilism in the name of a total art, "an art that is not different from life, but an action in life," exposed consequently to the unexpected, chance and precariousness. For Body Art, the body – that of the artist, that of the other, whether it is moving or still – is the basic fact. Land Art or Earth Art, with its ecological awareness, is a return to nature, leaving its footsteps or more or less temporary creations. Nancy Holt's *Sun Tunnels* (1976) in the Utah desert are orientated according to the solstices and their surfaces are pierced with holes corresponding to the constellations in order to reflect the changes of day and night. Others, like Christo and Jeanne-Claude wrap monuments and sites in cloth in order to reveal some of their unusual aspects.

This type of intervention is a so-called "installation." Installations are the assembly of heterogeneous objects, calling on the active participation of the viewer to discover the relationship between them and the space in which they are found. They are not designed to last, but may be modified when

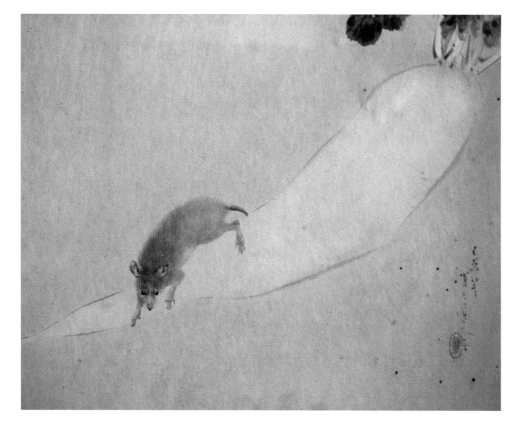

Watanabe Seitei or Shotei (1851-1918),
Rat on a Radish.
Ink on paper.
H: 24.5cm x L: 35cm.
Japan. Winter 1892.

the artist uses perishable materials such as flowers and leaves or introduces virtual images. All these tendencies, which manifest the fleetingness of things, bear witness at a deep level to the awareness in the West that the economy of profit and power threatens to destroy the planet.

Others, living closer to nature, managed to build a civilization more respectful of life, such as the oldest people on earth, the Aborigines of Australia. According to scientists, they arrived in Australia over 50,000 years ago when the lowering of sea level during the Quaternary ice age put Southeast Asia into contact with the islands. According to the Aborigines, their ancestors emerged from underneath the earth in human and non-human forms (the Rainbow Serpent, the Crocodile Man): traveling across the country, they created all things and taught their descendants the laws, rites and symbols before returning underground. It was the *Tjukurpa,* translated as Dreamtime. The word does not designate the imaginary phenomenon that occurs during sleep or that we construct with our desires, but a "supernatural" reality. It was not only the time of Creation, but also an undefined time, a time of past, present and future existence, when man lived in harmony with the universe.

Art is closely linked to this concept. It depicts the myths and their participants, the sacred sites, the ceremonies, the chants and the dances through which the culture is transmitted from generation to generation. The oldest vestiges are the cave carvings and paintings of Arnhem dating back 40,000 years, thus much older than those of Lascaux

and Altamira. They are still produced, as is painting on the body, eucalyptus bark and sand. Sculpture is less widespread: boomerangs, throwing sticks and water vessels in the desert, and the ironwood funerary poles of the Tiwi of the Bathurst and Melville Islands as well as all the utilitarian and ceremonial objects in stone, wood, fibers and feathers as well as jewelry made of bone, shell and seeds. Depicting dreams, singing and dancing them, is the continuation of the tradition of the ancestors so that the world can go on. Everyone, boy (after his initiation) or girl (after puberty), becomes the guardian of the dreams of his or her paternal lineage and the assistant of the dreams of his or her maternal lineage. The themes and ways of representing them are determined by filiation and cannot be treated without the authorization of their owner. Thus, through art, the individual affirms his authority over his domains, his knowledge of the subject, the earth and Dreamtime, and his ability to innovate.

After arriving in 1788, the British declared Australia *terra nullius,* no one's land, despite the presence of a million Aborigines whom they began to physically eliminate to seize all the resources. The assimilation policy introduced in the 20th century had the same goal in another form. However, Aborigines organized themselves and resisted. In 1963, they won their first victory northeast of Arnhem: their bark paintings were recognized as legitimate property deeds. In 1967, they obtained the right to vote and in 1972, limited autonomy in their territories.

Art has served the political struggle. It asserts the Aboriginal identity, the vitality of

Qi Baishi (1863-1957).
Squirrel and Grapes.
Ink on paper.
H: 121cm x L: 33.5cm.
China.

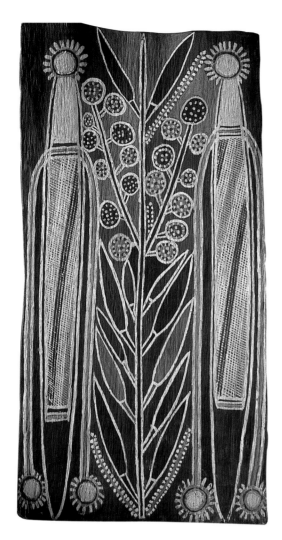

Burandai (1914). *"Bunimbir" (Morning Star) Funeral Ceremony.* **Painted on bark. H: 63cm x L: 33cm. Australia, Milingimbi region.**

its values and spoke of the genocide perpetrated by the Whites. The 1988 celebration of the 200th anniversary of colonization gave rise to a counter-demonstration by the artists of Ramingining (Central Arnhem): a *Memorial* of 200 *dupun,* decorated hollow funerary poles, one for each year of occupation, was erected (National Gallery of Australia, Canberra).

Australian Aboriginal art is now very lively. It has been recognized as such and no longer as an element of ethnography and has a place in the great museums of the worlds. To its materials – bark, sand, rock – and traditional colors – the red and yellow ochre of the earth, gypsum white, black from charcoal and manganese – have been added canvas, cardboard, silk and acrylic paints which are

resistant to the heat and dust of the desert. Traditional symbols are still used, but only the artist understands all of their meaning. Thus, he may paint the sacred aspects of a dream that remained closed to the understanding of the uninitiated.

Aboriginal painting is schematically figurative, narrative and symbolic. The common thread is the affirmation of an identity drawn from tradition, whatever the diversity of regional and individual styles. It seeks to reflect the essence beyond appearances, an approach many Western artists rediscovered in the 20th century. Some of the first known paintings were called "X-ray paintings" because they represented the internal anatomy of animals as if it were X-rayed. On other occasions, natural forms have been pared down to the graphic. Geometric figures – diamonds, rectangles, circles full of dots and parallel, oblique, intersecting lines of different colors – create rhythm.

In *Bunimbirr* ("morning star"), Burandai depicts a funeral ceremony through which the soul of the deceased rises from mother earth like the morning star before being reborn later. Two totems, each bearing the three morning stars, surround a shrub whose berries feed the *mokoy,* a wooden statuette that shelters the souls between death and the funerary rites.

Blitner's *Mimi Spirit Dreaming* illustrates the combat of two of these spirits of the rocks with a snake and a crocodile. With three colors – ochre, brown and white – he evokes the mystery of a mythical cave. Ochre is the color of the earth and of the mountains of the central desert dominated by the immense

monolith of Uluru (Ayers Rock). This sacred rock spreads over a hundred kilometers from east to west, changing color according to the time of day and the season, particularly during sunsets whose magnificence is unequalled in the tropics. Uluru has preserved the traces of the Ancestors, sites where they traveled, made springs gush forth and taught the rules of the law commemorated in cave paintings.

In East Asia, landscape painting was given the role of expressing the universal rhythm and the inner conscience. A major art since the Song dynasty (10th-13th centuries), its way was prepared by poetry. Poetry, initially regulated by Confucianism which made it, like painting, a tool for moralizing in the service of the state, was emancipated after the fall of the Han dynasty (220). Combining Taoist and Buddhist influences, it sang of nature, freedom, escape into the mountains and on the waters, love, friendship, separation, drunkenness, war and peace, all themes that reappeared in painting. Many of the literati wrote poetry and painted because the instrument was the same: the brush. Calligraphy, poetry and painting formed a whole, all three relying on writing and pursuing the same goal: restituting the cosmic breath and individual experience. Poetry is a form of painting through the images evoked by ideography and a song because of the meter inherent in a monosyllabic (phrasing) and tonal language. All the silence of the night is evoked in this quatrain, *Night on the Quay of the Maple Bridge,* by Zhang Ji (8th century):

The moon wanes, the crow caws, mist covers the sky;

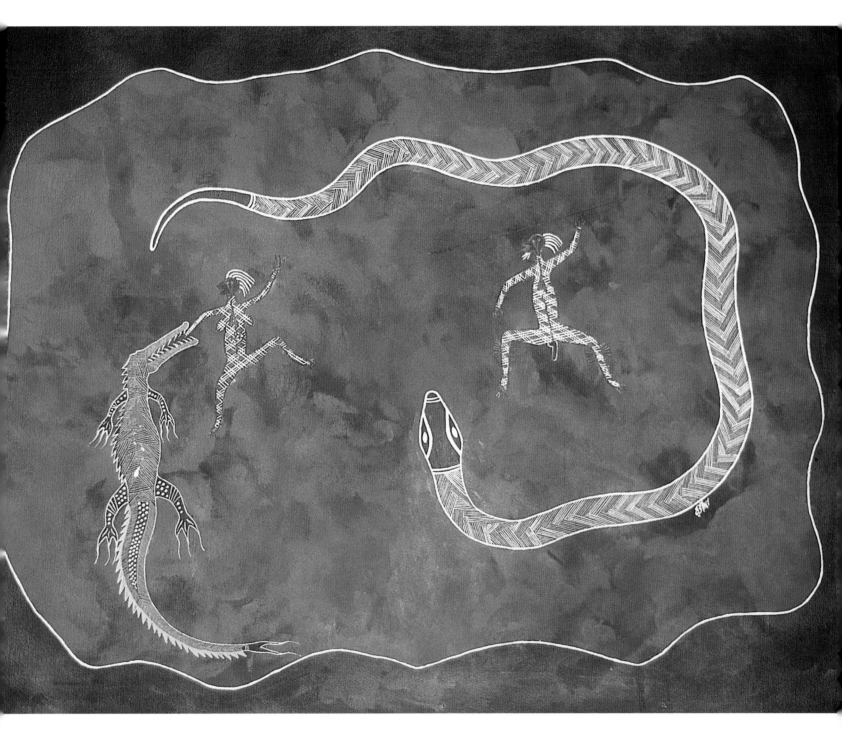

E. Blitner, *Mimi Spirit Dreaming*.
Ochre, brown and white
pigments on canvas.
H: 76.5cm x L: 102cm.
Australia, Arnhem Land, 1996.

Tetsuzan (1775-1841).
Two Puppies.
Ink on paper.
H: 32cm x L: 44cm.
Japan.

The maples of the bank and the fires of fishermen respond the sleep of sadness.

Outside the walls of Kusu, from the temple of Hanshan,

In the middle of the night the sound of the bell reaches the boat of the voyager.

"The poem is an invisible painting; painting is a silent poem." This statement has had a longer lifespan than that of Horace's *Ut Pictura Poesis*. It became more and more common to inscribe a poem on a scroll, then commentaries and collectors' seals. The profusion of all this elements had a devastating effect on the harmony of several paintings such as Zhao Mengfu's *Autumn Colors* or Ni Zan's *Landscape from the Rongxi* (National Palace Museum, Taipei).

Indeed, what is a landscape if there is no void? This is one of the major differences between East and West. On one side, the word simply refers to a stretch of the country; the void is a space where there is no one, where anything can happen. It causes anxiety and is the reason why fantastic art has made it one of its most powerful means. "Nature abhors a vacuum": is this statement not characteristic of this attitude? In the East, landscape is called "mountains and water" *(shan shui),* which refers to a way of looking at the universe whose two complementary and dynamic poles are the female yin and the male yang linked together by the void from which they emerged and from which the vital energy originates. Taoists assimilate it to

the Way (Tao or Dao) as stated by Laozi in his *Daodejing:*

From the Way is born the One
From the One, Two
The Two engenders Three
The Three produces ten thousand beings.

This Tao, this void, is called the Invisible or the Formless, the Inaudible or the Noiseless, the Impalpable or the Bodyless. But it is also the supreme plenitude as the valley holds all things and makes them grow: it is the mysterious feminine. The Tao is the void that contains everything, the unity that encompasses plurality and the unchanging that creates change. Man must remain in harmony with this eternal principle, "the pivot where affirmation and negation converge, where the other and oneself cease to oppose each other" *(Zhuangzi, II).*

In painting, the mountain symbolizes yang, the water yin, but in the Chinese dialectic, yang contains yin and yin contains yang, which means that each tends to turn into the other, causing the perpetual flow of things. These are also the poles of sensibility. As Confucius said, "the good-hearted man is enchanted by the mountain, the quick-witted man enjoys the water." When representing them, the painter does not aim for external resemblance, but for the reality that is "beyond words," expressing all the while his own emotions and thoughts. "Outside, I imitate the way of creation; inside, I capture the source of my soul" wrote Zhang Zao during the Tang dynasty.

The unpainted space is the void. It links the mountains and the water; through it the painter and the viewer enter into communion with the Whole, the Essence of Life, the Tao. It is in seizing it that "a stroke of three inches drawn vertically may represent a height of a thousand feet, and the ink spread horizontally over a few li may embody a distance of a hundred li" (Zong Ping, 375-443).

The intermediary between the earth, which is yin in nature, and the sky, which is yang in nature, man appears in the landscape in his place, that is, very small. It is again the void that manifests his relationship with nature. Wang Wei (420-478) wrote: "Height of a mountain: ten feet; height of a tree: one foot; height of a man: a hundredth of a foot."

Buddhism only intensified this attitude. After its arrival in the 1st century, it rapidly became Chinese, all the more so as many of its concepts are close to those of Taoism from which it borrowed the terms of Dao and Wu to translate them. Undoubtedly, the Buddhist void does not have the same meaning. Buddha's mantra, "form is nothing but void; void is nothing but form," signifies that nothing exists separately from others, but through its relationships with them, relationships that are constantly changing. Form is "void" because it has no independent existence, and the void is "form" because it contains everything. This mantra is related to the Buddhist law of conditioned production (everything has a cause). The Chan tendency (dhyana in Sanskrit: meditation) was the most successful because it was the closest to Taoism. Its principles are defined in the following quatrain, attributed to its founder Bodhidharma (6th century):

A particular transmission outside teaching
Not based on the scriptures
Directly pointing to the human mind
To see one's own nature and become
Buddha.

In the 7th century, the doctrine split into two currents, one in the North, another in the South. Both admit that the nature of Buddha is everywhere and that everyone can reach Illumination. The first advocates a gradual method of exercises, the second detachment, "not thinking" which consists not of thinking of nothing (this would still be attachment to this nothing), but of letting one's thoughts come and go freely like flowing water, until Illumination arrives, suddenly and totally. This "suddenism" prevailed. Chan was introduced to Japan (Zen) in the 12th century.

The influence of Chan on the painting of landscapes and "flowers and birds" was not very different from that of Taoism, its goals and methods were only, according to Osvald Siren, "carried to a further stage of subjective impressionism. Monochrome ink-painting became in the hands of the Chan masters the most subtle and immediate expression for intuitive glimpses or reflections of their creative minds" (Siren, 91). Many great artists were monks, but as in poetry it is difficult to say in a landscape painting what it Taoist and what is Buddhist. The distinction is easier for portraits or narratives. Generally speaking, China is more Taoist and Japan more Zen.

What they have in common is the overall conception based on a few principles that have been repeated by all the authors.

The first, as already mentioned, is to capture the cosmic breath and the movement

Clouds-eagle.
Undeciphered seals.
Silk.
H: 83.5cm x L: 27cm.
China or Japan, 17th c.

211

of life. The union of ink and brush is that of yin and yang which makes the Multiple emerge out of the One and the Invisible out of the Visible.

The second is "the idea precedes the brush." Contrary to the European painter who places his easel in front of the landscape, the East Asian painter absorbs aspects of nature at length to capture their essence, the spirit *(shen)* that is present in a dragonfly, grass or a stone on the path. It is "from inside" not "from outside" that creation takes place. Lengthy contemplation allows the elimination of the accessory to keep only the essential. Zhuangzi recounted how Duke Yuan wanted to have a few images painted. Many scribes rushed to offer their services, licking their brushes and grinding their ink[1], they remained standing. Much later, another arrived without hurrying. He received the instructions and left. The duke's messenger found him seated, legs crossed and naked to the waist. "Here is a real painter!" said the duke *(Zhuangzi, XXI)*.

The third principle is derived from the preceding one. He who follows the Tao and harmonizes his spirit to the universal rhythm will reproduce its qualities of naturalness and spontaneity. A single brushstroke will suffice to express his feeling and seize the truth of a boundless space. Zhang Yanyuan (9th century), whose influence was considerable on all the historians and critics of painting, wrote:

---

1. Ink, made out of charcoal obtained from old pine trees, was considered invigorating. Moreover, the pine tree is the symbol of longevity because of its evergreen foliage.

Shokei (fl. c. 1478-1508),
Eagle Holding a White Egret
in its Claws beside a stream.
Ink and colors on paper.
H: 92cm x L: 46cm. Japan.

212

"Starting a painting with the deliberate intention of producing a good painting, is risking failure. Success is more likely when one puts one's thought in movement and moves one's brush without deliberate intention. For then the hand will not get cramped and the mind will not be blocked. The painting is without one knowing why it is good" (Cheng, *Souffle-Esprit,* 1989, 24).

Finally, art is suggesting rather than describing in detail, in practicing ellipsis, the implied as in poetry. According to Zhang Yanyuan:

"In painting, one should avoid the concern of accomplishing a work that is too industrious and finished in the drawing of shapes and the noting of colors, as well as flaunting one's technique too much, thus depriving it of its mystery and its aura. That is why one must not fear the unfinished, but rather deplore that which is too finished… For the unfinished does not necessarily mean the unaccomplished, the fault of the unaccomplished lies indeed in the fact of not recognizing that something is sufficiently finished" (Cheng, 1989, 20-21).

Here are two examples of the art of suggestion that are often cited. The Emperor Huizong of the Song dynasty liked to test artists by proposing verses from Tang poetry as subjects for painting. Once, he proposed the following verse: "Near the bridge, tall bamboos surround an inn." All the painters tried to depict an inn hidden behind bamboo except Li Tang who only painted bamboo near a bridge, with a banner floating among the bamboo announcing the presence of the inn. His painting was chosen. Another time,

another famous verse was proposed: "After returning from the ride of the horsemen among the flowers, the horses' legs are perfumed." The emperor chose a painter who, unlike the others who all sought to paint horses surrounded by flowers, contented himself with drawing some butterflies chasing trotting horses (Cheng, 1989, 32-34).

I particularly like the *Solitary Fisherman in His Boat* by Ma Yuan (active between 1190 and 1224) in the National Museum, Tokyo. The fisherman is alone in his boat leaning toward his line, which he observes. He is surrounded by an immense sky, which blends into the water barely disturbed by a few waves. The space is empty but it contains the infinite life. What does it matter to the man that he is alone. He is attentive to the only present moment.

A contemporary of Ma Yuan, Xia Gui was a master of mist and rain. In his *Twelve Views from a Thatched Cottage* (Nelson Gallery and Atkins Museum, Kansas City), the void dominates the landscapes that unfurl on the horizontal scroll. The diluted ink makes the riverbank, pine trees, the village roofs and the boats that return or already balance on the mooring emerge from the mist.

It is rare to find an imaginary landscape. This is one. It may even be qualified as Surrealist because the artist has made an immense white bird, wings spread, emerge out of the fog between two chains of mountains. In the distance, lines of dark green clouds traverse the horizon. Here the void is no longer the unpainted space but that which, as Fan Ji wrote (Qing dynasty), "in the shape of smoke, mist, clouds or invisible breaths,

carries all things, leading them into the process of secret mutations."

Through contact with the West, contemporary painters modified their touch and colors, but their inspiration often remained "traditional." The great principle "of the cosmic breath and the movement of life" still prevails as in Zhang Daqian's (1899-1983) *Landscape,* which renews the theme of the man of letters traveling in his boat on water depicted by the void because of the modernity of the colors and the brushstrokes: in the foreground, quiver clumps of rushes; mountains spread out into the distance.

Lin Zixiao also treats a traditional theme: a flock of wild geese flying above reeds. The calm of the autumn landscape is rendered by a series of parallel lines on several planes; the ink fades and vanishes into the distance. One thinks of the verses of Liu Yuxi (772-842):

"From what country does the autumn wind arrive
Which in its melancholy accompanies the wild geese?"

The European influence is more noticeable in this *Untitled* work of Li Yongcun, but abstraction has not eliminated the feeling of nature. On the contrary, it gives it new forms. There are no longer mountains nor, at first sight, void. But the painter has kept the three-plane perspective that the eye regards successively from top to bottom, the ink fading in the distance. While he uses no "wrinkles" *(cun)* to model the contours of objects, splashed ink *(po mo)* in more or less black spots mixed with a bit of brown suggest the banks of a tranquil river (in white) with swaying reeds (in vertical lines). The union of

water (yin) and earth (yang), and of light and shade, still evokes the harmony of the silence and the rhythm of space and time.

In Japan, the spirit is turned even more towards the concrete than in India and China: the Absolute is nothing other than the world of phenomena. According to Shinto, the original religion of the Japanese, spirits live in all things: a mountain, a tree or a stone. Buddhism was assimilated from this foundation. The great monk Dogen (13th century) stated, "Impermanence is the Buddhahood. The impermanence of grass, trees and forest is verily the Buddhahood. The impermanence of the person's body and mind is verily the Buddhahood. The importance of (land) country and scenery is verily the Buddhahood" (Nakamura, 352). This attitude only reinforces the Japanese love of nature, a love less metaphysical than in Taoism or Hinduism: Zen insists on the truth of the present and the necessity of plunging into it as the past and future are illusions. The goal of meditation is not to attain satori (Enlightenment), but to penetrate into the flux of life "which is nothing special." Zen has had a great influence on all aspects of Japanese culture. Painting owes its highest qualities to Zen: economy of means, spontaneity, immediacy, the direct effect, the symbiosis with humble and ordinary things and the sense of the passing of time. Very early on, the Japanese sensibility expressed itself through notions without equivalents in China:

– *miyabi,* the taste for delicate things: "the blossoming of the plum trees, the subtle perfume of a rare wood, the harmony of the colors of a robe";

– *aware,* the melancholy when faced with the fleeting: birdsong, the sound of spring rain, the falling of a petal;

– *okashi,* the pleasure in simple, everyday things according to the season: moonlight, sunset, snow;

– *yugen,* the feeling of mystery, notably in Noh where masked actors and a chorus accompanied by a flute and three drums create an unreal spectacle where this world and the other world are confused;

– *wabi-sabi,* the beauty of humble and imperfect things with the patina of use and time.

Consider these two screens, a Japanese form, both consecrated to the landscape. The first, in ink highlighted with light colors, represents a landscape of mountains and water. In the left foreground, a horseman mounts towards the temple hidden among the trees; on the right, a boatman plunges his pole into the waters to advance; farther away, on a boat near a riverbank at the foot of the mountains, two old men play chess. The void of the right with its water and sky, where a round moon rises, balances the mountains of the left with their leafy trees and the roofs nestled within. A "classic" painting whose format allows it to be spread out over a large space in which the Japanese touch is revealed in the treatment of the inks and the colors of the trees and buildings, and the costume of the traveler. The second screen appears to be more decorative with its silver crescent moon above the clouds and the willows sprinkled with gold. However, the long bands of clouds, the gold squares and flakes, in contrast to the dark

214   **Li Yongcun (1949).**
Untitled. **Ink on paper.**
H: 132cm x L: 40cm.
China

green of the trees, offer an almost abstract and dreamlike vision from which emanates a sentiment of mystery and the fantastic.

This *yugen* is also found in the woodblock print, which usually glorifies female beauty and famous sites. In this scene, in which a boatman and his passengers enveloped in their straw coats move away from a village at the foot of a pagoda, Hiroshige illustrated with a few dull colors all the melancholy of the rain. The painter often depicted the rain. His most famous print on this theme is one of the *Fifty-three Stages of the Tokaido:* the storm that surprises travelers at Shono. Tight oblique strokes and dark colors reveal the storm's sudden violence, which bends the bamboo and makes passersby flee. Here the widely spaced strokes suggest a light rain during a peaceful night.

However, as in China, monochrome painting is the preferred means of expressing "images of the soul." With a few blotches of "splashed ink" and reserves, Shoshu made emerge out of a landscape of shores and a lake at the foot of a mountain lost in the mist the "truth of solitude," the meaning of the essence of Zen. This is also evoked by this other scroll, which depicts a simple circle *(enso).* A symbol par excellence of Zen because it has no beginning or end or because the beginning coincides with the end, it also represents the full moon whose light illuminates Enlightenment. The painter draws it with a single trait because Enlightenment is sudden or it does not occur. The bridge also has a particular meaning. It is one of the figures of *ma,* a Japanese concept that identifies space and time, which

other cultures separate. *Ma* designates the interval or distance between two objects placed beside each other or two actions, sounds or gestures occurring one after the other. It is the foundation of aesthetic creation, whether it is a question of a sacred site, a garden, the tea ceremony, music, a play or a work of art. The bridge is "that which links two things above *ma.*"

In Europe, landscape painting appeared much later and, until the advent of Romanticism, was almost always subordinated to the portrait or mythological or religious narrative. The cosmic sentiment that Chinese landscape is imbued with is absent. The only striking example of this period

was Bruegel's *Return of the Hunters* (Kunsthistorisches Museum, Vienna). This oil on panel from 1565 depicts a winter landscape with a village whose white roofs spread to the foot of the mountains on the right. The gray-green of the sky echoes that of the frozen ponds where men, women and children are skating. A lone crow flies in the icy air and makes the snow appear whiter and the sky vaster. Other crows are perched in the bare-branched trees. On the left, in the foreground, the tired hunters return, their dogs following them, tails lowered. No other painting better renders the silence of the winter, disturbed only by the skating and the heavy steps of men sinking into the snow.

J.M.W. Turner was the veritable creator of European landscape painting and, in his unfinished canvases, the closest, although using different means, to East Asia. His *Sunrises* (boat between two promontories, Norham Castle), *Landscapes* (with water; with a river and bay in the distance), his *Val D'Aosta* are, despite their titles, stripped of all naturalism. These quasi-abstract blotches of subtle colors which shade into each other – yellows, ochres, browns and blues – evoke in an intensely poetic way the unreal moments when the mist blends into the water, the clouds into the earth. "Formless and empty": this comment by a contemporary who thought himself a critic is considered by today's connoisseur as the most pertinent praise of these masterpieces.

This transcendent dimension is also found in the most Romantic canvas of Germany and perhaps of the 19th century, Caspar David Friedrich's *Monk Beside the Sea* (1810, Galerie der Romantik, Berlin). The man wearing dark clothes is tiny, alone on the seashore, faced with the immensity of the agitated water under the blue sky swathed in mist. Is he meditating about the destiny of man and his relationship with the Creator? "The divine is everywhere, even in a grain of sand," wrote Friedrich. A reflection which would not be disavowed by a Zen Buddhist who would, however, reject the word "divine" and would not abandon himself to passion or tragedy and temper his emotions with humor.

The difference between Friedrich and the Impressionists is his search for the inner truth or the part of eternity concealed within a landscape. The Impressionists were essentially preoccupied with seizing the beauty of the moment, the changes in the light, the vibrations of colors and the mobility of reflections of water and leaves.

There is less searching and more dreaming in the work of the naïve painters. Henri Rousseau painted his admirable *Charmeuse de Serpents* in 1907 (Musée d'Orsay, Paris). In a fantastic landscape of dense foliage and high grass in lighter colors, on the bank of a river shining in the light of the round moon, the black silhouette of a woman stands out against the sky. At the sound of her flute, the snakes undulate around her and the pink flamingo bends to hear her. From the painting emanates a mysterious nocturnal poetry accompanied by the silent melody of the flute and the peaceful quasi-monochrome green.

One of naïve paintings most original centers is in Haiti where a vigorous school of painting flourishes, the only one in the Caribbean and, up until recently, in Africa. It is probably not a coincidence that this island was the first independent Black republic (1804) whose cultural cohesion was founded on voodoo. Although all the artists use local reality as a starting point, the subjects are varied: evocations of the struggles for liberation, village and urban scenes, feasts and dances, still life, voodoo and Christian themes, and fantastic or realistic visions, sometimes treated with humor, sometimes with detail or devotion, most often with the help of vivid colors which reflect the exuberance of the tropical sun and vegetation. These painters are illiterate peasants, street vendors, taxi drivers, civil servants, voodoo priests and lawyers. Some claim to be inspired by the *loas* (spirits); others are faux naïfs working for tourists. Voodoo, which forms the island's identity, does not always appear as in the work of Jean-Louis Senatus who prefers magical landscapes, generally in monochrome. He called this painting *Rêve d'amour*: couples stroll or lie down in an enchanted forest where horses graze. They contemplate a sky traversed by layers of cloud similar to superimposed mountain chains. A large red flower rises in the air.

The imaginary took on a metaphysical dimension in the works of Giorgio De Chirico from 1909-1919 in which he sought the absolute through the odd association of heterogeneous objects. De Chirico was marked by Nietzsche and especially Schopenhauer who himself was influenced by Buddhism: "All the nostalgia of the infinite," he wrote, "is revealed to us behind the geometric precision of the place. There are unforgettable movements we live when such aspects of the world, whose existence we did not even suspect, suddenly appear, unveiling to us mysterious things that are there, within our reach, at each instant, without our too short sight being able to distinguish them, our too imperfect senses to perceive them... One should not forget that a painting must always be the reflection of a deep sensation and deep signifies strange, and strange means not known or quite unknown." De Chirico's paintings are urban landscapes with deserted streets and petrified architecture where man is only present in the form of statues or faceless mannequins.

Tanyu (1602-1674).
Egret in Reeds.
Ink on paper.
H: 117.5cm x L: 60cm.
Japan.

The same is true of the works of Paul Delvaux, along with an icy eroticism, in which naked women with wide staring or absent eyes stroll like sleepwalkers across gardens and cities "in a light of ore" (André Breton). René Magritte brought together banal objects in dreamlike spaces to load them with unexpected meaning and give the sensation of the unusual. The obvious is no longer obvious although poetry is always present. Thus, *L'Empire des lumières* (1954) shows a house beneath trees in a night pierced by the reflection of a street lamp in a pond, but one discovers that the sky and clouds are lit by daylight. Conversely, elsewhere a blue sky with passing clouds dominates nocturnal countryside. Yves Tanguy's landscapes are purely dreamlike, peopled with larval or mineral forms bathed in abyssal or moonlight, where there is not distinction between earth and sky (*Le soleil dans son écrin*, 1937, Peggy Guggenheim Foundation, Venice).

However, there is also the mystery of the everyday. A "metaphysical" painter like De Chirico, Giorgio Morandi produced sober and bare still lives: few shapes and colors, dull tones that invite meditative contemplation. If we compare them to those of Paul Cézanne, who was his first master – for example, his *Nature morte* of 1900 (National Gallery of Art, Washington) – the differences are obvious: in Cezanne bright colorings ("When color is at its richest, shape is at its fullest."), the white and green of the jug contrasting with the reds and yellows of the apples, the firmness of the contours outlining the volumes, the strength of the composition, the horizontal lines of the chest of drawers balancing the vertical lines of the drawer and the window. The painting is "full," but poetry and mystery are missing.

They attain their apogee in the still lives of East Asia. The most famous example is the monk Muqi's *Persimmons* (13th century, Daitokuji, Kyoto), painted in more or less concentrated ink, five in one row, and a lone sixth in front of them. Empty space occupies four-fifths of the work. Ink demonstrates its superiority over color in the evocation of the invisible and silence.

What is never seen in the East are the bloody hunting scenes so frequent in European still lives of the 17th and 18th centuries. The thirst for killing for pleasure that they denote only arouse repulsion where Taoism, Hinduism and Buddhism have accustomed people to not consider man as a species superior to other beings, as everything can change its form in the cycle of rebirth; all are equal in the universal flux. If we set aside the sketches of animals which humorously or ironically caricature humans, such as the scrolls of the *Choju-giga* (12th century), the representation of animals is characterized by tenderness: the lying gazelle scratching her muzzle with her leg in the *Descent of the Ganges* in Mahabalipuram (7th century), Sosen's female monkey watching over her child, Rosetsu's deer in the snow, Tetsuzan's puppies and Qi Bashi's squirrel. Tanyu's egret emerging from the mist arouses a quasi-metaphysical feeling. Tsunenobu's gibbon trying to catch the reflection of the moon in the water illustrates the Buddhist theme of illusion, of taking the visible for the real. A couple of birds, one in a cage, the other outside looking at it with love, symbolizes marital fidelity. Only the wild beasts look ferocious, as they do everywhere: the eagle is a favorite subject in Japan as is the tiger in Korea. But, do they not have the right to live? Did they choose to be an eagle or a tiger? Only man in the Bible assumes domination of the fish, birds, mammals, grass and trees because he is supposed to be created in the image of his God, claiming the right to kill for his own pleasure.

"Once upon a time, Zhuang Zhou dreamt that he was a butterfly fluttering about happy with his fate and not knowing he was Zhou. Suddenly, he woke up and realized he was Zhou. He no longer knew if it was Zhou who was dreaming of being a butterfly or a butterfly dreaming it was Zhou" (*Zhuangzi, II*).

On his deathbed, the Viet monk Man Giac (11th century) recited the following stanza to those around him:

The spring is going, the flowers fall
The spring comes back, the flowers bloom
The earthly things pass before my eyes
Old age has already arrived on my hair
Do not say that all flowers wither with spring
Last night, a prunus bough blossomed in the courtyard.

Life does not last. Beauty does not last. At least it will have illuminated a few instants of our passage on this earth.

Renzan (1805-1859).
Bridge in Mist.
Ink on silk.
H: 95cm x L: 35cm.
Japan

Bibliography

Akiyama Terukazu, *La peinture japonaise,* Genève, Skira, 1961.

Akurgal E., Mango C., Ettinghausen R., *Les Trésors de Turquie,* Genève, Skira, 1966.

Alleton V., *L'écriture chinoise,* Paris, PUF, 1984.

Alleva (d') A. *Le monde océanien,* tr. L. Echasser, Paris, Flammarion, 1998.

L'art de la plume : Brésil, Musée d'ethnographie, Genève - Museum national d'histoire naturelle, Paris, 1985-1986.

Barbier, J. - P., ed., *Arts de la Côte d'Ivoire dans les collections du Musée Barbier-Mueller,* Genève, 1993, 2 vol.

Barou J. P., *L'œil pense. Essai sur les arts primitifs contemporains,* Paris, Payot, 1996.

Bastin M. - L., *Introduction aux arts d'Afrique noire,* Arnouville, 1984.

Bazin G., *Paradeisos ou l'art du jardin,* Paris, Chêne, 1988.

Berlaut A. et Kahlenberg M. H., *Walk in Beauty. The Navajo and their Blankets,* Boston, New York Graphic Society, 1977.

Berlin M. et Kay P., *Basic Color Terms : Their Universality and Evolution,* Berkeley, University of California Press, 1969.

Bernal I. et Simoni-Abbat M., *Le Mexique des origines aux Aztèques,* Paris, Gallimard, 1986.

Beurdeley M. et C., *La céramique chinoise,* Fribourg, Office du Livre - Paris, Vilo, 1974.

Billeter J., *L'art chinois de l'écriture,* Genève, Skira, 1989.

Blier S., Beauty and the Beast : Ibo, in D. Fraser, ed., *African Art as Philosophy,* New York Interbook, 1974, p. 107 - 113.

Blofeld J., *Le bouddhisme tantrique du Tibet,* tr. S. Carteron, Paris, Seuil, 1982.

Boisselier J. et Beurdeley J.-M., *La sculpture en Thailande,* Paris, Bibliothèque des Arts, 1974.

Brion M., *L'Art fantastique,* Paris, Albin Michel, 1961.

Caruana W., *Aboriginal Art,* Londres, Thames and Hudson, 1993.

Chandogya Upanishad, tr. E. Senart, Paris, Les Belles-lettres, 1930

Chang L., *La calligraphie chinoise,* Paris, Club Français du Livre, 1971.

Cheng F., *Souffle-Esprit. Textes théoriques chinois sur l'art pictural,* Paris, Seuil, 1989.

Cheng F., *Vide et plein. Le langage pictural chinois,* Paris, Seuil, 1979.

Chiang Yee, *Chinese Calligraphy,* Londres, Methuen, 1961 (1938).

Colloque sur l'art nègre, Société africaine de culture, Paris, 1967.

Colour, A Mitchell Beazley Artists House, Londres, Marshall Editions, 1980.

Coomaraswamy A., *La danse de Çiva,* tr. M. Rolland, Paris, Rieder, 1922.

Coran, tr. Denise Masson, Paris, Gallimard, Folio, 1996.

Le Courrier de l'Unesco : La Beauté, décembre 1990 ; A la poursuite de l'éphémère, décembre 1996, Paris.

Courtney-Clarke M., *Tableaux d'Afrique. L'art mural des femmes de l'Ouest,* Paris, Arthaud, 1990.

Crossman S. et Barou J. P., *Peintures de sable des Indiens Navajo,* Paris, 1996.

Crossman S. et Barou J. P., *Tibet. La Roue du temps,* Paris, 1995.

De l'art nègre à l'art africain, Paris, Arts d'Afrique noire, 1990 (art. de M. - L. Bastin, A. Gnonsoa, C. Faik-Nzugi Mudiya).

Delange J., collab. *Arts africains,* Musée Cantini, 1970, Marseille.

Ducourant B., *L'art du dessin enseigné par les maîtres de Dürer à Picasso,* Paris, Bordas, 1989.

Duverger C., *La Méso-amérique, Art et anthropologie,* Paris, Flammarion, 1999.

École Nationale Supérieure des Beaux-Arts, *Groupes, mouvements, tendances de l'art contemporain depuis 1945,* Paris, 1990.

Faik-Nzuji Mudiya C., L'art plastique africain comme extension de l'art corporel, in *De l'art nègre à l'art africain.*

Focillon H., *La vie des formes,* Paris, PUF, 1934.

Fong Wen et al., *Images of the Mind,* Princeton Art Museum, Princeton University, 1984.

Forman B., *Batik Ikat, Arts suprêmes de l'Indonésie,* Paris, Cercle d'art, 1988.

Frey E., *The Kris. Mystic Weapon of the Malay World,* Singapore, Oxford University Press, 1986.

Gabus J., *L'objet-témoin. Les références d'une civilisation par l'objet,* Neuchâtel, Ides et Calendes, 1975.

Gabus J., *Art océanien,* Musée d'ethnographie de Neuchâtel, 1970.

Giedon-Welcker C., *Contemporary sculpture,* Londres, Faber, 1961.

Gillow J. and Dawson B., *Traditional Indonesian Textiles,* London, Thames and Hudson, 1992.

Gillow J. et Barnard N., *Textiles traditionnels de l'Inde,* tr. M. Hechter, Paris, Thames and Hudson, 1991.

Gittinger M. et Leedom Lefferts Jr. H., *Textiles and the Tai Experience in Southeast Asia,* Washington, The Textile Museum, 1992.

Grand Atlas de l'architecture mondiale, Paris, Encyclopaedia Universalis, 1988.

The Great Japan Exhibition : Art of the Edo period 1600-1868, Royal Academy of Arts, London, 1981-82.

Groslier, B.P., *Angkor. Hommes et pierres,* Paris, Arthaud, 1956.

Grube E., *The World of Islam,* Londres, Hamlyn, 1966.

Guiart J., *Océanie,* Paris, Gallimard, 1963.

Hahner - Herzog I. et al., *L'autre visage. Masques africains de la collection Barbier - Mueller,* Paris, Adam Biro, 1997.

Harris J. ed., *5000 ans de textiles,* Londres, Parkstone, 1994.

Hegel, *Cours d'esthétique,* tr. J.-P. Lefebvre et V. von Schenck, Paris, Aubier, 1995.

Hempel R., *L'âge d'or du Japon : l'époque Heian 794-1192,* Paris, PUF, 1983.

Hersak D., *Songye : Masks and Figure Sculptures,* Londres, 1985.

Huyler S., *Peintures sacrées de l'Inde,* Paris, Arthaud, 1994.

Itoh Teiji, *Jardins du Japon,* tr. E. Peschard-Erlih, Paris, Herscher, 1984.

Itten J., *Art de la couleur,* Paris, Dessain et Tolra, 1993.

Jimenez M., *Qu'est-ce que l'esthétique,* Paris, Gallimard, Folio, 1997.

Joplin C. F., ed., *Art and Aesthetics in Primitive Societies,* New York, Dutton, 1975.

Kandinsky W., *Du spirituel dans l'art et dans la peinture en particulier,* Paris, Gallimard, Folio, 1949.

Keswick M., *The Chinese Garden,* Londres, Academy Ed., 1978.

Khatibi A et Sijelmassi L., *L'art calligraphique arabe,* Paris, Chêne, 1980.

Koren L., *Wabi-Sabi for artists, designers, poets and philosophers,* Berkeley, Stone Bridge, 1994.

Kuck L., *The World of the Japanese Garden,* New York - Tokyo, Weatherhill, 1980.

Labbe A. J., *Religion, Art and Iconography : Man and Cosmos in Prehispanic America,* Santa Ana, Calif., 1982.

Lambert J. C., *La peinture abstraite,* Lausanne, Ed. Rencontre, 1967.

Leach B., *Le livre du potier,* tr. M. Scalbert-Beltaigne et B. Lhôte-Sulmont, Paris, Dessain et Tolra, 1974.

LEACH B., *A potter's book,* London, Faber and Faber, 1976 (The Buddhist quatrain in epigraph is quoted by Yanagi Soetsu in his introduction).

LE FUR Y., *Résonances,* Paris, Musée Dapper, 1990.

LEYS S., *Essais sur la Chine,* Paris, Laffont, 1998.

LI KI, *Mémoires sur les bienséances et les cérémonies,* tr. S. Couvreur, 2 vol., Leiden, Brill, Paris, Les Belles Lettres, 1950.

LINHARTOVA V., *Sur un fond blanc, Ecrits japonais sur la peinture du IXe au XIXe siècle,* Paris, Le Promeneur, 1996.

LÉON-PORTILLA M., *La pensée aztèque,* tr. C. Bernand, Paris, Seuil, 1985.

LOMMEL A., *Prehistoric and Primitive Man,* Londres, Hamlyn, 1966.

MC NAUGHTON P., *The Mande Blacksmith. Knowledge, Power and Art in West Africa,* Bloomington-Indianapolis, Indiana University Press, 1988.

MALRAUX A., *La métamorphose des dieux,* Lausanne, Guilde du Livre, 1957.

Manuel du jardin du grain de moutarde, voir R. Petrucci.

MASSOUDY H., *Calligraphie arabe vivante,* Paris, Flammarion, 1981.

MATISSE H., *Écrits et propos sur l'art,* Paris, Hermann, 1972.

MEYER A., *Art océanien,* Paris, Gründ, 1995, 2 v.

MUKERJEE S. C., *Le Rasa. Essai sur l'esthétique indienne,* Paris, 1926.

MURASE M., *L'art du Japon,* Paris, Livre de poche, 1996.

Musée Cernuschi, *Japon, saveurs et sérénité. La cérémonie du thé dans les collections du Musée des Arts Idemitsu,* Paris-Musées, 1995.

Museo Nacional del Banco Central del Ecuador, *Sala de archeología,* Quito, 1996.

Museo Nacional del Banco Central del Ecuador, *Sala de oro,* Quito, 1998.

NAKAMURA H., *Ways of thinking of Eastern peoples : India, China, Tibet, Japan,* tr. angl., Honolulu, The University of Hawaï Press, 1978.

NEWTON D. et al., *Sculpture. Chefs-d'œuvre du Musée Barbier-Mueller,* Paris, Imprimerie nationale, 1995.

NIANGORAN-BOUAH G., *L'univers akan des poids à peser l'or,* Abidjan, NEA, 1984-7.

Orfèvres lointains. Collection Ghysels. Texte de F. Borel, photographies de J. Bigelow Taylor, Paris, Hazan, 1995.

PAPADOPOULO A., *L'Islam et l'art musulman,* Paris, Citadelles et Mazenod, 1976.

PASTOUREAU M., *Dictionnaire des couleurs de notre temps. Symbolique et société,* Paris, Bonneton, 1992.

PERROIS L., *Arts du Gabon,* Arnouville, 1979.

PETRUCCI R., *Encyclopédie de la peinture chinoise, XVIIe-XVIIIe siècle,* Paris, Laurens, 1918.

PHILLIPS T., ed., *Africa. The Art of a Continent,* Londres, Royal Academy of Arts, 1995.

Philosophes taoïstes : Laotseu, Tchouangtseu, Lietseu, Paris, Gallimard, La Pléiade, 1980.

RAHULA W., *L'enseignement du Bouddha,* Paris, Seuil, 1961.

RAMBACH P. et S., *Jardins de longévité : Chine, Japon,* Genève, Skira, 1987.

RANDHAWA M. S., *Kangra paintings of the Bihari Sat Sai,* New Delhi, National Museum, 1966.

RAWSON P., *Erotic art of the East,* New York, Putnam's Sons, 1968.

RAWSON P., *La peinture indienne,* tr. G. Lambin, Paris, Tisné, 1961.

READ H., *Art and industry,* Londres, Faber, 1934.

READ H., *A concise history of modern sculpture,* Londres, Faber, 1964.

READ H., *Art and society,* Londres, Faber, 1967.

READ H., *The meaning of art,* Londres, Faber, 1968.

READ H., *Education through art,* Londres, Faber, 1970.

REID J. W., *Textile masterpieces of Ancient Peru,* New York, Dover, 1986.

REYNOLDS J., *Discourses on art,* ed. by Robert W. Wark, Yale University Press, 1975.

ROBINSON B. W., *The art of the Japanese sword,* Londres, Faber, 1961.

RODIN A., *L'art.* Entretiens réunis par P. Gsell, Paris, Grasset, 1924.

ROY C., *Arts of the Upper Volta,* tr. F. Chaffin, Meudon, Chaffin, 1987.

RUBIN W., ed., *Le primitivisme dans l'art du XXe siècle,* Ed. fr. par J.-L. Paudrat, Paris, Flammarion, 1991.

RUSSELL J., *Henry Moore,* London, Penguin Books, 1958.

SAHAGUN, *Histoire générale des choses de la Nouvelle-Espagne,* tr. D. Jourdanet et R. Siméon, Paris, Masson, 1880.

SCARRE C. ed., *Timelines of the Ancient World,* London, Dorling Kindersley, 1993.

SEGY L., *African Sculpture Speaks,* New York, Da Capo, 1975.

SILBURN L. ed., *Le bouddhisme,* Paris, Fayard, 1977.

SIREN O., *The Chinese on the Art of Painting,* New York, Schocken, 1973.

SMITH L., HARRIS V., CLARK T., *L'art japonais. Chefs-d'œuvre du British Museum,* Londres, Parkstone, 1994.

STEPHAN L., PAUDRAT J.-L., KERCHACHE J., *L'art africain,* Paris, Mazenod, 1988.

STOKES D., *Desert dreamings,* Melbourne, Rigby, 1993.

STONE-MILLER, R., *L'art des Andes,* tr. F. Lévy-Paoloni, Paris, Thames and Hudson, 1996.

TALADOINE E. et FAUGÈRE-KALFON B., *Archéologie et art précolombiens : la Mésoamérique,* Paris, Manuels de l'Ecole du Louvre, 1995.

TANIZAKI J., *Eloge de l'ombre,* tr. R. Sieffert, Paris, Publ. Orientalistes de France, 1977.

THOMAS M., MAINGUY C. ET POMMIER S., *L'art textile,* Genève, Skira, 1985.

TOWNSEND R., ed., *The Ancient Americas. Art from Sacred Landscapes,* The Art Institute of Chicago-Prestel, Munich, 1992.

Trésors du Nouveau Monde, Bruxelles, Musées royaux d'art et d'histoire, 1992.

VANDIER-NICOLAS N., *Art et sagesse en Chine : Mi Fou (1051-1107),* Paris, PUF, 1963.

VANDIER-NICOLAS N., *Esthétique et peinture de paysage en Chine des origines aux Song,* Paris, Klincksieck, 1982.

VANDIER-NICOLAS N., *Peinture chinoise et tradition lettrée,* Paris, Seuil, 1983.

SECKEL D., *The Art of Buddhism,* Londres, Methuen, 1964.

VAN LIER H., *Les arts de l'espace,* Paris, Casterman, 1971.

VARENNE J., *Le tantrisme, Mythes, rites, métaphysique,* Paris, A Michel, 1997.

VÉQUAUD Y., *L'art du Mithila,* Paris, Presses de la Connaissance, 1976.

VERGER-FÈVRE M.N., *Étude des masques faciaux de l'Ouest de la Côte d'Ivoire, Arts d'Afrique noire,* Nos 53 et 54, 1995.

WATTS A., *Le bouddhisme zen,* tr. P. Berlot, Paris, Payot, 1978.

WILLETT F., *L'art africain,* tr. C. Ter-Sarkissian, Paris, Thames and Hudson, 1990.

WILLETS W., *L'art de la Chine,* adapt. fr. de Daisy Lion-Goldschmidt, Lausanne, Edita-La Bibliothèque des Arts, 1968.

YANAGI S., *The Unknown Craftsman,* adapted by B. Leach, Tokyo, Kodansha international, 1972 ; *Artisan et inconnu,* tr. M. Beltaigne, Paris, L'Asiathèque, 1992.

ZAHAN D., *Sociétés d'initiation bambara : Le N'domo, le Korè,* Paris-La Haye, Mouton, 1960.

Index

Page numbers in italic refer to illustrations.

A

Aboriginals, 46, 76, 207-8, *208, 209*
Abstraction, 34, 43, 58, 61-2, 93, 106, 107, 145, 152-3, 163-4, 168, 172-4, 177, 197, 211, 213, 215
Açoka, 159
Adornment, 15, 17-8, 28, 33, 46, 65, 76-8, 89, 114, 119, *126,* 127, *128,* 128, 167, 174, 207
Afghanistan, 47, 152
Africa, 7, 8, 12-3, 15-6, 18, 24-5, 33-4, 36, 41-3, 45, 61, 68, 71, 76-7, 92-3, 97, 101, 121, 128, 132, 134, 141, 145, 147-8, 152, 167, 171-2, 174, 176, 180, 190, 205-6, 217
Anyi, 33, 78
Ajanta, 89, 147
Akan, 33, 68, 121
Akbar, 109
Akhenaton, 78
Alaska, 127
Alberti L. B., 151
Alexander of Macedonia, 161, 171, 207
Algeria, *99,* 132
Altaï, 114
Altamira, 12
Amaravati, 185
Ambrosio P., *81, 85*
Amerindia, 13, 17-8, 24-5, 33-4, 36, 43, 45-6, 65, 93, 101-2, 114, 127-8, 132, 134, 148, 171, 188, 190, 193-4, 205
Anatolia, 25, 114, 118
Andalusia, 117, 141, 152, 156
Andes, 34, 94, 124, 127, 134, 172, 194, 197
Angkor, 36, *82,* 89, 156
Angola, 42
Antilles, 217
Anvers, 131
Apollo, 36
Arabs, 46, 76, 101, 109, 117-8, 139, 142, 171
Architecture, 15, 17, 23, 36, 43, 46, 57-8, 72-3, 113, 131, 141-2, 147-8, 151-2, 156, 159, 161, 193-4, 197, 217
Ardebil, 118
Aristophanes, 79
Aristotle, 10
Arms, 75-6
Arnhem, 207, *209*
Arp H., 84
Arras, 117
Art nouveau, 151
Arts and crafts, 151
Ashanti, 33, 77, 92, *93*
Asia, 8, 13, 18, 25, 28-9, 31, 33, 39, 41, 46, 56-7, 73, 78, 89, 91, 101, 121-2, 131, 145, 155, 159, 162, 167-8, 185-6, 206, 208, 211, 215, 218
Athens, 65, 79, 80, 135
Atlantic Ocean, 36, 152, 162, 194
Attar F., 63
Australia, *6,* 13, 43-6, 76, 206, 207, *208, 209*
Austria, 117
Autun, 148
Avalokiteshvara, 186, *187, 189,* 203, 204
Aztecs, 25, 45, 188, 190, 193-4

B

Babylon, 160
Baghdad, 109, 141, 168
Bali, 124, 172
Balthus, 84
Bamana (Bambara), *32,* 134, 174, 177-8
Baroque, 147, 151, 161, 200
Basel, 190, 193
Batak, 124
Batalha, 151
Baudelaire, 46
Bauhaus, 106, 151
Baule, *31,* 33, 92, *178,* 178
Baya, *99*
Behzad, 109
Beijing, 159, 163
Belgium, 65
Bembe, 145, *150*
Ben Jr., B., 205
Bena Luluwa, 93
Benares, 180
Bénin, 33, 92
Berberes, 121, 128
Berlin, 41, 215
Bernini, 200
Beti, *80*
Bhartrihari, 89
Bible, 161, 218
Bidyogo, 178
Bihar, 31
Blitner E., 208, *209*
Bobodioulasso, 152
Bodhidharma, 211
Bonampak, 194
Boni, 77, *78*
Borobudur, 36, 159
Botticelli, 84, 93
Boucher F., 84
Buddha and Bouddhism, 10, 31, 33, 36, 41, *44-*5, 55, 63, 71-74, 76, 89, 91, 101-2, 113, 117, 122, 124, 138, 139, 157, 159, 163, 172, 180-2, *184, 185,* 185, *186,* 186-7, *188,* 190, 201, 203-4, 208, 210-1, 213, 217-8
Bukhara, *113, 117*
Bourges, 80
Brahma, 97, 199
Brancusi, 23, 25, 61-2
Brasilia, 151-2
Brazil, 128
Breton A., 13, 217
Bruegel, 58, 131, 215
Brunelleschi, 151
Bruxelles, 117, 124
Buitron Rojas A., 96
Bulgaria, 13
Bura, *20,* 24, *25*
Burandai, 208, *208*
Burkina Faso, 13, *20,* 24, *25,* 43, *74, 79, 80,* 92, *122, 152*
Burma, 28-9, 181, 185, *186*
Burundi, 77
Bushongo, 176
Bwa, 177
Byzantium (Constantinople), 17, 31, 101, 105, 109, 115, 146, 148

C

Cairo, 41
Calder A., 147
Calligraphy, 16-7, *50,* 52-3, 63, 73-4, 109, 131, 135-6, 139, 141-2, 152, 156, 163, 208
Cambodia, 7, *82,* 89, 124, 142, 156, 181, 185-6
Cameroon, 43, 78, *80*
Canada, *65*
Canberra, 207

Carolines, 45, 174
Casablanca, *52,* 62
Catal Hüyük, 114
Caucasus, 119
Ceramics, 15-18, 23-4, 36, 41, 45-6, 49, *50,* 53, 57, 61, 63, 65, *68,* 71-74, 77, 89, 102, 105, 141-2, 152, 172, 194, 197
Cézanne, 58, 217-8
Chad, *15, 20, 21,* 24
Chancay, 119, 127
Chartres, 106, 186
Chavin de Huantar, 28, 127, 194
Chevreul, 98
Chicago, 151, 194
Chimu, 127
China, 2, 12, 15-18, *16, 22,* 23-25, 29, *29,* 31, 33, 36, 39, 43, 45-6, 49, 50, 52-3, *54, 55,* 61, 63, 68, *69, 70, 71,* 72-3, *84, 85, 88,* 89, 91, 97, 100-102, 104, *108,* 109-110, 112, 114-5, 117, 122, 124, 127, 131, 135, *137, 138,* 138, 139, *140,* 141, 145, 147, *154-*5, 159, 161, *161, 162,* 164, *164, 168,* 181, 185-6, *195,* 207, *211, 211,* 213-4, *214,* 215, 218
Chojiro, 18
Chokwe, 42
Chola, 199
Christ and Christianity, 12-3, 45, 80, 85, 101-2, 105, 131, 148, 161, 180, 186
Christo et Jeanne Claude, 206
Colima, 45
Colombia, 93, 94
Confucius and Confucianism, 17, 28, 45-6, 55, 71, 91, 208, 210
Congo-Brazzaville, 36, *153, 171*
Congo-Kinshasa, *12, 13, 67, 74, 77, 77,* 93, *130, 131, 132, 133,* 179, 180, *181*
Constable, 106
Cook Islands, 174
Cordoba, 152
Corregio, 84
Cortés H., 124
Costa L., 151
Costa Rica, *30, 63,* 65
Crete, 105, 134
Ctesiphon, 118
Cubism, 13
Cupisnique, 28
Cuzco, 197
Cyclades, 25, 142, 145, 168

D

Dada, 13, 206
Damascus, 117, 153
Dan, 43, *47,* 92, 180
De Chirico, 217
Denmark, 104
Delacroix, 84
Delhi, 110, 185
Delvaux P., 84, 218
Diqis, *30*
Djenne, 24, 152
Dogen, 213
Dogon, 16, *65*
Donatello, 147
Dongson, 62, 122, 124
Dorset, 65
Drawing, 10, 15, 17, 31, 33, 49, 55, 57, 167, 172, 206, 212
Dresde, 84

Druet R., *134*
Dubrovnik, *103*
Dubuffet J., 13
Duchamp M., 13, 206
Dunhuang, 186
Dürer A., 124
Dutch, 106

E

Easter Island or Rapanui , 43, 93, 174
Ecuador, 33, 36, *38,* 57, *59,* 96
Êdê, *49*
Edo (Tokyo), 46, 75, 91, 139
Egypt, 12, 15, 23-4, *24,* 25, 33, 42, *51,* 58, *66,* 68, 78-9, 101-2, 105, 114-5, 122, 135, 141, 145, 147-8, 160, *166-*7, 168, 171-2, 205
Eichendorff J. von, 6, 167
Eishi, 91
Eitoku, 113
Ellora, 147
England, 102, 161, 207
Epidauros, 148
Ernst M., 8, 84
Eroticism, *23,* 58, 80, 84-5, 91-93, 200, 217
Eschylus, 148
Etruria, 105, 135, 148
Europe, 15, 17, 24-5, 41, 43, 45-6, 56-58, 63, 65, 71, 97, 101-2, 112, 114-5, 117-8, 122, 128, 132, 134, 138, 142, 148, 161, 174, 180, 200, 203, 205, 212-3, 215, 217-8

F

Fan Ji, 213
Fang, 176
Fanti, 92
Fauves, 13
Fayoum, 171
Fes, *117,* 121
Fiji, 43
Firdowsi, 109
Flemish, 106
Flores, *17*
Florence, 84, 117
Flores, *17*
Fon, 33
Fontainebleau, 84
Fostat, *51*
Fragonard, 84
France, 12, 15-6, 24, 61, 84, 102, 117, *134,* 151, 161
Friedrich C. D., 215
Fu Baoshi, 162, *165*
Fujiwara no Teika, 73
Functions, 8, 15, 17-8, 28, 76, 92, 97, 147, 172, 177

G

Gabo N., 58, 145, 147
Gabon, 180, *183*
Gan Wuguan, *54*
Gardens, 73, 98, 131, 142, 147, *157, 158,* 160-4, *160, 161, 165,* 215
Gauguin P., 106
Genoa, 117
Geneva, 128
Géricault, 132
Germany, 23, 215
Ghana, *40,* 92, 95, *95,* 121
Giacometti A., 8, 180
Ginkakuji, *157,* 164
Giorgione, 84
Giza, 147
Goeritz M., 58
Gothic, 147
Goya, 180
Granada, 152, 156, 162

Grebo, 176
Greece, 7, 10, 12-3, 15, 17, 25, 41-2, 57-8, 65, 71, 78, 84-5, 102, 105, 115, 131-2, 135, 148, 161, 185
Gu Kaizhi, 56
Guanacaste, *63*
Guatemala, 34, 119, 127
Guerrero, 93
Guilin, *162*
Guinea Bissau, 178
Gurgan, 102
Guro, *9,* 92
Gurunsi, 77-8, *80*

H

Hadda, *45*
Haïti, 93, *95, 202,* 217
Hammershoi W., 104
Han, 29, 55, *70,* 71, *85,* 91, 114, 124, 145, 208
Han Zhuo, 110
Hanoi, 31, *160*
Hariri, 109
Harunobu, *86,* 91, 114
Hasegawa Tohaku, 113
Hatchepsout, 148
Hawaii, 43, 174
Hegel, 12, 18, 23, 34
Hemba, 177
Hepworth B., 58
Herat, 109
Hideyoshi, 18, 72
Hinduism, 76, 85, 89, 122, 156, 185, 197, 199-201, 213, 218
Hiroshige, 12, 114, *200,* 214
Hôan, 215
Hokusai, 12, 114
Holbein, 118
Holt N., 206
Hon'ami Koetsu, 139
Hopis, 127
Horace, 208
Huaguang, 55
Huari, 127, *132,* 135, 197
Huaxtecs, 25
Huê, 73
Humayun, 109

I

Iatmul, 172
Iberia, 151
Ibn Battuta, 118
Ibn Muqla, 141
Ibo, 43
Ife, 24, 33, 92
Ifugao, *123*
Ijo, 177, *177*
Ilkhans, 109
Imhotep, 147
Impressionnists, 12, 98, 106, 114, 217
Incas, 114, 127, 197
India, 12, 17-8, *19,* 23, 29, 31, 36, 41, 45, 58, 62, 73, *83, 85, 87,* 89, 97, 102, *104,* 109, 110, *114,* 115, *115,* 118, 122, *126, 129,* 135, 147, 156, 159, 163, 171, 180, 185-6, 197, 199, 200, 205, 213
Indonesia, *14, 17, 37,* 41, 76, *78, 116, 118*
Ingres, 52, 57, 84
Inuits, 43, 65, 68
Iran, 17, 31, *31,* 41, 61, 63, *100,* 102, *102,* 107, 109, 115-6, *118,* 118-9, 141-2, 145, *146, 148, 149,* 152, 161-2, *169,* 185
Iraq, 111, 142, 144

Ise, 159, 205
Isfahan, *50,* 109, 118, 156, 162
Islam, 16, 43, 45, 102, 107, 109, 115, 117-8, 122, 128, 135, 141-2, 151-2, 156, 161-2, 185
Italy, 80, *81,* 106, 117, 200
Itsukushima, 160
Itten J., 106
Ivory Coast, *9, 15, 31,* 43, *47, 68,* 78, 121, *175, 178,* 180, *182*

J

Jade, 16, 25, 28, 39, 41, 61, 68, *69,* 71, 93, *124,* 127
Japan, 8, 10, 12, 17-8, 24, 29, 36, 39, 43, 46, *56,* 63, 72-3, 76, 86, 89, 91, 104, *105,* 107, 113, 115, 117, 122, 131, 135, 138, 139, 141, 143, *153, 158,* 159, 163-4, 167, 171, 181, 185-6, *196, 197, 198, 200, 201, 203, 204,* 205, *206, 210, 211, 212,* 213-5, *215, 216,* 218, *219*
Java, *37, 41,* 62, 76, 122, 124, 159
Jayadeva, 85
Jia Dao, 162
Jiang Kui, 53
Jogjakarta, 124
Johnson P., 151, 159
Jomon, 171
Junayd, 109
Judaism, 78, 161, 186
Jugendstil, 151

K

Kalimantan, 124
Kamasutra, 85
Kandinsky, 98
Kangra, 89
Kano, *56, 107,* 113, 160
Kant, 13
Kasai, 121, *133,* 134
Kashan, 118
Kashmir, 162
Kashu, *197*
Katsura, 160
Kayapo, 128
Kenya, 42
Kenzo Tange, 151
Khajuraho, 23, 85
Khartoum, 78
Kiamba, *130-1*
Kiev, 151
Klee P., 134, 167
Klimt G., 84
Kline, 113
Konarak, 23, 85
Kongo, 176
Koran, 45, 62, 107, 109, 141-2, 162
Korea, 18, 29, 31, *31,* 36, 39, 63, 72, *73,* 74, 89, 113, 115, 159, *163,* 181, 185-6, 214, 218
Korin, 113
Koryo, *31,* 72-3
Kran, *175*
Krishna, 85, 89, 97, *104,* 110, 197, 200
Kuba, 121, *132, 133,* 134, 176
Kuna, *120-1,* 127
Kushan, 185
Kwele, 36, 174
Kwere, 42
Kyongju, *163*
Kyoto, 74, 117, 139, *157, 158,* 159, 160, 164, 218

L

Ladakh, *184*
Lahore, 162
Lao Pakou, *108*
Laos, *8, 10,* 124, 181
Laozi, 210
Lacquer, 29, 118
Lascaux, 132, 207
La Tolita, 33
La Tour G. de, 180
Lê, 73
Leach B., 10, 17, 18
Leconte de Lisle, 80
Léon, 151
Leonardo da Vinci, 57-8, 104, 167
Liang Kai, 56
Liberia, *15*
Li Bo, 56, 162
Libya, 132
Li Rihua, 50, 55
Li Tang, 213
Li Wei, 138, *140*
Li Yongcun, 213, 214
Lin Zixiao, *195,* 213
Liu Yuxi, 213
Lobi, *43,* 77-8, *79, 122*
London, 131, 147
Longmen, 186
Lotto, 118
Luba, 93
Luristan, *31,* 33, 39, 46
Ly, 72, *72*
Lyon, 117

M

Madagascar, *11,* 121
Maghreb, 128, 141, 152
Magritte R., 65, 218
Mahabalipuram, 218
Mahabharata, 33, 36, 122, 199
Malanda, 145, *153*
Mali, 24, *32, 65, 176,* 177, *179*
Malraux A., 7, 34
Mandalay, *186*
Manet, 84
Mangbetu, 12-13
Man Giac, 218
Man Ray, 85
Maori, 25, 174
Maragha, 109, 132
Marka, *176,* 177
Marlik, 145, *148, 149*
Marquesas Islands, 174
Masks, 15, 18, 25, 33, 41, 43, 45, 47, 68, 71, 93, *150, 166-7,* 168, 171, 171-180, 193-4, 206
Massoudy H., 142, *144*
Mathura, 185
Matisse, 52, 98, 100, 106-7
Matraki, 109
Maty, 174
Mayas, 25, 34, *34,* 45, 142, 171, 194
Ma Yuan, 213
Mecca, 118, 152
Medina, 152
Meissen, 24
Melanesia, 43, 172
Mende, 178
Merina, 121
Mesopotamia, 16, 23, 33, 58, 105, 114, 147, 160
Mexico, 13, 65, 127, 174, 188, 190, *193*
Mezcala, 45, 93, 174, *193*
Michelangelo, 21, 84
Micronesia, 43, 93, 174
Mies van der Rohe, 151
Mi Fei, 162
Ming, 39, 72

N

Naïves, 107, 217
Nature, 7, 8, 10, 12, 52, 63, 73-4, 76, 109, 131, 151, 159, 161-2, 164, 167-8, 190, 194, 197, 205-6, 208, 211, 213
Navajos, 42, 127, 205-6
Nazca, *62,* 65, 127, *132,* 197
Nefertiti, 41, 78
Nepal, 49, 180-1, *190, 191,* 201
Nervi P. L., 151
Newton, 97
New York, 136, 145
New Zealand, 43, 174
Nguyên, 73
Nicoya, 25, *63,* 65
Niemeyer O., 151
Nietzsche, 217
Niger, 43, 46
Nigeria, 24, 92, *92, 177*
Nikko, 46
Nishapur, *50,* 102
Nizami, 109
Ni Zan, 208
Nok, 24
Nubia, 148
Nukuoro, 93, 174
Nuna, *74, 77*

O

Oceania, 7, 13, 17-8, 24, 36, 42-3, 45-6, 68, 93, 101, 172, 176
Olmecs, 25, 45, 93, 194
Orvieto, 80
Osaka, 46, 75
Ottomans, 109, 117, 141

P

Pacific Ocean, 25, 43, 124, 127, 197
Pacioli L., 57
Painting, 10, 12, 15-17, *18,* 36, 41, 43, 46, 49, 50, 52-3, 55, 57-8, 63, 72-4, 84-5, 89, 91, 93, 100-1, 104-6,
109-110, 112-3, 118, 22, 131-2, 135-6, 142, 145, 147, 163, 167, 199, 201, 203, 205-8, 210-1, 213 -5
Pakistan, *23*
Palenque, 171
Paminggir, *118,* 124
Pan Marta, 147
Panama, 62, 120-1, 127
Pantheon, 148
Papua, 18, *122*
Paracas, 114, 127, 194
Paris, 61, 117, 128, 134, 142, 145, 193, 203, 217
Parthenon, 57, 79, 148
Pazyryk, 114, 118
Persepolis, 39, 148
Peru, *17,* 18, 24, 25, *28,* 33, 60, *62, 64,* 114, 122, 127, *132,* 134, *193*
Peuls, 18, 46
Pevsner A., 58, 145
Phidias, 148
Philippines, 122, *123*
Picasso, 7, 34, 52, 58, 65, 84, 106
Pissaro, 12
Plato, 10, 57, 79, 80
Plucker (conoid), 8
Pollock J., 136
Polykletos, 57
Polynesia, 43, 174
Pompeii, 135
Praxitelus, 79, 80
Pueblos, 127
Punjab, 89
Punu, 180, *183*
Pygmies, 121
Pythagoras, 12, 57

Q

Qajars, 109
Qataban, 171, *173*
Qi Baishi, *55,* 65, 138, *140, 207,* 218
Qimbaya, 93, *94*
Qin, 135
Qing, 28, *71,* 71-2, 110, 112, 159, 163, 213
Quetzalcoatl, 65

R

Rabat, 121
Radha, 85, 89, *104,* 110, 201
Rajasthan, *83, 110,* 206
Ramayana, 23, 33, 122, 199
Rasic M., *103*
Ravenna, 106, 151
Rembrandt, 7, 84
Remojadas, *193*
Renaissance, 7, 10, 15, 57-8, 84, 135, 151, 161
Rennes, 180
Renzan, *219*
Reynolds J., 52
Reza Abbasi, 109, 118
Rhythm, 46, 50, 62, 98, 104, 121, 131, 134-6, 138-9, 141-2, 145, 147-8, 151, 153, 156, 159, 160, 162, 164, 199, 208, 211-3
Rodin, 7, 57-8, 199
Romanesque, 148
Romania, 61
Rome, 10, 13, 41, 80, 102, 105, 115, 148, 151, 161, 171, 185, 200
Rosetsu, *204,* 218
Rothko M., 106
Roublev A., 186
Rousseau H., 217

Rubens, 84, 131
Rumi, 144
Ruskin, 107
Russians, 117, 188
Rwanda, *8, 77*
Ryoanji, *158,* 164

S

Saadi, 109
Sadiki S., 53, *62*
Safavids, 109, 118, *118*
Sakuta Yoshi, 105
San, 24
Sanchi, 159, 185
Santa Cruz, 78, 127
Santo Domingo, *193*
Santorin, 65, 135
Sao, *20, 21,* 24
Sara, *15*
Sassanids, 115, 117-8
Schöffer N., 147
Schopenhauer, 217
Sculpture, 13, 15-8, 23-5, 29, 31, 36, 41, 43, 45-6, 49, 57-61, 72, 85, 89, 92-3, 131, 135, 137, 142, 145, 147, 156, 158, 174, 186, 199, 203, 207
Scyths, 118
Seals, 16, 135
Seine, 28
Sei Shonagon, 139
Senghor L. S., 145
Sen no Rikyu, 73-4
Senatus J. L., *202,* 217
Senufo, 33, *68,* 77, 92, *93,* 179
Seoul, 186
Sepik, 68
Sesshu, 113, *196*
Sesson, 113
Seurat, 97-8
Shah Abbas, 156
Shah Jahan, 156, 162
Shang, 31, 33, 53, 71, *71*
Sharaku, 7
Shilluk, *76,* 77
Shinto, 113, 159, 168, 172, 205, 213
Shokei, *212*
Shosen in, *107*
Shoshu, *201,* 214
Shiva, 85, 97, 199
Siberia, 28
Sierra Leone, 178
Simil, 93, *95*
Sinan, 109
Sind, 18
Slavs, 148
Soami, 164
Somalia, 46, *77,* 78
Song, 17, 53, 56, 71-2, 72, 131, 164, 186, 208, 212
Songtsen Gampo, 204
Songye, *67,* 179, 180, *181*
Sosen, *203,* 218
Sotatsu, 113
Soto J. R., 147
Soulages, 113
Spain, 36, 84, 106, 127, 180, 190
Sri Lanka, 29, 181, 185
Srinagar, 162
Stonehenge, 142
Sudan, *76,* 77-8
Suger, 106
Sukhothai, 186
Sukracarya, 185
Sulawesi, 8, *14, 78, 78*
Sultanabad, 142, *146*
Sumatra, 118, 124
Sumba, *116,* 124
Sun Guoting, 53
Surakarta, 124
Surrealism, 12, 172, 206,
213
Suse, 61
Su Shi, 52-3, 55, 136
Suzhou, *161,* 163
Suzuki Shonen, 139, *143*

T

Tabriz, *100,* 109
Taino, 171, *192*
Taipeh (Taiwan), *160,* 210
Taj Mahal, 147, 156, 162
Tamil Nadu, 206
Tamna, 171, *173*
Tang, 28, 53, 56, 71, *84,* 91, 132-6, 135, *138,* 145, 213
Tang Tai, 112
Tanguy Y., 218
Tanizaki J., 39
Tanyu, 160, *216,* 218
Tanzania, 91, 92
Taoism, 17, 56, 63, 89, 136, 141, 159, 162, 167, 208, 210-1, 213, 218
Tara, 89, *191,* 203-4
Tatlin, 58
Tehran, 39
Teotihuacan, 25, 45, 147, 171, 193
Tetsuzan, *210,* 218
Textiles, 15-8, 31, 41, 45-6, 53, 65, 102, 110 to 121, *110 to 121,* 124, 127, *132, 133,* 134-5, 141, 194, 197, 205-6
Thaïland, *45,* 74, 124, 181, *185,* 185-6, *186*
Thule, 65, 68
Tiahuanaku, *64,* 127, 135, 197
Tibet, 89, 181, *184, 189, 190,* 201, 203-5
Timor, 48-9, 62, 124
Tinguely J., 145, 147
Tintoretto, 84
Titien, 84
Tiwi, 207
Tlemcen, 152
Tlingit, 127
Tokugawa, 46, 91, 117
Tokyo, 91, 113, 151, 213
Topkapi, 102
Toraja, 8, *14, 78, 78,* 124
Torin, 141, *141*
Tosa, 113
Totalik A., *65,* 68
Totonacs, 25, 194
Tournai, 117
Toussian, 177
Trân, 72-3
Trobriand Islands, *26-7, 170*
Truong Van Y, *90*
Tsunenobu, 218
Tunis, *12*
Turkmenes, 119
Turner, 106, 215
Turkey, 41, 109, 118-9, 141
Tyr, 102

U

Uighurs, 115
United States, 115
Ur, 115
Urbino, 84
Urubu, 128
Uruk, 135
Utamaro, 91, 200
Utzon J., 151
Uzbeks, 112

V

Valdivia, 36, *38*
Van Gogh, 7, 12, 58, 106
213
Vanuatu, *33,* 45
Vasari, 106
Vatsyayana, 85
Vaux-le-Vicomte, 161
Velazquez, 7, 84
Venice, 84, 117, 128, 151, 217
Versailles, 161
Vicus, *24*
Vienna, 124, 215
Viet Nam, 29, 31, 36, 39, 49, 62, 72, 74, 77, 89, *90,* 91, 101, 115, 122, *160,* 164, 181, 185-7, *187,* 218
Vili, 176
Vishnu, 85, 97, 122, 199, 200
Vladimir, 151

W

Wakamba, 41, *42*
Wang Wei, 167, 210
Washington, 218
Watanabe Seitei (Shotei), 206
Wayana, 128
Wè, 43
Wei, 186
Wen Tong, 136
West, 10, 13, 17-8, 31, 39, 41, 49, 52, 57, 78, 84, 91, 93, 101-2, 106-7, 117, 132, 159, 161, 163, 185, 206, 213
Weston E., 85
Woodblock prints, 12, 46, 91, 105-6, 113, 118, 213
Wu Changshuo, 138, *139*
Wuxi, 163

X

Xia Gui, 213
Xie He, 110, 135, 138
Xinjiang, 31, 115

Y

Yamato, 159
Yanagi S., 8, 10
Yang Guifei, 91
Yangshao, *22,* 24, 36, 53
Yangzhou, 163
Yasunobu, 56
Yelwa, 24
Yemen, 76, *173*
Yi, 72
Yiman, 172
Yohure, 46, 92, 180, *182*
Yoruba, 41, 68, 122
Yuan, *16,* 72
Yungang, 186

Z

Zaire, 177
Zanskar, *126*
Zapotecs, 45, 193
Zaramo, 78, *91,* 92
Zen, 36, 46, 55, 73-5, 163-4, 206, 211, 213-5, 217
Zeshin, *105*
Zhang Daqian, *101,* 213
Zhang Ji, 208
Zhang Yanyuan, 212-3
Zhang Zao, 210
Zhao Mengfu, 208
Zhejiang, 74
Zheng Xie, 131, 164
Zhi Wan, *138*
Zhou, 29, *29,* 33, 68
Zhu Mo, *138*
Zhuangzi, 136, 210-2, 218
Zong Ping, 210
Zulus, 76-7
Zuñis, 127

Miniatures, *19, 87, 100,* 107, 109, 110, 118
Miro, 106
Mithila, 31, *35*
Mixtecs, 25, 194
Mochicas, *17,* 33, *60,* 93, *193,* 194
Moctezuma, 124
Modigliani, 84
Moguls, 29, *87,* 109, 118, 129
Moholy-Nagy L., 147
Momoyama, 113, 198
Mondrian, 98, 110, 142
Monet C., 98
Mongolia, 31, 115, 181
Monte Alban, 171
Moore H., 7, 13, 58, 62
Mopti, 152
Morandi G., 217
Morocco, *34,* 36, *52, 53, 117,* 121
Mortlock, 174
Moscow, 148, 188
Mossi, *13,* 92, 145, *152,* 177
Movement, 16, 46, 50, 58, 79, 105, 131, 134, 136, 139, 141-143, 147, 213
Mumuye, *92*
Munich, 107
Munkala, *171*
Muqi, 218
Murasaki Shikibu, 139

By the same author

Le Viêt-Nam, Histoire et civilisation, Paris, Éditions de Minuit, 1955. (épuisé)

L'Asie du Sud-Est, dans *Encyclopédie de la Pléiade, Histoire Universelle,* tome III, Gallimard, 1958.

L'économie de l'Asie du Sud-Est, Paris, PUF, 1958 ; 2e édition, 1964.

Les relations économiques sino-soviétiques, 1949-1958, Cahiers de l'Institut de Science économique appliquée, Paris, 1959.

Histoire de l'Asie du Sud-Est, Paris, PUF, 1959, 2e édition, 1967. (Traduction italienne, farsie, japonaise).

La pierre d'amour, Paris, Éditions de Minuit, 1959.

Conflits de cultures en Asie du Sud-Est, dans UNESCO, *Histoire du développement scientifique et culturel de l'humanité,* vol V : *XIXe siècle,* tome II, Paris, Robert Laffont, 1969.

La propagation de l'innovation dans le domaine du caoutchouc en France, Cahiers de l'Institut de Science économique appliquée, n° 134, série AD, n° 2, février 1963.

L'industrie de l'enseignement, Paris, Éditions de Minuit, 1967.

Traduction : Dang Tran Con et Phan Huy Ich, *Chant de la femme du combattant,* Gallimard, 1968.

Il Sud-Est asiatico contemporaneo, Firenze, Sansoni, 1974.

Jeunesse exploitée, jeunesse perdue ? Paris, Presses universitaires de France, 1978.

L'éducation comparée, Paris, Armand Colin, 1981.

Histoire du Viêt-Nam des origines à 1858, Paris, Sud-Est Asie, 1982.

L'éducation : Cultures et Sociétés, Paris, Publications de France, 1991.

Marx, Engels et l'éducation, Paris, Presses Universitaires de la Sorbonne, 1991.

Culture, créativité et développement, Paris, L'Harmattan, 1992.

Éducation et Civilisations, tome 1 : *Sociétés d'hier,* Paris, UNESCO-BIE-Nathan, 1995.

Aigrettes sur la rizière. Chants et poèmes classiques du Viêt Nam choisis, présentés et traduits du viêtnamien, Gallimard, 1995.

In collaboration with

Groupe d'études de l'IEDES, *Alphabétisation et développement économique,* Paris, Études Tiers-Monde, PUF, 1964.

L'enseignement en Afrique tropicale, collection Tiers-Monde, PUF, 1971.

Das Moderne Asien, Frankfurt, Fisher, 1969.

Inde et Extrême-Orient contemporains, Paris, Bordas, 1971.

L'Histoire du XXe siècle : l'Asie du Sud-Est, 2 vol., Sirey, 1970-1971.

L'éducation en milieu rural, (avec P. Rakotomalala), UNESCO, 1974.

M. Debesse et G. Mialaret, *Traité des sciences pédagogiques,* tome VI, PUF, 1974.

I Propagonisti della Rivoluzione, Asia, volume 3 : *il Sud-Est,* Milano, Compagnia Edizioni Internazionali, 1974.

G. Mialaret et al., *Le droit de l'enfant à l'éducation,* Paris, UNESCO, 1979.

« Culture et développement », n° spécial de la *Revue Tiers-Monde,* Paris, janvier-mars 1984.

Pour un bilan de la sociologie de l'éducation, Cahiers du Centre de recherches sociologiques, Université Toulouse-Le Mirail et CNRS, n° 2, mai 1984.

Université et développement au Rwanda, Kigali, PNUD, septembre 1984.

Clés pour une stratégie nouvelle du développement, Paris, Éditions ouvrières-UNESCO, 1984.

Stratégies du développement endogène, Paris, Presses de l'UNESCO, 1984.

G. Mialaret et al., *Introduction aux sciences de l'éducation,* Genève-Paris, UNESCO-Delachaux et Niestlé, 1985.

C. Coquery-Vidrovitch et A. Forest, eds., *Décolonisation et nouvelles dépendances. Modèles et contre-modèles idéologiques et culturels dans le Tiers-Monde,* Presses universitaires de Lille, 1986.

Le Viêt-Nam post-révolutionnaire. Population, économie, société, 1975-1985, Paris, L'Harmattan, 1987.

A. Ruscio, ed., *Le Viêt-Nam. L'histoire, la terre, les hommes,* Paris, L'Harmattan, 1989.

L.F.B. Dubbeldam et al., *Développement, culture et éducation,* Annuaire International de l'éducation, 1994, UNESCO-CESO, 1995.

« Pluralité et éducation : politiques et pratiques », *Revue francophone d'éducation comparée,* n° 48, mai 1995 (Colloque de Montréal, 1994).

Acknowledgements

This book could not have been written without the work of many researchers, of which I unfortunately know only a part, which may have led to the occasional error. Nor would it have been possible without information from the experts, merchants, craftspeople, local people and photographers I met on my travels, who are too numerous to be named. I am especially grateful to Atemi Ohta Shann, Lu Gao and Georges Condominas who respectively identified some Japanese and Chinese paintings as well as the Edê heron for me; Chrisoula Petridis who translated the book into English; and Bruno Leprince, who collaborated with me not only on the design, but also on the whole production process. My wife Hông Anh, along with her knowledge and advice, was my companion during its writing and I wish to express to her my affectionate appreciation.